# FIRST and LAST
# *Seasons*

# DAN McGRAW

DOUBLEDAY New York London Toronto Sydney Auckland

# FIRST and LAST
## *Seasons*

---

# A FATHER, A SON,

### *and*

## Sunday Afternoon Football

PUBLISHED BY DOUBLEDAY
a division of Random House, Inc.
1540 Broadway, New York, New York 10036

DOUBLEDAY and the portrayal of an anchor with a dolphin are trademarks of
Doubleday, a division of Random House, Inc.

*Book design by Bonni Leon-Berman*

"(Remember Me) I'm The One Who Loves You"
Words and Music by Stuart Hamblen
Copyright © 1949 by Chapell & Co.
Copyright Renewed
International Copyright Secured. All Rights Reserved.

Library of Congress Cataloging-in-Publication Data

McGraw, Dan, 1959–
First and last seasons: a father, a son, and Sunday afternoon football /
Dan McGraw.—
1st ed.
p.   cm.
1. Cleveland Browns (Football team)   2. Football fans—United
States.   3. Fathers and sons—United States.   4. Terminally ill—
United States.   I. Title.
GV956.C6   M34   2000
796.332'64'0977132—dc21
00-034031

ISBN 0-385-49833-0
Copyright © 2000 by Dan McGraw
All Rights Reserved
Printed in the United States of America
October 2000
First Edition

1  3  5  7  9  10  8  6  4  2

For Meredith

# CHAPTER ONE

# Shallow Happiness

As my father stood before me that morning, his ill-fitting boxer shorts shit-stained and hanging down below his Value City pajama shorts, his hands shaking with a palsy as he tried to support himself with spindly arms on the metal hospital bed frame, his legs withered and pockmarked with bluish black sores, and his faded pajama top barely covering the grotesque distended bulge hanging from the left side of his abdomen, I noticed his trademark smile. It was the famous Dick McGraw smirk. To those who didn't know my father very well—and most people didn't (his choice)—his smirk was pure arrogance, a punk smile that smarted of superiority. But having seen this expression my whole life, I knew differently. It was a smile that said everything is okay, one that exuded confidence, an unspoken sign that I understood to mean that he had not a care in the world. That morning it communicated his independence, a look that said he was in charge of this final part of his life, even though he was losing control of his body. And as the ambulance drivers filled out their forms, made condescending small talk, and tried to pull up his underwear, I noticed a certain dignity in him.

On this hot August day in Cleveland, Ohio, he was being taken to the hospice to die. He knew it and I knew it. We had spent months talking about what he would do when the end was near, how he wanted to die, how he wanted to do this on his own. It wasn't that he had given up or wasn't praying for a miracle. Oh, he had prayed, all right. "Gee, God, I'll never be bad again," was how he described his conversations with the Lord. But he was ready now. Yes, he was afraid, and yes, he wasn't quite sure what came next. When he decided to give up the pointless chemotherapy treatments, he explained to me he wasn't giving up. He was giving in.

Eight months earlier the surgeon had cut him open to see why he had rectal bleeding and abdominal pain. My dad was familiar with bleeding and pain. He had had a small tumor on his colon removed four years earlier and had undergone painful chemotherapy and radiation treatment. But for the most part, he had had a pretty normal life during the four years after the surgery. When they opened him up in January 1999, the surgeon actually said "Oh shit" upon seeing the condition of my dad's insides, and closed him up immediately. The cancer was running through his abdomen like mad, with a tumor the size of an orange blocking his colon, and "seeding" of smaller tumors on his liver, pancreas, and stomach. Just to make sure there was no silver lining, the surgeons opened up a hole in his side and fitted him with an ileostomy bag, a device that would take the solid waste from his large intestine directly out of his body.

He awoke from his surgery scared, aware of the bag attached to his left side, and confused over what had been described to him as "routine" exploratory surgery. None of the doctors would look him in the eye when they did their postop. My father had spent a good part of his career as a lawyer dealing with malpractice cases, so he knew the psyche of the medical profession. They wouldn't tell you anything unless you made them, and in a meeting two days after the surgery, the oncologist was wishy-washy about the prognosis. Maybe two years, they told him. My father knew better but tried to keep it to himself. He never used the word "terminal" or "inoperable"—he preferred not to burden anyone with unnecessary truths—but the diagnosis was merely a formality. He would be dead by Christmas, maybe Thanksgiving.

He hated that bag. The only time I saw him discouraged was when he was wearing it. When he had friends over, he would joke about it, calling the stoma on his side Rosebud and telling stories of someone called Shit Bag Sullivan, a guy with an ostomy device from the old Irish neighborhood who worked on the railroad. Shit Bag Sullivan, as lore would have it, would sit in the caboose and fling his fecal matter at passing train cars. I never knew if Shit Bag really existed or was just another one of those Irish saloon stories my father had grown up with. But regardless, the thought of a man cruising through life while flinging crap at the world had a certain universal appeal. And my father was certainly one who enjoyed flinging figurative crap.

But in private he was deeply depressed about that bag. As a man who favored scatological humor, he couldn't shit or fart anymore. He was always very weird about farting. He referred to breaking wind by the Latin word *flatus*. That was what made him, though, using his schooling in the classics and moving it to the realm of farting.

A few months before the hospice morning, he delightfully recounted sitting on the bowl to take a piss and passing a small piece of crap that had somehow avoided both the bag and the tumor blocking his colon. He called it his renegade turd, and proudly discussed it as if he had given birth. I told him he should write a children's book about his exploits, *Dicky and the Renegade Turd*. Might give Captain Underpants a run for the money. But aside from the occasional jokes, that bag devastated him. He stopped going out, even to a quick dinner at my brother's bar. He was embarrassed by the smell. And the damn thing gurgled and popped at strange times. Mostly he hated having someone else help change it. It made him feel that he was no longer in control of one important facet of his body.

I helped steady him as the ambulance drivers decided how to get him out to the ambulance. He hadn't spoken or stood up in days, but his grip was strong on my arm. I sat him down on the edge of the bed, and I put some old ratty slip-on tennis shoes on his scaly feet. He put both of his arms around me to stand up again, finally making it on the third try. We had never been very affectionate physically toward each other. Ours was a family that shook hands rather than hugged—typical Irish Catholics in that regard. But I held him as tight as I could, smelling the shit and death that surrounded him. His body was decaying piece by piece, starting at the extremities and working inward. When I was a kid, my dad smelled like Mennen Skin Bracer and Pall Mall cigarettes. Now he smelled of decay, a little bit like Lake Erie in the midst of an alga bloom on a hot August day—half-alive, half-dead.

I steadied him on his feet, and we moved slowly outside, down two steps and to the door. I could feel the football-sized tumor pressing against my side from his abdomen as I held him. It was hard and moved between us, pushing into my ribs. Each step was laborious and halting, my right arm around his shoulders, his right arm reaching across my body to hold my left forearm. We stopped at one point, and I asked if he was doing okay. He just smiled and held my arm tighter, motioning to keep moving.

We lifted him onto the ambulance stretcher, and the smirk was still there. As they strapped him to the gurney, I noticed relief had passed over him, and the smirk turned into a more genuine smile I had seen only a few times in my life. He seemed actually happy to be going to die. This did not puzzle or upset me. He had told me over and over again how he had had a great life. He was the father of six grown children, all of whom were doing well in life. And after my mom died of her own cancer in 1975, my father eventually married his present wife, Theresa, who had eight children of her own. Having so many children was quite appropriate for him, as he was a child at heart himself.

I had asked him a month earlier if he was afraid to die. "Of course," he told me. "But I don't have any choice. I'm going to fight this as best I can, but there comes a time when you have to accept things. When there is nothing else you can do, there is nothing else you can do. I guess I'll have to see what happens next."

He was sixty-nine years old, young in some people's eyes, but to him, it was enough. That was one of his favorite words: enough. When people would ramble on nonsensically, he would just hold up his hand and say, "Enough." He had a living will now that also said, "Enough." It stipulated that no extraordinary means be used to save his life. He made sure he made it to enough before this hot August morning. He had met with all of his children, guys he had gone to second grade with, high school friends, and business associates—almost like an athlete doing a farewell tour of all the stadiums he had played in. And he really loved every minute of it, holding court with his old friends while they talked about the time they beat those colored boys in baseball down at Rockefeller Park or the time that Mad Dog Galvin passed out face-first in a pizza or the time the bartender passed out at the Shamrock and all the greenhorns in the neighborhood helped themselves to free booze.

But in the past few weeks he had grown tired of the visitors. He was pulling into himself. The metastasis was withering his extremities. And his strength, paradoxically, was moving toward his torso, where the cancer ruled. His glib personality was pulling in, too. It was time to prepare, to weed out all that was unimportant in his last days. His final act was his, and his alone. "Dying is the last thing I am ever going to do," he told me one day, "and I am going to do this on my terms."

And just before they were about to load him into the ambulance, I thought of a little private joke we had shared through the years. "It looks like you have finally found shallow happiness," I whispered in his ear. He rolled his eyes and he almost laughed, looking at me with a genuine love I hadn't seen much in my life from him.

"Shallow happiness" was a code phrase we had for the ultimate in human enlightenment, or unenlightenment, as it were. I'm not sure where it came from, but the basic premise is that those with nothing to worry about have found a true happiness, something the rest of us, with various cares and worries, could never attain. It was anti-enlightenment, anti-intellectual, anti-attachment. It could be found in the faces of the mentally retarded, porno stars, TV weather forecasters, drooling middle linebackers, the drunken Irish, drugged-out rock stars, death row inmates. My dad used to tell me that the ultimate in shallow happiness would be if he was confined to a wheelchair, senile beyond repair, drooling on himself with his fly permanently down. "A burden to my children," he used to joke. "Hopefully you."

I don't know if my dad saw it this way, but I began thinking that maybe the concept of shallow happiness wasn't such a joke after all. Maybe it is an essential phase to go through, the act of letting go of all earthly things, of being content with your life, of not caring about what is unimportant. We spend our lives building and adding parts—jobs, spouses, careers, a piece of dirt in the suburbs, the best car. Even though he had made a lot of money in his life, material things had never engrossed my dad. His clothing was often bought at discount stores, Sipowicz-style short-sleeve dress shirts for work that he collected for ten dollars each. He lived within a stone's throw of Lake Erie most of his married life, but unlike our neighbors, he never bought a boat. He was a high-powered lawyer, but rode the bus to work every day, regaling us at home with the ongoing saga of the cross-dresser with the hairy chest who insisted on wearing see-through blouses. To him, ideas were important. People came in a distant second. Material possessions barely registered on his radar screen.

They closed the door on the ambulance and took my dad off to die. I was to follow in my car, help him get set up in the hospice. I went inside and grabbed a bag of his personal items. There were a dozen or so prescriptions on the kitchen counter. I didn't think he'd need them anymore, but I packed them up just the same. Then something caught my eye. Tucked in the corner of the kitchen counter was a small bag of marijuana. He had played around with marijuana to combat nausea and a lack of appetite from the cancer, usually to no avail. I figured he wouldn't be needing it where he was going. I hadn't smoked pot in fifteen years, but I figured someone might need to kill some pain over the next few weeks. Maybe I was looking for my own version of shallow happiness.

I had not planned to come back to Cleveland and help my dad die, certainly not to steal his pot as I put him in an ambulance. But coming home does strange and dark things to a person; we tend to revert to our former role in life. In my case, I was the family fuckup, the prodigal son who would never turn down a good time, never turn away from a drink or a smoke or a line, always finding a way to fail when success was easily in my grasp. Cleveland had taught me failure, and I was quite good at it back in the day. As happens to most kids whose parents dominate, my life never really got going until I was far away from my father. Maybe I had to get out from under the city's shadow; maybe I had to get out from under his.

But the more I thought about it, I really wanted to come back, at least for a short time. Before his operation, before that surgeon had uttered his "oh shit" diagnosis, I had decided it might be a good time to make it back to my hometown. I was thirty-nine years old and had successfully fled Cleveland for a career in journalism ten years earlier. But there was something about Cleveland that kept pulling me back. I couldn't quite put a finger on it—why I thought it might be fun to spend some time with my dad in Cleveland. Like all fathers and sons, we had had our tough times, butting heads over unrealized expectations and failing to have a clear understanding of who we were as individuals. But in recent years we seemed to be getting closer to some sort of understanding; we talked on the phone often and seemed to genuinely enjoy each other's company. Point-blank, he was a fun guy to talk to. Told great stories. Was well read. Appreciated fart-and-shit humor.

These were the things I loved about my father: his witty banter and the unassuming way he could put you at ease, the high-minded discussions of great books, the way he would lend you money, but only after he beat you up on the phone for ten minutes. Other components of his personality—the obstinate insistence that his was always the right way, his distance from any real emotions, his unwillingness to confront serious family problems—still bugged me. My relationship with him was much like my relationship with my hometown. There were things I hated about Cleveland: the parochial attitude of many of its residents, the way just about every ethnic group disliked the others, the dirt and the grime, the way things never seemed to change. On the other hand, Cleveland was one of those places that have a built-in insanity to them, a place where beer drinking and sports are religion, a place where a burning river seemed not so strange, a screw-the-rest-of-the-country attitude that makes you feel proud. And, in my consistent attempt at inconsistency, I also liked the fact that things in Cleveland never seemed to change. For in Cleveland, it seemed to me, throwing crap at the world as it flies by seems perfectly normal; the rest of the country, after all, had been throwing crap at Cleveland for quite some time.

My plan was to write a book about the Cleveland Browns coming back, after being shamelessly moved from town by Arthur B. Modell three years earlier. I would look at the history of the storied franchise, their return from the dead, and how their season would shake out. My interest was twofold. I thought I could make a quick buck on Browns fans eager to buy anything to do with the team, and also I could spend some time with my dad in his later years. Few of us that have moved away from home ever get a real chance to spend any quality time with our parents as they get older. When we visit, everything seems rushed, and most of the time is wasted in talking about the weather or sports or local neighborhood gossip. This was going to be our chance to just hang out, without the pressures of time or careers or family. The timing worked out well, as my career had pretty much stalled, and I was anxious for a midlife crisis. I was about to turn forty, and my marriage had been on the rocks for about ten years. Getting back to Cleveland seemed like a perfectly natural thing to do.

I had been a writer for *U.S. News & World Report* since 1993, based in Fort Worth, Texas, covering whatever came along, a generalist if there ever was one. Covers on billionaire moguls one week, briefs on crime stories the next. I had worked my way up from nothing—no training in journalism schools, no internships, just a succession of jobs and firings, always using freelance writing to make an end run on the Ivy League writing establishment. What I brought to the business was my ability to see things a bit differently, a bit more obtuse than the average spare writer; mostly I broke the rules because I didn't know them. As I broke more rules—and by that I mean not following the pack mentality of my business—I found myself being sucked up into a meaningful career path. I never felt that I had much to do with it, though. I did good work when I failed and good work when I was thought of as a fine writer. Timing and luck had everything to do with it.

In the course of my career, I managed to find myself at three tragic events of the 1990s: the Branch Davidians at Waco, the Oklahoma City bombing, and the massacre at Columbine High School. It has been said that journalists are essentially tourists at other people's tragedies, a truism if there ever was one. Along with the rest of the media pack, I would parachute into each of these terrible events, gather the necessary facts and sources, write the best account I could under the circumstances, and then move on to the next tragic event. It was easy to become callous toward the work, but there were emotional moments. In Oklahoma City a man in his fifties, a rough-and-tumble oil worker with steely forearms, cried in my arms as he talked about his dead two-year-old granddaughter. When I told him I was going to call my three-year-old daughter in Texas, he asked if he could talk to her. He told me he just wanted to hear a child's voice.

But at Columbine High School, in April, I became unraveled by it all. Fresh off the news that my father had inoperable cancer,

I was in no mood for anything when I made my way to Denver. In the few years I had been in journalism, the entire landscape had changed. There were more satellite trucks, more TV talk shows, more live stand-ups than Waco or Oklahoma City ever had. On the lawn at the high school, journalists far outnumbered sources. Still and video photographers were pushing into kids' faces, trying to get that one good shot of fresh-faced teenagers crying on each other's shoulders. One kid complained to me that he had unwittingly become part of a logo for MSNBC.

There was just too much at Columbine. It wasn't even that the tabloids were trawling for interviews with thousand-dollar deals. It wasn't just the fact that Katie Couric was talking to the father of one of the dead kids, holding his hand and sobbing. It wasn't that a TV station from Tulsa was going live from the high school lawn and then kicking it back to the weatherman in the studio back in Oklahoma. It wasn't that every news organization had begun the blame game, trying to find a "villain" in this horrible event, when in fact there were two—Eric Harris and Dylan Klebold—right before their eyes. It wasn't Dan Rather giving his wistful look on cue. What happened at Columbine more so than at the other disasters-of-the-week was that the community became overrun with us media types at the same time they were trying to come to grips with their tragedy. Were you in Klebold's bowling class? What was he like? What was his average? Did he have any pets? Was he really evil? Who was his girlfriend? I felt as if I were doing research for Jerry Springer.

I began to feel that I was indeed the intentional tourist at the latest tragedy. And we in the media became much like the dog in the old joke who licks his balls. Why did the thousand-member media horde descend upon Littleton? Because they could.

I spoke to my dad from my hotel near the high school on one

of those nights. He loved to live vicariously through me in these circumstances, proudly telling his friends that I was in the middle of it all, watching press conferences on TV to see if he could get a glimpse of me. I think some smug high school kid who had already cut a deal with ABC had just turned me down for an interview. Even though I felt for the kids in that school, some of them were becoming too slick in their dealings with the media. The whole experience was turning my stomach. I called my dad just to chat, but he could tell I wasn't too happy with what was going on.

"What's the problem?" he said after a few minutes of small talk.

"I really don't know why I am here," I answered. I complained that I was on the low rung of the pecking order. *Time* and *Newsweek* were better known than *U.S. News,* and besides, this was very much a TV story. Hell, even the local media guys had more clout. And wasn't everyone missing the obvious?

"Why does everyone look for so much greater meaning in these things?" I complained to him. "Every single story like this becomes some greater national self-examination process. *Time* will probably have an essay that this whole event marks the end of some era. As if the national psyche has been permanently scarred and everyone who ever met these two guys could have done something to prevent it. Maybe two fuckheads decided to shoot up their school and that's the end of it. Everyone here wants to assign blame. The gun nuts. Permissive society. Bad schools. Sometimes shit and death just happens."

"Shit and death" was another one of our code phrases. John Irving used it in his novel *The Hotel New Hampshire* to describe the school colors of the Dairy School: brown and gray. In Cleveland those were the colors of the Cuyahoga River and the sky from November through March. Shit and death. That's what life boiled down to sometimes. And that's what I saw in Littleton that week. Media overkill. Kids burying friends. Shit and death.

He agreed with the media overkill. "There is so much coverage," he said, "but they don't tell you anything." But he was also a pragmatist, and a father who was not shy about offering advice. "Just get back to work," he told me. (It reminded me of the advice he gave me in high school when the priests at St. Ignatius found out I was skipping mass to get high with my friends in the alleys around school. "Just go to fucking church," he told me after our meeting with the assistant principal.)

"So when are you coming to Cleveland?" he asked, changing the subject.

"Speaking of shit and death," I responded. I told him I had arranged for a leave of absence from *U.S. News* and would be there in June. But I needed to talk to him about something.

"You know how this book is supposed to be about the Browns?" I asked. "Well, I think it's changed—I mean the focus of it all."

"How so?"

"Well, it's turning out that the book will be about us, you dying and all. My editor thinks that mixing in the football with personal experience from our relationship—you know, about how sports and shit bind together fathers and sons—how that might be a good read. You know, football, drinking, and death. That sort of thing."

"Football, drinking, and death. I think I know where I fit in. What do you need me to do?"

"Well, I thought we could tape some conversations over the summer, try to figure out who we are—that sort of stuff. Maybe watch some football. Basically I want you to help me write this book."

I knew this would hook him. He was perhaps the best-read man I had known, an expert on Shakespeare, Thomas Wolfe, Hemingway. He even claimed to have understood most of James Joyce's *Finnegans Wake*.

"Have you spoken to your brothers and sisters about this?"

I told him I had, approaching each of my five siblings and getting their reservations or approval. All said they were fine with it, as long as it didn't turn into a circus.

"I don't know how to ask this," I proceeded carefully, "but how long do you have?" He had been evasive about his prognosis from the beginning, saying he had a year or two, but I knew it was less. You don't get opened up and closed right away, with a shit bag on top of it, if you're going to last awhile.

"I'll be dead before the year is out," he said without emotion.

"I guess that means that you'll never see the book published," I told him. "You can say anything you want."

"You mean I can trash people and not have to worry about it?" He laughed. "Count me in. By the way, what's good for you?"

"Whatya mean?"

"I mean, what's good for the book? What's the best time for me to die?" He gave a little chuckle, letting me know he was going to have fun with this project.

"Well, sometime after Thanksgiving would be good, enough time for us to talk and see the Browns play."

"I'll do my best."

We made our way from his condo, our own little two-car funeral procession, my dad and I, minus the lights and purple flags. The destination was the Hospice of the Western Reserve, a health care facility in the former Marianist Brothers residence at St. Joseph's High School. The hospice was right on the lake, next to the football field where we played as kids, encircled by the cinder track where I ran the half-mile and bordered on the other side by the St. Joe's gym, where my dad coached us in CYO (Catholic Youth Organization) basketball. The hospice was also next to Euclid General Hospital, where my mom worked as a nurse and where I was born.

It was right in the middle of the neighborhood where we grew up, sitting at the junction of East 185th Street and Lake Erie, and it seemed appropriate that my dad was coming home. When we were kids, and later as adults, East 185th was the center of our lives. Running through an ethnic neighborhood dominated by Eastern European immigrants—Slovenians, Croatians, and Lithuanians mostly—the street was a mishmash of meat markets, bakeries, and most important, bars. A rite of passage in our neighborhood was "the crawl," which consisted of knocking down a shot and a beer in each of the twenty or so bars and bowling alleys that lined East 185th in the two miles or so between Interstate 90 on the south and Lake Erie on the north.

As we drove down East 185th, I couldn't help but feel a part of my life gushing within me and settling uncomfortably in my soul. He was the one who was dying, but my life was flashing before my eyes. We passed Muldoon's Saloon, which used to be called the Dugout, where we drank illegally before softball games on Sunday mornings. Past the Horseshoe Bar, one of the best punch palaces in history, a place where I got in a fight with some Italian boys from Collinwood when I was eighteen. Past the Triple Crown Lounge, once called the Two-Cro's Tavern, named not for birds but for the two Croatians who owned the place. A friend of mine got busted for selling cocaine in that place.

Down past Oliver Hazard Perry Elementary School, where I went to kindergarten under the guidance of Miss Kimmack. Down past Fritz's, now called Uncle John's, once the joint with the best Friday fish fry.

On we went, past Chervin Wallpaper and Paint, where my brother got me a job sweeping the floors when I was a sophomore in high school. The owners fired me when I flooded their basement and ruined their wallpaper stock. Past Maxim's Pizza, where I would run to on Sunday mornings after church, clutching the two quarters my dad had given me to put in the collection plate at Holy Cross Catholic Church. The choice between pizza or baseball cards and missionaries in Central America seemed like an easy decision. Past the Lasalle Theater, now closed, where I saw my first movie, *The Night of the Grizzly,* in which a Gabby Hayes–type character got mauled by some menacing bear. Past Flynt's Lasalle Tavern, now called Magoo's, but back then owned by the Flynt firefighter brothers, and the scene of great political arguments with the Hurley clan. Down past Setina's Meats, one of the best places for Slovenian sausage in the neighborhood, now boarded up with plywood. Jackshaw Chevrolet, since sold, where everyone in the neighborhood bought their cars. McGarry's Bowling Alley, the Village Bar, Telich Insurance, all businesses that sponsored our Little League teams.

East 185th was a bit tacky, but it was my favorite place in Cleveland. It still operated on the premise that every bar had its own clientele, no matter how similar all the joints were. If you frequented Muldoon's, you saw the same people; ditto the Village. Not that there was any real difference in any of them. But a man could define himself in many ways, and if you grew up around 185th Street, you defined yourself by what saloon stool you chose to sit on at least four nights a week.

My cell phone rang. It was a guy we nicknamed Lance Romance. I had met him in some bar on 185th, in the early 1980s. Lance had grown up in Orwell, about an hour east of Cleveland, and had moved to Cleveland in his teens to get away from "Hooterville," as he liked to call his hometown. We called him Lance Romance because he was always trying to pick up as many chicks as possible. Shortly after we met, we rented a place called the Backhouse, a three-bedroom flophouse downtown that was behind a bar and down the street from a fully functioning whorehouse. Rent for the place was eighty-five dollars a month. Our main occupation in those days was going to rock concerts, getting laid, and selling decent quantities of cocaine and marijuana. I say that not to brag or feel bad about it; it was just what we did.

"What are you doing, man?" he boomed. He liked to yell into the phone, talking quickly and without pauses, generally taking control. As he talked, I realized we were supposed to go to the Browns game that night in Canton. After three years of having no pro football due to Art Modell's little rape act on the fans of Cleveland, the city was finally getting its football team back this night. The Browns were playing the Dallas Cowboys in the Hall of Fame game, a national audience from ABC's *Monday Night Football* would watch, and all the Cleveland media were gushing about the wonder of it all. I had two media passes, and Lance and I had decided to make a road trip of it.

"I'm on 185th Street," I told him.

"What bar are you in front of?"

"Just passed some new place called Maglio's. I think it used to be called Someplace Else. Not sure what it was before that."

"I don't think I ever got drunk there," he said. "Very odd, for 185th Street."

"I don't know if I'll be able to make it tonight. My dad is in an ambulance and I'm taking him to the hospice."

"How's he doing?" Lance asked.

"Pretty much circling the drain."

"That's pretty harsh, my friend. Is everything okay?"

"Well, some people think he's going to pull out of this, but I don't expect him to last the week. I get through by expecting the worst, dealing with it that way. But he's in pretty good spirits. He knows what's going on, even though he's pretty jacked up on morphine."

"I remember when your dad found me down in your basement banging that chick at the bottom of the stairs." Lance laughed. "Kicked me out of the house and stole my beer."

"Whenever he told the story, he always said he waited until you were finished before coming downstairs. He said he waited about two minutes, which was about one minute longer than you needed."

"Your dad always could tell a story, even if there wasn't much truth in it," Lance said. "The great Dick McGraw, Irish storyteller."

"That's where I get it from, son."

"So you're not going to the game. Any chance I can get the passes from you?" Leave it to Lance to get to the heart of the matter.

"I don't think I'm going to make it back to my house to get the passes. I've got to stay here until my brother gets over to the hospice, and I thought I'd maybe see if my dad wanted to watch a bit of it on TV."

"Let me know if you need anything," he said. "I'll be down at the Tree House later if you want to get a beer. Call me if you're up for some drinking later."

"Sounds like a plan."

I hung up the phone as we drove into the hospice parking lot. My dad was still smiling as they wheeled him out of the ambulance, and we made our way to his room. The hospice was a cheery place, decorated in mauves and muted greens, rather new and fresh, and it neither looked nor smelled like death. In fact, it had an antiseptic quality to it, but not in a fake way. It was the first time I had been inside, but I was satisfied with the accommodations. In the center section was a lounge with a piano and comfortable-looking furniture, with four wings in a cross-pattern coming off the center. My dad had been to the hospice several times before, and he liked it there. Unlike the staff at the hospitals he had been in, the hospice staff treated him like an adult. There was none of that singsong condescending chatter that nurses in hospitals use to make life easier on them. The hospice was a place to die, and the staff asked the patients what they wanted and gave it to them.

A few orderlies moved him into his bed and asked me to leave for a few minutes. The first thing they had to do was clean him up, change that awful bag, and sort out his medicine. When I came back in, the smell was so bad that we had to open up the doors of his room to the patio outside. They had put a diaper on him so that he needn't get up from his bed to piss. Pissing for him had become a major routine in the past week. My brothers and I had to hold him up while we held a bottle for him. With his kidneys failing, though, he could usually just squeeze out a few drops.

He was comfortable and his eyes were rolled back in his head. They took him off all of his other medicine except for the morphine. He had wanted to die as painless a death as possible. He was where he wanted to be. I tried to get him to eat some lunch, but he pushed all the food away. He didn't have to say, "Enough." He fell asleep quickly, resting comfortably, his mouth agape, the smile gone.

After sitting with him for about an hour, I walked outside and stood on the cliff facing Lake Erie. My earliest memories in life were about being tossed in the lake by my mother. She was a strong swimmer who believed the best way to teach a child was to toss him in water at around age two and let the waves wash him back to shore. She taught all of us six kids the same way, just around the time we learned how to walk. Tossed us in. Sink or swim.

Lake Erie held a certain comfort for me. When I was three or four, we would gather rocks from the beach and paint them, giving them to my father as paperweights for his office. He kept dozens of them through the years, rocks that would sit on the bookshelf behind his desk, even after we were all grown. He used to joke that the stiff breezes in his office necessitated a complicated paperweight system to keep his law practice going.

The lake was filthy when I was a kid in the sixties. We lived about two miles east of the sewage treatment plant. I remember being about six years old, standing on the T-pier over at Beachland Park, wanting to swim but looking into water that was the color of coffee with cream. Raw sewage floating by. Down near my feet was a sheep's head floating, a lamprey eel sucking out its insides.

When my mom died from Hodgkin's disease—I was fifteen at the time—I left the house and made my way to the beach, crying and thrashing and throwing driftwood around. Within a short time I felt a certain peace that I had never felt before. There was a calming effect in the sound of the waves on the pebbled beaches, the smell of dead fish and alga blooms, seagulls flying overhead, freighters on the horizon, seaweed clinging to the piers. But what I found most interesting about Lake Erie was how it generated nothing on its own, but reflected everything around it. In November when the skies were gray, Lake Erie was also gray, and the piercing wind whipped up the waves and cut right through your heart. In the summer, when the skies were blue and the wind gentle, Lake Erie was peaceful and bright blue, too, sailboats moving on the horizon and kids finding smooth stones to skip across the calm waters.

As I stood on the cliff behind the hospice, I looked on the horizon to one lone freighter making its way to port in Cleveland ten miles to the west, probably dropping off some iron ore or coal for the steel mills. The sun was dead in the sky toward the west, the lake bright blue, with a shine and shimmer on each wave. The winds were from the south, fairly strong in the late afternoon, and the gusts were hitting the waves coming from the northwest, stalling them on the way to the shore. The waves were two or three feet about a hundred feet out, but the closer to shore they got, the smaller they were, dying as they got to a viscous black alga bloom near shore. The waves away from shore seemed to be bobbing up and down without much direction. Lake Erie looked as if it were boiling.

I turned my back to it. There was Euclid General Hospital a hundred yards to the east, where my father first held me. There was the football field, where the St. Joe's team was practicing—actually they were now Villa Angela–St. Joseph's, the result of a merger with the girls' school down the road. Just beyond the goalposts was the gym, where we spent all day Saturday playing basketball in the CYO leagues. I finished fourth in the city in the half-mile on the cinder track surrounding the field. It was now overgrown with weeds.

It is in these moments that we expect some comfort, an epiphany of feeling that might wash over us and bring us back to shore. I felt none of that as I stood there. I was numb. For all of the brave faces and jokes my family and I had used to avoid what was going to happen, I found myself ill prepared for the endgame. My father was my hero. He was also my nemesis. He was an over-powering figure in my life; virtually every major decision I had ever made came with the baggage of what my father might think. He could disarm you with his humor, but his wit often had a meanness to it that would cut right through you. He was a man I loved most of my life, but there were many times I hated him.

When I came back to his room from my lakefront repast, he was still lying in the bed, jacked up on morphine, his breathing irregular. His eyes were closed, but he was not sleeping. Just as his organs and body systems were failing one by one, so, too, was his consciousness, his personality. Just a few hours before, he had that smirk, that defiant expression I loved. When I went back in to see him, he had none of that. I had always derived a lot of my happiness from him when I needed to—shallow happiness included—but now there was little. The man who was my father was slipping away—literally and figuratively—and there was nothing anyone could do.

Nearly everyone was there. My brothers, Mark and Brian, were at his bedside. My dad's baby, Mary Margaret, now thirty-two, was holding his hand. Grandchildren were held over his bed so he could kiss them. My sisters Sheila and Kathleen were making their way up from Columbus. My stepmother, Theresa, and many of her kids were there, too. But I always hated so much family around. I had to get away; I had had enough. I needed a drink.

My brother Mark owns a bar about a mile down Lake Shore Boulevard from the hospice, a bar named Mark's Time-Out Grille. Mark had bought the Time-Out about five years earlier and turned a dead old-man's joint into a place that was packed on most evenings. It was a place that was a little rough around the edges by some people's standards, but for me it was perfect—twenty TVs, great pizza, cheap beer, and a number of good Cleveland characters that were always fun to talk to.

I made my way to the Time-Out from the hospice, not knowing if I just needed a drink, if I needed to get away, or if I needed to talk with friendly strangers. The place was packed. At the bar were the usual guys: Jocko, Racist Ed, Joanie the Cop, Horst, TC the Bookie, Lithuanian A1, Ralph the Fishman, and assorted others. I settled on a stool between Max, who owned an upholstering company, and Crowley, who lived above the bar and worked for my brother as a handyman, mopping floors and cleaning toilets and such.

"I heard your dad's not doing very well." Max was a burly Croatian, a few years younger than my father, but on this day he looked about twenty years younger. He drank Miller in bottles, usually settling in every day about 6 P.M. and leaving by nine.

"Things don't look good, Max. Clock's running down."

"That's too bad. I always liked your dad."

My dad had come into the bar often before he got real sick, before the shit bag had kept him at home, and the regulars knew him pretty well. "Hey, Sheila, get Danny a beer."

Crowley also offered condolences, although it was hard to understand him. He was a slight, wiry man, always sitting at the barstool farthest from the door. By this time, Crowley had been drinking for a few hours, the cheap Canadian whisky and ginger ale that he favored. Crowley, who was also a few years younger than my dad but looked twenty years older, operated on the three-and-nine rule. If you caught him somewhere between his third and ninth drinks of the night, he was quite charming and coherent; before that he was sullen; afterward, unintelligible. He also smoked a couple packs of Marlboro Lights every day, and by evening, nearly every sentence was interrupted by violent hacking. But Crowley was among the most likable creatures of my brother's bar. "I may be a drunk," he once told me, "but I'm not an asshole." If only more people could be so accurate in their self-assessments.

When I was halfway into my twenty-three-ounce Bud Light draft, another came forward. "That's on Crowley," Sheila told me. Crowley held up his drink, proclaimed something unintelligible, though most likely witty and appropriate, then hacked and went to the men's room.

I sat there for a few hours, talked football with Max, listened to Crowley hack and wheeze, and drank as much beer as I could. Just about everyone in the bar was dressed in brown and orange, waiting for the Hall of Fame game that night and the return of the Browns. For three and a half years these people had protested and wailed. They had paid for a $300-million new stadium—

mostly from a tax on booze and cigarettes, which for Clevelanders is akin to putting a tax on mother's milk. But even though
these blue-collar fans were paying for a stadium that most would
never be able to afford to get into, it seemed not to matter. When
the Browns kicked off to the Cowboys just after 8 P.M., everyone
in my brother's bar stood and cheered. Football was back in
Cleveland. The city had done the impossible. They had brought
the Browns back from the dead.

I made it back to the hospice during the second quarter. My dad
was sitting up in bed watching the game. There were about six
people in the room, and it looked a little like the old days, like a
typical Sunday afternoon at the McGraw house. In our world, life
would generally stop when the Browns were on TV, and though
my dad was not what you would call a fanatic about the Browns,
he would rarely miss a game. He had seen the greats play: Otto
Graham, Marion Motley, Jim Brown, Paul Warfield. And he had
watched the Browns lose in every way possible, from Brian Sipe's
interception in the frozen 1980 play-off game, to John Elway's
improbable drive in the 1984 AFC championship game. He had
seen the Browns when they were great, he had seen them when
they sucked, and like most Clevelanders, he always came back for
more. It was almost like it was in our bloodline. As familiar as the
steel mills and the desperate winters. As familiar as the waves
crashing on the lake. As familiar as sheep heads and lamprey eels.
    Halfway through the second quarter, rookie quarterback Tim
Couch came into the game. The heralded passer from the University of Kentucky was the first overall pick in the college draft
by the new Browns and was generally thought of as the man who

would bring football glory back to Cleveland. Most people at my brother's bar wondered if Couch had the intelligence to lead the team. After all, he was a hillbilly in their eyes, and hillbillies ranked just above blacks in the reverse pecking order of Cleveland life. But after missing his first pass, Couch completed ten in a row against the Cowboys. I mentioned to my dad that Couch looked pretty bad during practices at training camp, but that he seemed to play better when the pressure was on. A little like Otto Graham, I nudged.

My dad rolled his eyes. "He looks good," he whispered in a barely audible voice.

And that was about it. By halftime my dad was back in his semiconscious state, and I decided it was time to call it a night from hospice duty. My brother Brian, the oldest boy in our family and a lawyer like my father, would spend the night. I had the next night, my sister Kathleen the one after, and brother Mark the night after that.

Before I left, I wandered around and found a little chapel that faced out on Lake Erie. I wasn't really the religious type anymore, regarding most of the Catholic religion I was raised in as little more than complex fairy tales. We had gone round and round on this through the years, my dad and I, never really coming to any sort of understanding why he believed so strongly and I so little. The part I never understood was how such a learned man, a man who studied philosophy and art and literature, could believe in such concepts as the Virgin Mary and purgatory and angels and such. He never quite understood how I could reject the faith that had been passed down in our clan for a thousand years.

I thought little of our disparity when I entered, though. There was an altar in front of a picture window that was filled with Lake Erie. I felt tears well up in my eyes as I thought about him down the hall, making his peace and moving on his journey. I was going to miss him terribly. The lights from a few freighters shone like beacons on the horizon, the moon highlighting the waves as they made their way to shore. I was crying pretty hard now, but I didn't really know why. I knew my dad was dying, and I knew I should be upset. But we had talked about this in that intellectual way we conversed, sure of ourselves, how we knew what was coming. My dad had talked about his own death in such matter-of-fact terms that I felt I was prepared for its inevitability. I knew now that I wasn't.

On the altar by the window was a guest book. There were notes in it, nearly exclusively from family members who wanted to write something after their loved one had died. Most were the garden-variety "Grandma's now in heaven" type of note, but one caught my eye. It was dated July 28, 1999, and was written in a messy handwriting I was very familiar with.

> *I am a patient—praying naturally only for myself, but this altar-by-the-sea has inspired me to pray for others. Please love them, God. Please love and understand all those who descended with me and from me, and all those who will descend with me and from me. Whoa!! This is becoming complex! In short, I pray for all—known or unknown—that my life has or will touch. Also, for a little help in sentence structure, spelling and syntax.*

It was signed "Richard J. McGraw—Age 69." As a postscript, he had written, "And especially for Aristotle," which I found out later was his pet name for my stepmother, Theresa (as in "Who do you think you are—Aristotle?" when she would try to do things like balance the checkbook).

And just like that, a broad smile came to my face. Here he was, suffering through painful cancer, confused on morphine, but still writing something that was inspirational. He was praying for himself, praying for others, and he was concerned about his wife. And hey, who couldn't use a little help with sentence structure, spelling, and syntax?

As I left the chapel, I felt a smile on my face that bordered on shallowness, the good kind. I was about to head back to my brother's bar for a few more pops when I noticed a little gold plaque on the wall near the door. The inscription read, "This chapel is a gift from Mr. and Mrs. Arthur B. Modell."

Thanks, Art. Maybe you aren't such a creep after all.

# CHAPTER TWO

# Sunday Afternoons

The carpet in our living room was bright green. I vividly remember that little detail because I spent fall and winter Sunday afternoons lying on my stomach on the floor, my chin in my hands, with elbows propping up my head, all the better to hear every word coming from the speakers of our Magnavox hi-fi console. My brother Brian, two years older, lay next to me, our legs tangled together as we jockeyed for position to get our feet closer to the furnace grate, the only source of warmth in our old drafty house.

On one of these Sundays, two days after Christmas, I don't recall being aware of a tree or new presents or holiday decorations. The only thing on my five-year-old mind on that cold and windy afternoon was the game on the radio, the 1964 NFL championship between the Cleveland Browns and the Baltimore Colts. And as I watched my father pace the living room, hanging on every word of play-by-play man Ken Coleman's frenzied commentary, I knew this Sunday afternoon was different. This was serious business, this championship game, and I could tell it was serious because my father was gleeful and somber and agitated, all at the same time. So I acted serious, too, keeping quiet, listening, getting excited only when he got excited. In all my five-year-old seriousness, I kept my mouth shut, put a weighty scowl on my game face, and tried to image the game at Municipal Stadium.

My dad would get up from his chair, move to the window, sit back down, get up again and fiddle with the volume or the AM tuner, clap occasionally, and then do it all over again. As the game went on, he would look down at my brother and me on the floor and say, "I think we're going to win this one, boys, I think we're going to do it." Then he would pace some more, lean on the mantel over the fireplace, throw his arms up in frustration, and then pace some more.

I was aware of the Browns at this age, though I didn't know much about them aside from the fact that they were "our" team. When we played football at our park down by the lake, Brian would pretend he was running back Jim Brown; our neighbor across the street, Jeff Ross, would be quarterback Frank Ryan; Michael Burger would be wide receiver Gary Collins. On defense, they would change their names to Dick Modzelewski or Ross Fichtner or Jim Kanicki. Whoever kicked off was Lou "the Toe" Groza. I was too young to pretend I was anyone good. The older guys took all the star players. I was the classic tagalong for my older brother, and the only way he and his friends would let me play was by being the center for both teams, snapping the ball between my legs and then getting out of the way. Still, I imagined myself as being one of the Cleveland Browns, just like my brother. When I came home after playing one day, I asked my dad who was the center for the Browns. He told me John Morrow. From then on, I was number 56, John Morrow.

The Colts were strong favorites to run the Browns into Lake Erie that day. On their roster were six future pro football Hall of Famers: Johnny Unitas, John Mackey, Lenny Moore, Gino Marchetti, Raymond Berry, and Jim Parker. Don Shula, who was born in nearby Painesville and had played football at John Carroll University in Cleveland, now coached the Colts. Years before,

Shula had played for the Browns under legendary coach Paul Brown from 1951 to 1955. Colt quarterback Johnny Unitas was the 1964 NFL MVP, and Shula, in his thirties and the youngest head coach in the league, had been voted Coach of the Year.

The Browns, on the other hand, had just four future Hall of Famers: Jim Brown, Paul Warfield, Leroy Kelly, and Groza. The Browns were quarterbacked by journeyman Frank Ryan, who at the time was studying for his Ph.D. in mathematics at Rice University. They were coached by sixty-five-year-old Blanton Collier, a mild-mannered man with horn-rimmed glasses. In the unenviable position of having to replace Paul Brown, the legend, just the year before, Collier was widely respected as a student of football, a soft-spoken gentleman from Kentucky who looked and acted like a grandfather. He was partially deaf, and could only understand the players and coaches on the Browns by reading their lips.

With an old codger as coach and at the mercy of one of history's finest quarterbacks, no one expected the Browns to give the Colts much of a game. Edwin "Bud" Shrake of *Sports Illustrated* cut to the quick: "It is yawningly conceded that the Eastern Conference champion Cleveland will be playing merely for the dubious pleasure of being thrashed by Baltimore on December 27. . . . To be realistic about it, the championship game of 1964 has already been played. Baltimore won it in October by beating Green Bay."

This was championship football before the games had Roman numerals and before they became national holidays. It was simple in those days: the winner of the Eastern Conference played the winner of the Western Conference. No wild card play-offs, no washed-up singers performing at halftime, no four-hour-long pregame shows. In fact, the TV broadcast was blacked out in

Cleveland. Even though the Browns had 130,000 ticket requests for the 80,000-seat Municipal Stadium, owner Art Modell refused to lift the blackout, reasoning that offering the game on free broadcast TV would somehow be unfair to the fans who had made it into the stadium. Sportswriters at the time theorized that Modell just wanted to sell standing-room-only tickets. Looking back now, it is easy to see how Modell's cavalier treatment of Browns fans on the championship Sunday in 1964 was a precursor of events that would unfold thirty years later. Insidious as it sounds, the only people in the country unable to watch the Browns and the Colts on TV in 1964 were the people living within seventy-five miles of Cleveland.

But I knew nothing about those things at the time. I was doing my best to be a Browns fan just like my father. I was listening intently to the game, hoping to hear my man John Morrow do something wonderful. But, then and now, centers do not make plays we hear about on the radio, aside from the occasional holding call or fumbled snap. Morrow must have played well that day, because I do not remember hearing his name.

It was a windy and cold day down at the stadium, and neither team scored in the first half, adding to uneasiness in our living room. My dad had ordered my mother to have dinner on the table during halftime. On game days my mother—like most Cleveland housewives of the era—would time Sunday dinner around the game, guessing as to when halftime might actually occur. But given the uncertainties of the clock in pro football, dinner was usually a little late or a little early, depending on time-outs, two-minute drills, and the like. Being a little late or a little early might lead to some arguing or cold stares, which would intensify if the Browns were losing. I am still amazed that my mother was able to coordinate the halftime scramble, as she knew nothing about football and my dad knew nothing about preparing a meal.

We ate in silence, quickly shoving the food in our mouths, and then the males in the family retook their positions in the living room (my sisters and my mother were either uninvited or uninterested). Quickly the game changed. Groza, then the oldest player in the NFL at age forty-three, kicked a forty-three-yard field goal early in the third quarter. My dad looked down at Brian and me on the floor and said with certainty, "Here we go, boys." And he was right. The next time the Browns got the ball, Jim Brown ran for forty-six yards and then Ryan hit Collins with a perfect TD pass on a post pattern. My dad was now jumping in the air. The Browns then forced the Colts to punt, and on their next possession, Ryan hit Collins again, this time with a forty-three-yard TD pass. Suddenly we were winning, 17–0.

In the fourth quarter Ryan and Collins hooked up for the third time. Groza hit a meaningless field goal near the end of the game for a final score of 27–0. And as the clock ticked off the final seconds, my dad was running around the room, jumping around, with an insane grin on his face—certainly shallow happiness in its most passionate form. Brian and I jumped around, too. We were now indoctrinated. This was certainly the way men acted when their team won a championship. We then tackled each other and fell to the floor, but before we broke anything, my father shooed us outside. Other kids were gathering in the street, having just experienced the same living room drama.

We tossed the football around. Kids were imitating Gary Collins running the post pattern; my brother Brian ran over guys like he was Jim Brown. I was still the center, still John Morrow, but now I was the center for the world champion Cleveland Browns. We played until our parents called us home from their front porches. And as we lay in our beds that night, Brian and I talked about every aspect of the game, replaying in our minds what we thought it looked like down at the stadium. How Gary Collins must have jumped in front of the goalposts. How Jimmy Brown was running over Gino Marchetti. How Lou the Toe would hike up his pants over his gut before knocking one through the uprights.

We didn't know it at the time, but we would never feel this way again. The 1964 Browns championship would be the last title any of us in Cleveland would celebrate in any major sport. Never again would the words "Cleveland Browns" and "world champions" be used in the same sentence. We would get close, for sure, but I would never again see my father as joyful as he was on that Sunday. We wouldn't even make it to the Super Bowl. Just shit and death and plenty of it. And plenty of Art Modell.

There is a scene in the movie *City Slickers* where the Daniel Stern character talks about how he and his father went through many rough times, times when they could barely speak to each other without fighting, but how baseball brought them together. There must be something in the male chromosome structure that allows us to yell and scream and beat each other up one minute, then calmly discuss a ballplayer's batting average or the merits of the prevent defense the next. My father and I were that way. We fought each other constantly—particularly in my teens and early twenties—but sports were always something we could come back to. And though we enjoyed all sports—basketball was the game we both played with the most skill—football was somehow different. Maybe it was the pomp and circumstance of it all, the momentous occasion each game would become, the weekly buildup to Sunday. I think I was always pulled more strongly to football because it was what we did on Sundays in the fall, as much a part of the day as church and *The Gene Carroll Show*. (Clevelanders remember *The Gene Carroll Show* as an awful amateur-hour variety show with baton twirlers and tap dancers and such. As a family, we would gather every Sunday at noon after church and make fun of the participants.)

My father loved to play catch with us in the backyard. He would be the quarterback, while Brian and I would run our routes. There was the cut-over (five steps down, then a right angle to the left), the post pattern (five steps out, then a diagonal to the left), and the buttonhook (five steps down, then turn around quickly). I loved the buttonhook, because my father always threw the ball a split second before I turned. To catch the ball on a buttonhook pattern, a certain trust factor was needed. The quarterback had to know where the receiver was going to stop, and the receiver had to hope the quarterback didn't throw the ball too early. I used to love to turn around and have the ball right there in my gut, sometimes knocking the wind out of me as I clutched it in my stomach.

We loved playing football, and we loved playing because we were Browns fans. It was a part of life, something that was not of your choosing. My father used to joke that he only belonged to two organizations in his life, and he was born into both of them: the Roman Catholic Church and the Democratic Party. He might as well have added Cleveland Browns fan. It has been said that the first words that a child from Cleveland learns upon emerging from the womb are "Pittsburgh sucks."

My dad had been watching the Browns since they first formed in 1946, winning their first All-American Football Conference championship that year. At the time, Cleveland had an NFL team, too, the Cleveland Rams. The Rams had a great quarterback in Bob Waterfield and actually won the NFL championship in 1945. But the NFL then was hardly what it is today. Football was a college game. In fact, when my father was in high school at Cathedral Latin School in 1946, their team drew 60,000 fans at Municipal Stadium for a game against Massillon High School. The Rams generally drew a third of that, playing in smaller venues around Cleveland and struggling to make ends meet. My father recalled seeing the Rams play at Shaw High in East Cleveland.

The Rams decided to move to greener pastures in Los Angeles after the 1945 season, mainly because the new Browns franchise had locked up Municipal Stadium for their games. Few in Cleveland cared. "I can't remember anyone really that upset when the Rams left," my dad recalled. "Not like it was when Modell moved the team. Everyone knew that the Browns were being put together and that Paul Brown would be the coach. Brown was a hometown guy and already a Cleveland legend."

The Browns were part of the newly formed All-American Football Conference, an upstart league ready to challenge the NFL. Paul Brown, who had coached at nearby Massillon High School and Ohio State, was such a Cleveland presence that they named the team after him. And he proceeded to create a powerhouse, signing players from his coaching days who were still serving in the military during World War II—heroes like quarterback Otto Graham, fullback Marion Motley, kicker Groza, receiver Dante Lavelli, and defensive lineman Bill Willis. Willis and Motley were black, superior athletes, and Brown took advantage of other coaches' prejudice to field the best players he could find. He was the first in pro football to consistently use black players on a pro football team. Brown was a winner and he knew better than anyone that a football player is a football player, no matter what color his skin.

Brown is best known today for his innovations to the game. He invented the face mask. He developed a complicated playbook—unheard-of at the time—and made his players study film of their opponents. He was the first to send in plays from the sideline, developing his "messenger guard" rotation of linemen who would ferry in the plays. He started what was later to be called the "taxi squad," a group of five players that practiced with the team but were not permanent members of the official roster. They were kept on the payroll of the local taxi company, whose owner—Mickey McBride—coincidentally owned the Browns.

The Browns won four titles in four years while in the AAFC, including an undefeated season in 1948. When they joined the NFL in 1950, they opened the season by beating the reigning NFL champion Philadelphia Eagles. They closed the season by beating the Los Angeles Rams for the NFL title. Football fans now don't realize what an achievement the 1950 season actually was. It was as if an expansion team had come in and won the NFL title. Or as if the Oakland Raiders had beaten the Green Bay Packers in the first Super Bowl. In many people's eyes it was a bigger upset than when Broadway Joe Namath's Jets hammered the Colts in Super Bowl III.

"The NFL at the time dismissed the Browns as a trap and pass team," my father said. "They would run traps for Motley and Graham and then throw the ball long to Lavelli and Mac Speedie. The NFL thought they were a gimmick. But what they were was the best team in the country. And after the Browns came into the NFL, everyone became a pass and trap team. Most of them still are."

In all, the Browns appeared in the NFL championship game every year from 1950 to 1955. Counting their four AAFC titles, the Browns won seven titles from 1946 to 1955. The fans of Cleveland became used to winning, and my father's generation took pride in the team's achievements. This period coincided with the city of Cleveland reaching its zenith. The factories were humming in postwar America, Cleveland was the sixth largest city in the country, and immigrants from all over the world were coming to Cleveland to work. The city had some balls to it, too. Factory workers forged steel during the week, and then the Browns pounded on their opponents on Sunday. Plenty more where that came from, pal.

Consider the year 1948 in Cleveland, the year my dad graduated from high school. The Cleveland Indians won the World Series. The Browns ran over the rest of the AAFC. The Cleveland Barons, the best minor league hockey team in the country back when the NHL had just six teams, won their league championship. And Cathedral Latin School, my dad's high school, won the city championship in football.

My dad sold scorecards for the Indians that year and just about every game at Municipal Stadium.

"As I look back now, it was probably the best year that Cleveland ever had. The war was over; my brother Howard came back from Europe. The Indians were drawing 80,000 at the stadium. I was graduating from high school. Everything was possible then. You have to realize how hard the Depression hit Cleveland, and then the war. No one talked about Cleveland then like they do now. We were one of the best cities in the country."

I asked him about the games back then—what it was like to go to the World Series. "I was digging ditches for the electric company during the World Series," he began incredulously. "I had to make money for college. It wasn't like it is now where the whole city stops because of a sporting event. We were digging holes for utility poles on Ninth Street, building the infrastructure of the city. Sure, we would sneak into a bar once in a while to watch the games on TV. But the TVs were only about a foot wide back then, and we couldn't really see anything. Our foreman would catch on and chase us back outside. But no one thought anything of having to work. That's what you did back then.

"I went to just about every Sunday Browns game, though," he continued. "The tickets were only fifty cents, and if we told them we were seventeen, we got in for a quarter. The bleachers were where a lot of the blacks sat, and we joined them there because it was cheap. When they would kick a field goal or an extra point, the ball would go right into the bleachers. They didn't have a net like they do now. The radio announcer would say there was a little-boy fight in the bleachers over the ball. But I remember seeing people pulling knives and beating each other senseless trying to get that ball. Most everyone was completely jakey anyway. Drunk and disorderly. I guess some things don't change that much.

"But the Browns back then didn't sell out every game. Most crowds were about 40,000 to 50,000. Pro football was still suffering from the stigma that a bunch of drunks and misfits played it. College players who got a degree wouldn't be caught dead playing pro football. Paul Brown changed that. He made football respectable. But for a long time, the Browns were so good that they had little competition, and looked at pro football as a lower class of competition."

When I was growing up in the 1970s and 1980s, I used to get sick of hearing my dad and his friends talk about 1948. It was Bob Feller and Joe Gordon and Kenny Keltner. Otto Graham and

Marion Motley and Dante Lavelli. It was always '48 this and '48 that, how great life was, the parties they went to, the girls they met. Of course, my dad and his buddies were young then, and life was full of possibilities. For those of my generation, though, possibilities dried up very quickly.

In April 1960, six months after I was born in 1959, the Cleveland Indians traded Rocky Colavito to the Detroit Tigers for Harvey Kuenn. Thus began a downward spiral that didn't see the Indians even contend for a title until the mid-1990s.

In 1961 a thirty-five-year-old advertising executive named Art Modell bought the Browns for $4 million. He fired Paul Brown in 1963, and the team won the championship in 1964 but haven't played in the big game since.

In 1962 the Browns drafted running back Ernie Davis, who had broken all of Jim Brown's records at Syracuse University and won the Heisman Trophy. Davis was diagnosed with leukemia before training camp started and died before the 1963 season.

After the 1965 season, Jim Brown went to London to film *The Dirty Dozen*. The shooting took longer than expected, and Brown missed the start of training camp. Modell threatened to fine Brown $1,500 for each week of training camp he missed. Brown decided to retire instead, ending his career as the greatest running back in NFL history after only nine seasons.

In 1970 Indians All-Star catcher Ray Fosse was flattened by Pete Rose in the All-Star Game during a bam-bam play at the plate. Fosse suffered shoulder injuries and was never the same. Also in 1970 power-hitting first baseman Tony Horton, who had hit twenty-seven homers the previous year, had a nervous break-down in August and never returned to the team.

In 1974 the Indians promoted ten-cent-beer night at the stadium. More than 20,000 people showed up (a large crowd in those days), got completely jakey, stormed the field, and caused the Indians to forfeit the game to the Texas Rangers. At one point, Rangers and Indians players were smashing unruly fans with baseball bats in the outfield.

On January 4, 1981, during a play-off game against the Oakland Raiders, with time running out and the Browns down by 2 and within field goal range, quarterback Brian Sipe tried to throw a touchdown pass to tight end Ozzie Newsome. A Raiders defensive back intercepted, and the play Red Right 88 will live forever in Browns infamy. After the interception, Coach Sam Rutigliano told Sipe, "I love you, Brian." Defensive tackle Lyle Alzado responded, "Fuck that 'I love you' shit. He just cost us a lot of money." Alzado later died of brain cancer.

On January 11, 1987, a week after the Browns won a double-overtime play-off game against the New York Jets, John Elway of the Denver Broncos drove his team ninety-eight yards in the closing minutes to tie the score in the AFC championship game. This is known in Cleveland sports history as "the Drive." The Broncos won in overtime, though replays showed the field goal was wide left. Earlier that season Pro Bowl safety Don Rogers died of a cocaine overdose at his bachelor party.

During the 1987 AFC championship game against the same Broncos, the Browns scored 30 second-half points to bring them within 5 points, 38–33. With time running out, running back Earnest Byner tumbled into the end zone for the apparent game-winning score. He forgot the ball at the 2-yard line. This is known in Cleveland sports history as "the Fumble." The Broncos went to the Super Bowl for the second straight year.

In 1988, in game five of a best-of-five series, Michael Jordan of the Chicago Bulls drained a last-second shot over the outstretched arms of Cleveland Cavaliers guard Craig Ehlo. This is known in Cleveland sports history as "the Shot."

In March of 1993, during spring training, promising Indians pitchers Steve Olin and Tim Crews were killed in a boating accident in Florida.

In 1995, after wrangling with Cleveland city leaders over who would pay for a new stadium, Browns owner Art Modell announced the move to Baltimore. Also in 1995 the Indians made the World Series for the first time since 1954. They lost in six games to the Atlanta Braves.

In 1997 the Indians were two outs away from winning the deciding game seven of the World Series against the Florida Marlins. The Marlins tied the score in the ninth, then went on to win in the eleventh inning, 3–2. This is known in Cleveland sports history as "the Collapse."

In 1999 the Indians were up two games to none in a best-of-five series against the Boston Red Sox. In game three the Indians were ahead 2–0, and Tribe pitcher Dave Burba was working on a shutout in the fifth inning when his arm broke down. The Indians proceeded to lose the game, and then the series, including a 23–7 thrashing in game four.

Those are the highlights of my career as a Cleveland sports fan. I purposely left out all the bad trades (Paul Warfield for draft rights to Mike Phipps), the bad draft choices (remember linebacker Mike Junkin, the mad dog in the meat house), and the truly bizarre (the Indians trading future Hall of Famer Dennis Eckersley because outfielder Rick Manning was having an affair with his wife). I will match this list with any sports fan in the country.

I've rostered this sports fan's nightmare not to elicit sympathy, but to give a frame of reference. Sports are important when we are kids. It's all we really care about, and we carry the memories of our childhood seasons into adulthood. We forge our identity with our city and with our friends, in part on the basis of our shared sporting experiences. And my generation's memories are all about losing and unfulfilled promise. When my father was growing up, Cleveland was a town on the make, a thriving industrial city, with sports teams that embodied the city's blue-collar might. They were winners. When I came of age in the seventies and eighties, the town was a polluted shell of its former glory. The jobs were leaving town in the tens of thousands, and many of Cleveland's citizenry had no choice but to follow them. More important, professional sports' importance to a community is usually inversely proportional to the civic health of a city. When my dad was growing up, the pro sports teams weren't the be-all and end-all of life. There were other things to do. But when I was growing up, we looked to sports to carve out an identity for our city, something we could hang on to when everything else was slipping away. It made losing all the more bitter.

When you look at photographs of the crowds at Browns games in the 1950s, you generally see men wearing coats and ties. A few people might have brown and orange stocking caps during the cold weather, but no one is wearing official jerseys or licensed NFL merchandise. The crowd looks almost gentle as they watched their team play. My father told me the look of that crowd is deceiving, but on the whole, the crowds at Browns games during the fifties and sixties were much different from the ones that enveloped me in the seventies and eighties. "There was always a lot of drinking," my dad remembered. "And the fights in the bleachers were violent, especially when those jakeys were fighting over the ball after extra points. But I guess it was nothing like you guys had when the bleachers got really crazy."

In our youths, going to Browns games was serious business. There were no cheerleaders. The orange helmet was the only franchise in the league without a logo. The team usually wore plain white jerseys and pants (Paul Brown believed that being dressed in white made the players look bigger to the opposition). The crowd was almost exclusively male. No self-respecting Browns fan would think of bringing his wife or girlfriend to the game. Ditto for kids. You didn't want to waste a ticket on them. Wives, girlfriends, kids were what you wanted to get away from. (It's funny, but teams and leagues now call for family-friendly stadiums with no smoking and curtailed drinking. At the same time, they make the games most "unfriendly" to families by charging prices for tickets that most families can't afford.)

But that's how we wanted it back then. No kids running around, women kept to the sideline. My father loved to tell a story about taking my mom to a game while they were dating in the fifties. He repeatedly asked her if she understood football, if she needed him to explain anything to her. Throughout the game she insisted that she understood football perfectly well. Then in the second half she asked him a question. "The only thing I don't understand is how do you tell which team has the ball?" My dad never took her again.

And who could blame him? The football spectacle was never glamorous in Cleveland. It was a matter of survival. Municipal

Stadium was dreary at best, bitter and wet, with wind blowing off Lake Erie in November, a muddy field built on landfill garbage, and the odor of stale urine and vomit. It was foul and rank, and we loved every inch of it. I remember a quote from former Pittsburgh Steelers great Jack Lambert, who went to college at Kent State in Ohio, about his take on Municipal Stadium. "The wind will be blowing off the lake, the snow will be swirling in our faces. It will be nasty. And I'll love it."

As they were for my father's crew, the bleachers were my crowd's choice spot to sit. Not because of the rowdiness that was later to become the "Dawg Pound," but because these were still the cheap seats and they were usually available later in the week. Contrary to the nostalgic belief of our time, the Browns rarely sold out the entire cavernous and cold stadium. You could usually walk up on game day and snag a few bleacher seats for eight dollars or so. And for eight dollars you were able to see one of the most amazing shows in sport—not the show on the field, but a stupefying drunk show in the stands.

The bleachers at the old stadium were at the open end, the east side of the field. The end zone came right up to the stands, and the seats were actually quite good for watching the game. You had a clear view of the plays setting up in front of you. You could watch the quarterback make the progression of reads, watch linemen open holes, see the field goals kicked directly in your line of vision. By my era, they had put netting between the bleachers and the goalposts, negating those little fights over the ball my father remembers so well.

I think the netting was symbolic, as the crowds in the bleachers were like animals that needed to be separated from the rest of society. I remember during one Browns-Steelers game when two Steelers fans climbed the flagpole in the bleacher end and tried to fly a Steelers flag. Soon two Browns fans had shinnied up the pole and were fighting with the Steelers fans fifty feet in the air. As the pole swayed back and forth, cops at the bottom of the pole motioned for the four to come down. Incredibly they obliged the cops. As each of the four slid down the pole, cops bopped them in the head with billy clubs and hauled them out of the stadium.

There were always drugs in the bleachers in my days, too. It was nearly impossible to sit for any length of time without a joint being passed down the row. Browns bleacher fans were particularly magnanimous about sharing their marijuana, as it was considered good form to pass the joint down the row without expecting its return. In a similar spirit the ushers in the bleachers usually turned a blind eye when fans brought their own booze. We often had a bottle of Jim Beam, a case of beer, and plenty of pot to last the afternoon. A friend of mine who was going through a divorce had his two young sons for the weekend and brought them to the game with our group one Sunday. The rest of us weren't too thrilled about it. But when we got to our seats, the two kids—I think they were five and seven—opened up their long coats to reveal that their father had stashed a six-pack of beer in each of the boys' inside coat pockets and had packed their shirt pockets with joints. "They never search kids," was his explanation. We voted him Father of the Year.

The bathrooms were particularly infamous in the old stadium. The men's rooms had the old-fashioned troughs, where we would stand four or five abreast and piss out the cases of beer we went through. One of the rites of passage of being a male in Cleveland was finally being tall enough to piss in the stadium bathrooms without being boosted by your father. I remember the first time I was able to do this; it was at an Indians game, and I was so proud when my little pecker made it over the lip of the trough.

At halftime of Browns games, the lines for the bleacher bathrooms were long, and people had little patience for waiting in line. First someone would piss in the sink, then a line would form behind him. Next would be the garbage can. Finally bleacher fans would just start pissing on the floor, and as the drains backed up, there was usually an inch or two of pee covering the floor. I always wore boots when sitting in the bleachers, regardless of the weather.

And the women in the bleachers were not immune to joining in the grossness. The lack of women's bathrooms in the bleachers caused some women to try to find an open stall in the men's rooms. But deviation spirals downward, and the women hardly civilized the space. No one seemed the least bit surprised when they bottomed out alongside the men.

I mention all this not to be disgusting—maybe a little—but to give the flavor of the era. Even though the Browns were usually competitive, the fans in the bleachers seemed more interested in debauchery than the game itself. There were games I attended that I had to read about in the paper the next day to find out who won. Maybe we were just medicating ourselves, as living in Cleveland during the seventies and eighties was hardly an idyllic experience. Graduating from high school or college did not guarantee any kind of job. I knew college graduates who were working as landscapers or drywall hangers. We were in the very depths of the Rust Belt depression, and we all knew that the American Dream was a cruel joke. As Clevelanders in our teens and twenties, we did what we knew best. We got fucked-up every chance we got.

And as I look back on those days, the memories of the games themselves reflected the city's dissolution. I was there when Sipe threw the interception on Red Right 88. I was there when Elway drove down the field in the last minute. The hated Steelers of the seventies were winning Super Bowls and kicking our ass every year. But we were resilient. If we were going to lose, we were going to have a good time doing it.

I suppose the times make the men more than the men make the times. When my father was in his twenties, he and his friends were getting married, beginning careers, starting families. The city was on top and their teams were winning. My friends and I, on the other hand, were going to college, not finding jobs, avoiding marriage, and getting drunk every Sunday afternoon. Like others of my generation, we were avoiding growing up. And we were becoming experts at losing.

When the Browns were playing away, or if the game was a sellout and on local TV, my brothers and our friends would usually watch the game at my dad's house. Unlike most parents, my dad very much enjoyed having teenagers and young people around him. He enjoyed the smart-ass conversations, the attempts at cleverness that teenagers like. He didn't mind us drinking in the house after we came of age, and usually expected a few beers as payment for allowing us to watch the game with him. My friends and I would brag to him about the craziness we might have witnessed on Friday night at the Euclid Tavern, and he would jump right in with his own war stories. You guys don't know what it is to go to saloons, he would say, and then launch into some story about the old days and how the old Irish drunks would roll into the street, stopping the streetcars.

When I was still living at home, my father was a stickler on attending Sunday mass, which was often difficult given that I usually closed the bars on Saturday nights. The last mass on Sunday at Holy Cross Church was at 12:30 P.M., which at most churches would be cutting it close for a 1 P.M. kickoff time. But Father Scully, an old Irish priest who grew up in my father's neighborhood, always said the late mass, and he had an unwritten guarantee that his mass would be over in time for the start of the Browns game.

Scully was a bit pompous, aloof, and condescending, the classic old-time autocratic Irish Catholic pastor. But this guy definitely had a wild hair up his ass. There were always rumors that he was, shall we say, ministering to the ladies of the evening downtown on Prospect Avenue. When I was an altar boy, I had to wake him up for his mass once because he was passed out drunk. He splashed Hi Karate aftershave on his face and hands so the parishioners wouldn't smell the booze and cigarettes when he passed out communion.

Father Scully refused to allow his parishioners to engage in the handshake of peace, reasoning that "peace" was an ambiguous term when his parishioners would fight each other in the church parking lot after services. But my favorite part of the Scully mystique was his two-minute sermon. It usually went like this: "Life was great in the forties and fifties, but those of you in this generation have lost your way. Let's stand for the creed." Typical message for Clevelanders. Life was great back then and it sucks now. Let's watch football.

After I moved out of my parents' house, I still came back home to watch games on Sunday. It was the only time during the week I could really talk to my father. We would discuss the latest John Irving novel. Catch up on gossip in the neighborhood.

We loved to make fun of the athletes. We would count the number of times the players would say "y'know" during interviews. During one game, NBC announcer Curt Gowdy was explaining the severity of the yardage penalized for grabbing the face mask. "It's five if you hold it, and fifteen if you jerk it." My father and I looked at each other, smiled, and grabbed our respective crotches.

There was a time in the early eighties when I found myself basically homeless. I had flunked out of Cleveland State University for the second time and was driving a cab. One night I made a bad left turn downtown and smashed head-on into an oncoming car. I wasn't hurt, and neither was the other driver, but when I came to work the next day, they fired me. The insurance company wouldn't carry me on its policy. As low points go in one's life, there is perhaps nothing lower than being fired as a cabdriver.

I never let anyone know I was homeless, and it went on for several months. I would crash at friends' houses during the week, staying late on purpose and asking them if I could sleep over because I didn't have a ride home. The bartender at the Euclid Tavern, John Cardinal, would let me sleep on the couch in his apartment above the bar. I used to sneak into the Sig Tau frat house at night and crash on their couches in the basement. I stole food from grocery stores, and I used a forged college ID to take showers in the Cleveland State gym. I tried to pretend that I was going to school and was still living in the old house where I had been evicted. It seemed that very few people caught on.

I had the habit of going to my father's house on Sundays for dinner, and when I was homeless, I never missed a Sunday. I would catch a bus out to his house, load up on some food, and wash my clothes for the week. When I would get there, my dad would give me twenty bucks and the keys to the car and tell me to get a twelve-pack of beer. He never asked for the change.

And for the most part, we avoided talking about my problems. He knew I was fucking up my life, but he let it pass. Instead, we would just talk football. He would talk of Otto Graham and the old days. I would talk about how Brian Sipe was just as good. We would jump up and down when the Browns scored a touchdown, curse the screen when they screwed up. He would give me some steaks or chicken to grill at halftime, and even though I was in my early twenties, I felt very comfortable playing son. Perhaps too comfortable.

One fall Sunday the Browns were playing at home—I can't remember whom they were playing—but the game had sold out and was on local TV. My brothers and my friends were going to the game, but I had no money and couldn't. It was just me and my father, at his house. My dad was mostly silent—he seemed bothered—and toward the end of the game, after dinner, I was drinking beer with him when he'd had enough and asked me point-blank, "Where are you living?"

I lied. "I'm staying with Lance."

"I hear you're not living anywhere, that you're drinking all the time, and you're crashing at different people's houses every night."

"I don't have a car, so I usually stay wherever I end up at night." That much was true.

"I'm not stupid. You are totally fucking up your life, and I'm not going to be the one who is going to bail you out again."

This much was also true. Whenever I needed money, he would help me out. It was always a few hundred here, a few hundred there, but he always helped me out. He paid college tuition for me every year, even though I often dropped all the classes before the semester was over. But he usually wrote the checks, after making me pay for it with a canned lecture, pointing out how screwed-up I was.

This time his face was stern. "How much do you need?"

"For what?"

"To find a place to live, for chrissakes."

I asked if I could move back home.

"No." Long silence.

"Well, two hundred will get me in this rooming house down-town." I had begun bartending a joint called the 2300 Club downtown, a hangout for cops and hookers and local factory workers. The owner had hired me to work the 6 A.M. to noon shift because I had a $200 bar tab, and the condition of my work-ing was that he would take half of my weekly paycheck—which was the sterling sum of $80 a week—until the debt was paid. With tips, I was making about $150 a week. The rooming house charged $150 a month, but I needed a $150 deposit to move in.

He wrote a check for $250. We watched the end of the game in silence. I don't remember who won. When the game was over, I went to the fridge and got another beer. I sat down with him and told him how sorry I was, how I was going to get my life together. He just looked at me and shook his head.

"Get out of here now. I'm not going to have you sit here all night and drink beer. Don't come back. I don't want to see you anymore."

I gathered up my belongings. My laundry was still wet. I stole some food from the basement refrigerator. I came upstairs and tried to say good-bye. I couldn't find him, but noticed the car was gone.

I walked down the street to the bus stop, past Holy Cross

School, where I had gone as a kid, past the church where I had been an altar boy. I sat at the bus stop, the same bus stop that I used to run to every day at 6 P.M. to meet my father on his way home from work. I waited for more than an hour for the bus, and cried the whole time. That night, I cashed my check at the 2300 Club and drank about thirty dollars' worth of beer. I moved into the rooming house the next day and slowly began to put myself back together.

A year later I wrote an exposé about the cab company that fired me, which was published in *Cleveland Magazine*. From there I was able to get full-time work writing, first for a trade magazine publishing firm and then later as a reporter with the *Lake County News-Herald*. And as I look back now, I can see that the bottom was that Sunday afternoon at my father's house when he told me he didn't want to see me anymore.

I honored his wishes. I stayed away. I never hated him for what he did. I admired him for confronting the issue. No one else did. After some time, I came back for various family functions and dinners, but before long I was in Texas, and watching football with him wasn't a part of our lives anymore. That's why watching the new Browns in the hospice with him was important for me, and for him, too, I think. As I looked at him on his deathbed, barely conscious but trying to stay alive, I thought back to all those games we watched, all those Sunday afternoons where we lived and died with the team. I thought of that game in 1964 when he was screaming and clapping and acting crazy. His hair was dark and wavy back then, he was athletic-looking and vibrant, life was full of possibilities. He jumped around like he was a kid.

We were winners then. We were innocents. It was so very long ago.

# CHAPTER THREE

# A Complicated Man

The new Browns won their exhibition game against the Cowboys. Kicker Phil Dawson hit a game-winning field goal in overtime for a 20–17 victory. It was perhaps the worst thing that could have happened to the team and the city. Players were quoted in the paper as saying that the play-offs were a realistic goal for the team. Veteran sports media types were predicting a 9-7 or 8-8 season. The bang-to-hype ratio was totally out of whack. Callers to the sports talk shows were severely upbeat. The local media were gushing with civic hosannas for the new Browns. The reasoning for such optimism was that the Browns were going to be unique among expansion teams. For one, they were the only expansion team, meaning they didn't have to share the NFL spare parts auction called the expansion draft with any other teams. Secondly, they were going to play one of the easiest schedules in the history of the NFL. The combined record of the teams on their schedule was just .353.

The Browns also had a number of other factors going for them. The biggest impediment to getting good in the 1990s NFL was the league salary cap, which in 1999 stood at $57 million. Teams that had dominated in the past—the San Francisco 49ers and the Dallas Cowboys, for example—were having trouble fitting their established star players under the cap. It was a yearly dance for those teams, prorating bonuses and restructuring contracts every off-season to get the team under the cap. The Browns were essentially starting with a clean slate and did not have to pay now for bad decisions in their past.

Avoiding long-term contract blunders is the determining factor for success in today's NFL. And the enemy of being great is not being bad, but being good. It has become apparent that the best way to develop a good team in the NFL is by being horrible the previous year. Hungry young draft choices making league minimum salaries are cheap raw material to build a franchise. Add the fact that young players are not allowed to file for unrestricted free agency until they have played four years in the league, and a new franchise has at least four years before it has to open up the bank in earnest. Signing free agent stars, while tempting because they can bring early wins to a new franchise, to long-term multi-million-dollar contracts can destroy a team before it even gets started.

The 1995 expansion team, the Jacksonville Jaguars, is the case study franchise for success in today's NFL. Jacksonville evolved from a 4–12 expansion season start to a place among the best teams in the league in fewer than five seasons. The Jaguars had forgone signing expensive free agents in their first few years and made their rookie draft choices play every down. The Carolina Panthers, on the other hand—their expansion counterparts in 1995—decided to roll the dice on being good early and signed veteran and expensive stars in their infancy in the league. Though the Panthers had more early success than the Jaguars and fielded a number of good, competitive teams, by 1998 their roles had reversed. In 1998 the Jaguars were 12–4, while the Panthers were 4–12.

The Jacksonville lesson was not lost on the new Browns management. By making shrewd draft picks, the new Browns would circumvent the salary cap dilemma that the more established teams had to contend with annually, at least for the first four years. And as they were the only expansion team to begin play in 1999, they did not have to outsmart another new franchise on draft day. The diligent draft strategy would also give the Browns tons of room under the salary cap, which enabled them to make use of the Carolina strategy, too. They had the room to sign some free agent veterans to round out their team and make them good early. With intelligent strategic management, the prevailing wisdom was that this team would be unique. It was an expansion team with a built-in history, a team with a select group of free agents that could contend from the time they strapped on their orange helmets and a team that would have the young talent to contend in the future, too.

But there was one major problem. The NFL had changed dramatically in the 1990s, from a game that used to thrive on size alone to a game that now thrived on speed. As players became bigger in the 1980s, the difference in size, especially on the offensive and defensive lines, was often the edge that brought teams championships. But by the 1990s the difference between the largest and the smallest players had become less dramatic. Strong safeties now weigh 230 pounds, linebackers 260. Defensive ends might go closer to 280. But what differentiates these players today is speed. Defensive units now look for players who are able to run sideline-to-sideline. Offensive linemen are now expected to be able to pull out in front of running backs, even if they weigh 320 pounds. Receivers are expected to play the vertical game, stretching defenses downfield. Even quarterbacks, who in the past were picked for their classic drop-back passing ability, are now being scouted for their ability to "make things happen." Tennessee Titans quarterback Steve McNair is the prototype of this new breed of QB, a guy who has a rifle arm but can also run a

4.5-second forty-yard dash. And McNair has the size to break the tackles of 300-pound defensive linemen.

The victory over the Cowboys made Clevelanders and the Browns players giddy. Local radio talk shows were full of callers talking play-offs in the team's first year. Corey Fuller, a cornerback who left the Vikings to sign a free agent contract with the Browns, said the team would do no worse than 8-8. "This isn't an expansion team," Fuller said. "Expansion teams are for cities that never had teams, like Jacksonville or Carolina. We are a team coming back into existence."

Maybe the sense of history and logic was lost on the fans and the players. This *was* an expansion team. It was stocked with castoffs from other teams and loaded with green rookies, and most of the experts said the Browns would be very bad. They had no speed. But this meaningless overtime victory in the first pre-season game colored the eyes of the whole city. We wanted this so bad that we saw what we wanted to see. We wanted to see a winner.

And despite the fact that Cleveland was able to keep the colors and the team records, the problem with starting a team from scratch is that the assembled players have no cohesion with one another. It's a sports cliché that says team chemistry is important, but it's a cliché because it's true. The biggest challenge facing these new Browns was carving out an identity, and for the men who now play in this era of mass free agency, the fact that Paul Brown once coached here or Otto Graham once threw passes here means nothing. Players today have no sense of history. They can't afford to. When the average life span of an NFL player is less than four years (it is an interesting fact that they are held hostage that long before they can demand a new contract, eh?), sentimental attachments to a city or franchise will deprive them of their fair market value. Players can only have a sense of whom they are playing next week and of what they have to do to keep earning a living.

By the end of a season, the very demanding and painful nature of an NFL campaign does give players their own common history. They'll form friendships and alliances with the other members of the team, and their experiences will either make them better or pull them apart. With free agency, though, chemistry is hard to maintain, as chances are that most of the guys won't be with the team a year or two down the road. So, despite the overwhelming outpouring of support from the fans, the uniqueness of the new Browns was lost on most of the players. They play for a business that has branch offices in thirty-one other cities. They go where the money is. History matters little today.

The NFL office has no sense of history, either. Executives from NFL Properties wanted the Browns to put some sort of logo on their helmets and to redesign their drab uniforms. The problem for the league is that it has all of these cool logos to sell, and one plain orange helmet that looks like a brightly colored M&M. It doesn't matter that the Browns are always near the top in merchandise sales. The NFL marketing guys wanted uniformity, and they couldn't stomach the Browns being different and logoless.

To the organization's credit, the new Browns held firm. When asked at a civic luncheon whether the Browns were going to change their uniforms to satisfy the league, new owner Al Lerner told the crowd: "If the league wants different uniforms, let them go out and buy their own team."

I made my way to the hospice about 3 P.M. the day after the exhibition opener. My brother Mark had spent the night, and he told me that my dad had taken a turn for the worse. His breathing was labored, and he hadn't communicated with anyone since seeing Tim Couch play on TV the night before. The pastor of Holy Cross Church, Rev. Robert McNulty (Father Scully had died some years before), was on his way to perform the last rites of the Catholic Church.

All of my brothers and sisters, most of my stepbrothers and stepsisters, my dad's wife, Theresa, his sister, Helen, his brother-in-law, John Robinson, and a few nieces and nephews were at his bedside. The nurses and orderlies working at the hospice were used to all of us by now. We had essentially taken over the place waiting for the end. The lobby area was overrun with pizza boxes and little children. We were like that, our family, slightly screwed-up and selfish most of the time, but able to rally when we needed to.

We didn't want my dad to go into the great beyond by himself. But I wondered how he felt about all of the drama. In many respects, he was a very private man who preferred to deal with crises by himself. He had told me he wanted nothing special when he died. In fact, in his will he had written that his church service should have "no eulogies, no bagpipes, no mimes." We had a good laugh when he showed me that. But I knew it masked a larger truth for him. He wanted to be left alone, left alone to die on his terms.

But I underestimated him. When Father McNulty came to the side of his bed with oil to anoint his forehead, my father opened his eyes and looked directly at the priest. McNulty and my dad had attended grade school together at St. Thomas Aquinas during the 1940s, and my dad instantly recognized his former classmate.

"Hello, Father," he said with respect. Those were the first words he had spoken that day. Then my dad looked around the room and focused his gaze on my brother Mark. "Take your hat off," he bellowed.

The guy certainly had regained some of his feistiness. And as the priest went through his prayers and anointed my father's head with oil, my dad had a smile on his face. Not quite shallow happiness, but a genuine affection for the sacrament. He was a big fan of the rituals of the Catholic Church, and at this moment I could tell he was wrapping himself in them. He wasn't one of those Catholics who think the world ended when the mass stopped being said in Latin, but he was big on incense and candles, the Forty Hours' Devotion, and the Stations of the Cross. The rituals comforted him.

When the last rites were completed and all the prayers said, I heard a voice from the back of the room. My Uncle John Robinson, in his late eighties and suffering from prostate cancer and dementia, decided to weigh in on the solemn occasion.

"Dick, it looks like it's time to tap the second keg," Uncle Johnny said quite loudly. He was not known for strange comments, but this one certainly baffled everyone in the room. I looked at my brother Mark, then at my brother Brian. They both shrugged their shoulders but were laughing quietly. I looked back at Uncle Johnny and he had a bemused look on his face. We tried to pin him down on what he meant, but old Uncle Johnny was a bit confused and incapable of explaining his pronouncement.

After we left the room, we came to the conclusion that Uncle Johnny viewed life as a two-kegger. Your first keg is your life, and then you get a second keg in the afterlife. My dad's first keg was now running on foam. And it was apparent that no amount of pumping the tap would get it going again. But the second keg was on its way. Not a bad deal, all told.

.   .   .

My relationship with my father was always complicated. For starters, I look just like him. I shared the thick, bushy eyebrows, the big Irish nose, the red face. And constantly hearing about our resemblance was unavoidable and tiresome. As he cast a very big shadow, I always felt serious pressure to live up to his accomplishments and his expectations of what his son should be. Looking like him but not achieving like him was a colossal burden for me. In my estimation he expected perfection, and I never felt that I could look into his eyes on even terms until after I had become an editor with *U.S. News & World Report.*

I also had a severe stutter when I was a kid, and I've never quite grown out of it. To this day, I have to make deliberate pauses and use verbal crutches to communicate. Most people don't notice, but I think about it every day. While working for *U.S. News & World Report,* I often do radio interviews to promote stories I've written. I've never been exceptionally nervous when being interviewed, however, and radio hosts have often commented on what a good guest I've been. By carefully choosing my words, and pausing when I get into trouble, I can usually sail through these live broadcasts. But an hour after finishing the interview and reporting about my performance to my father on the phone, I'd struggle to get my words out. I've never quite understood why my stuttering is so conditional. I'm sure some psychotherapist would have a field day with me. I know what the symptoms are. My father made me nervous. But I also felt comfortable around him. You figure it out.

My parents never put me into speech therapy during my school years, even though I had trouble speaking a complete sentence during that time. Catholic schools didn't "waste" money on speech therapists during the sixties and seventies, and I was expected to get over it by strength of will. My father's only advice during those years was "slow down."

I don't blame my stuttering on him. I think it's more complicated than that. But I always wondered why my parents did so little about it. It was a question that had always nagged at me, an open wound that had only recently begun to close. There were so many days and nights in my life when I prayed that I might be able to speak. In fact, I was inadvertently aided when I covered a Promise Keepers rally—the men's Christian movement founded by former University of Colorado football coach Bill McCarthy. I found myself surrounded by born-agains praying for "the devil to be cast out of this young man's mouth."

When I came back to Cleveland in June, after I had told my father about his larger role in the book, one of my first conversations with him was about my stuttering. I had to find out how he felt about it. I mean it must have really killed him. He was a lawyer and a skilled orator and he had a son who could not speak. I never knew whether he didn't care, or perhaps cared too much.

"Why didn't you put me in speech therapy?"

"We thought you would grow out of it."

"But I never did."

"You sound okay now." He was agitated. And, sure, I have come a long way. I'm not Mel Tillis, by any stretch. But I still have my moments. In fact, the biggest problem I have is saying my last name. My father's name.

I decided not to let up. "Did you know how hard I had it in high school?"

I told him about the time I had to give a speech in class during my freshman year. The speech was supposed to be six minutes long, and I hadn't prepared much for it (the fear of stuttering was obviously overcome by academic laziness). I had two minutes of material and stuttered my way through the other four. My classmates used to cringe when I was put behind the lectern.

I also told him about the time I had tried out for the high school spring musical. Like most stutterers, I can sing comfortably. But the director of the play wouldn't allow me to be onstage— even as a part of the chorus without any lines. Even when I was quarterback on my peewee football team, the coaches had reservations about allowing me to play because they thought I would freeze up while calling signals.

In high school I tried to avoid the problem by not raising my hand in class. I also started drinking and smoking pot heavily. I think I started abusing intoxicants because it let me play the fool more effectively. As long as people were laughing at me, I thought I might as well be fucked-up. The problem was that my stuttering became much worse when I was drunk. In fact, the only time I really stutter badly now is when I have been drinking heavily.

But the stuttering also led to my being more comfortable expressing myself in the written word. I found that, by writing, I could choose the words I wanted to convey my thoughts, rather than only using words I was comfortable speaking.

"I felt that the best way for you to get over it was by doing it on your own," he finally responded. "And besides, you should have prepared better for your speech."

"I don't know if you notice it or not, but I still stutter around you more than around anyone else."

"I didn't know that . . . Are you blaming me?"

"No, I'm just trying to understand."

"Maybe it's just one of those things we'll never understand."

I let it go. He was obviously uncomfortable with the line of questioning. All I know is that stuttering became less of a problem for me after I started to have some success in the world of journalism. And that wasn't until I was about thirty years old. Obviously I became more confident when I moved out of his shadow. Before I left Cleveland, I was more comfortable playing his fool than succeeding in life. And what better fool to play than a stuttering drunk. It took me a very long time to break out of that role.

My dad's life was the great American success story. He grew up in the Irish ghetto of Cleveland—St. Thomas Aquinas parish—a blue-collar area near East 86th and Superior Avenue, full of just-off-the-boat Irish. He was born in 1930, the beginning of the Great Depression.

His mother, Marie Frain, was born in county Roscommon, Ireland, in 1890. Roscommon was a poor rural area near the Northern Ireland border, and the Frain family could not afford to keep Marie. The Frains already had three children—a son who was needed to help on the farm and two daughters who were born blind. Marie was sent to live with an aunt and uncle in Cleveland, Ohio. She made the trip by herself at age nine. She never saw her parents again.

Her aunt and uncle owned a bar on Woodland Avenue across the street from the Van Dorn Iron Works. They also ran a rooming house for other off-the-boat greenhorn Irish. Marie worked in the bar during the day and helped cook and clean at the rooming house at night. She never finished the third grade. Her past made my grandmother a tough old broad, an amazingly strong woman who later became the president of the St. Thomas PTA. The position was considered one of the most powerful in the ward, just behind the councilman and the parish's pastor.

My dad's father, Fred McGraw, was born in 1884 in Mount Gilead, Ohio, about one hundred miles south of Cleveland. His family worked on the railroad. When Fred came of age, he traded his family's blue collar in on a white one. He landed a job at Western Union as a telegraph operator and moved to Cleveland. Between 1905 and 1908 Fred traveled with the Cleveland Indians, sending back the play-by-play of the game to the radio guys back in Cleveland who re-created the games from his missives. My grandfather would send "fly ball out to left field." The play-by-play over the radio would then sound something like this: "There's a long fly ball, deep to left field. He's at the wall, he leaps and catches it."

My dad's devotion to "sentence structure, spelling, and syntax" came indirectly from his father. When he worked at the Western Union office, Fred sent cables for many of the illiterate Irish. He became very adept at correcting their grammar and spelling, even though he, like his bride, had never gone beyond the third grade. He passed his proficiency in language to his youngest son, and my father then drilled it into us. It's weird how those things work out.

And speaking of illiterates, there is strong evidence that my ancestors coming over from Ireland could not read or write. In Ireland there is no surname "McGraw." Over there, the *th* sound in the name "McGrath" is not pronounced. Thus "McGrath" is pronounced as "McGraw." When these McGraths came through Ellis Island, the immigration officers would ask them to spell their last name. Many would shrug their shoulders. So the immigration people would write their name as it sounded to them, and a host of illiterate McGraths became McGraws.

My dad had two older brothers—Howard and Jack—who were teenagers when he was born, and a sister, Helen, who was twelve. I always suspected that he was an accident. "From the time he was born, he was always the center of attention," my Aunt Helen told me. "You should have seen how it was when he took his first steps. You would have thought it was the Second Coming. Everyone in the neighborhood soon knew that little Dickie McGraw was walking."

The Irish neighborhood in those days was, by necessity, an insular community. My grandmother used to tell me that she remembered seeing signs in storefronts that read, "Irish need not apply." The Irish were seen as a race of beer-guzzling boneheads, with thick hides and ham-handed fists, ready to punch anyone who got in their way. They had too many children, were too involved with the Catholic Church. Though some of that attitude had changed by the time my father came of age, his times were still very much defined by race and ethnicity. The Irish still had something to prove in Cleveland in the 1930s and 1940s. They had to prove that they were capable of more than just menial labor.

Adults surrounded Dickie McGraw from the day he was born. During the Depression his great-aunt and -uncle moved in with the family. His father was often busy with work, and "Uncle"—retired and on a pension—would take my dad to baseball games and movies. Friday nights were for boxing matches at East 55th and Hough Avenue. "Uncle had nothing else to do, so we went everywhere together," my dad would tell me. Uncle also had an on-again, off-again drinking problem. One night, according to family lore, Uncle either shot or was shot by a relative while they drank Four Roses in the basement.

Fred McGraw died of heart failure in 1941. Just eleven at the time, my dad had little memory of his father. The family suffered hard times after his death. My father worked thirty hours a week as a soda jerk at Sam Levine's drugstore from the age of nine until eighteen. The summers of his youth were spent selling scorecards at League Park, then the home of the Indians. He paid his own way through Catholic grade school, high school, college, and eventually law school. He was the first in his family to graduate college.

His brother Jack was the man he looked up to most. Jack was a witty and talented fellow, a 6'4" basketball player who received a scholarship to John Carroll University. But like many of his contemporaries, Jack developed drinking problems and became an infamous mail carrier for the post office. It is rumored that he once shot a dog on his route.

I found an old letter that my Uncle Jack had written to his boss. He was trying to get my dad on the payroll during a holiday rush in the 1940s. The letter is addressed to Mr. James L. Collins, Assistant Postmaster, Cleveland:

Dear Sir:

As a personage of importance in the Cleveland Post Office, I throw myself with all due humility at your feet and beg that you put my brother, who is of sound mind and health, on the U.S. payroll at Christmas time. He is a good boy, the Lord only knows, if somewhat simple.

Understand, however, that he does not have to have a supervisory position. He is very democratic and will do anything a white man will do, that is, with the exception of using an electric razor. He draws the line there, and I believe that there is no job at present in the postal system that would require a man to use an electric razor. So much for his ability.

In the event that you meet with any opposition by sundry people, that is, if anyone should be horrified at the thought of two McGraws in the post office, just drop the subject and hand in your resignation. I will give you full authority to do so. If this is not enough, see your ward leader. And so with complete confidence in your ability to increase postal revenue,

I remain,

Sincerely,

John J. McGraw

Superintendent of Empty Sacks

East Cleveland Branch

Jack's letter confirmed my hunch that my family history is one of smart-asses. There was a certain arrogance in my father's blood, and he combined it with his own internal aloofness. He truly felt that he was better than most people, but his philosophy contained a host of contradictions. He was a self-proclaimed man of the people, but in reality he had little use for the travails of the common man. He was an intellectual who at one time taught James Joyce, but he was also a man who enjoyed fart humor. He never joined any clubs or organizations; such conventions were beneath him. "Why would I want to join an organization and be defined by those people in it?" he once questioned me. "When you do that, you lower yourself. You should be defined by who *you* are, not some club you belong to."

One day several years ago, I came to his house for a visit. He was sitting in his reclining chair reading, as he always did. On his lap was Proust's *Remembrance of Things Past*. And on the TV was *The Jerry Springer Show*. When I remarked at the weird combination of entertainment he had going on, he just looked, took stock, smiled at me, and broke into his version of an old country-western song: "Oh I wish I was in hillbilly heaven. . . ."

My dad was a difficult man to get to know. He was always the life of the party—sometimes I thought that my friends would rather watch a football game with him than with me. He was full of bravado. But there was also a certain sadness in him, especially in his later years, when he was more prone to brooding. He had little patience with his grandchildren. He had given up in many ways. And he was dying at a fairly young age.

My dad's arrogance and aloofness were rooted in his childhood. Aside from growing up in a house full of adults, he was independent at a very early age. He was responsible for contributing to the support of his extended family and for his own care after his father died. Working so hard as a child taught him that his life was his responsibility and not to expect others to make his path for him. He was a very intelligent child. I found a report card from 1943 when he was in the eighth grade at St. Thomas Aquinas. Every grade was an A. But his grade in behavior was marked "very poor." It was as if I were looking at my own report card from the eighth grade.

When he grew older, he became the ring leader of a select group of cronies from Superior Avenue. They called him Muggsy. An old friend of my father's, Jim O'Day, now a retired banker living in Pittsburgh, recalls that my dad was responsible for finding bars that would serve them liquor when they were fourteen years old. "One night we hopped on a streetcar, then transferred to another, then got on a bus that took us to this bad neighborhood over on Kinsman," O'Day told me. "Kinsman was already turning black at that time and wasn't the best neighbor-hood. We walked into this little joint, all of us pretty scared about going into a strange bar. But he was right. We were welcome and we got to drink there all night."

He was a late bloomer in sports—the scale by which boys are weighed—mostly because he was small in grade school and high school. At St. Thomas he played "lightweight" basketball and football. These teams were decidedly second-rate to the "heavy-weight" teams that were fielded. He was a center on his football team and came to be known for being an undersized, yet tough, lineman. As a basketball player, he played forward, again under-sized, yet known as the guy who played good defense inside and forcefully grabbed rebounds.

He was cut from his freshman basketball team in high school, which for him was a crushing event that he still remembered more than fifty years later. One day we commiserated our similar fates. I had been the last cut on my freshman high school basket-ball team at St. Ignatius. At the time, I was only about 5'4", but I thought I was good enough to make the team as a third-string guard. By the time I graduated, I was 6'3" and could dunk a bas-ketball. But as often happens, coaches keep tall players on fresh-man teams, even if they have no ability. The hope is that these big clods will develop into something by the time they are seniors.

"I'll always remember this," I told him. "They kept Mike Ryan because he was six-foot-four. It just killed me. I played so well during tryouts."

"Earl Gentile," he replied.

"Who?"

"Earl Gentile was the guy who kept me off the team. He was a football player who was about six-four in his freshman year. I never had a chance."

It's funny, but some of these seemingly meaningless twists and turns in our lives have great import on what happens to us later. My father became interested in subjects other than sports after he was cut from the freshman team. He joined the theater group at his high school, and it prepared him for his later life as a lawyer. Soon after he passed the bar, he became known as one of the best trial lawyers in Cleveland. His contemporaries often described his closing arguments as "legal theater."

As for me, after I was cut, I started hanging out at the high school yearbook office. My brother Brian was an editor on the book, and I went to the office after school to wait for a ride home. Soon they had me writing captions for pictures, then headlines, and before long I was writing copy. By the time I was a senior, I was editor of the yearbook. It was my first foray into journalism, and quite frankly, I learned more on that job than in any college class.

My father decided to attend law school after college, not because of any great love of the law, but because they offered him a scholarship. Attending law school also deferred his military service for a few years. He served in the air force after law school, and one of his cases as the base lawyer in Madison, Wisconsin, was to bust a private for marijuana possession. The MPs vacuumed the man's pockets and found a few seeds. With my father prosecuting, the man was sent to the stockade for ten years.

After his service he became a trial lawyer in Cleveland and thoroughly enjoyed his work. As the product of a tough immigrant neighborhood, full of saloon brawls and street fights, he relished the intellectual combat of the legal profession. "I realized very early on that the courtroom was the only place in our society where fighting was officially sanctioned by our culture," he told me. "It was always me against the other guy. I used to think of it as a street fight. That's why I was good at what I did."

He started out defending the Cleveland Transit System, mostly in accidents that involved the company's buses. He continued in civil trial work his entire career, eventually having his own law firm and becoming among the top trial lawyers in Cleveland. He made six figures back when that meant something, and retired with a million dollars in the bank. But even though he had interests in politics, and certainly could have written his own ticket in more lucrative practices such as corporate law, he never switched from defending insurance companies. "Money was never important to me," he said. "I never had an entrepreneurial bone in my body. I did what I liked. I didn't do too badly at it, either."

He was a curious sort of lawyer, often quoting Shakespeare and Hemingway during his closing arguments. But he was never stuffy, never looked down at juries. He prided himself on being able to read the minds of blue-collar jurors. Reading them and convincing them were his bread and butter. He rarely lost a case.

When I was in the third or fourth grade, my mother brought me downtown for Christmas shopping, but for one reason or another, she had to drop me off at the courthouse so that I could ride home on the bus with my father. I sat in the back of the courtroom and watched him perform.

The case involved a man who was injured during a Cleveland Barons hockey game. Back in those days, they did not have Plexiglas around the rink. Instead, there was chicken wire that extended three or four feet above the boards. A man sitting in the first row had put his face directly against the chicken wire so that his nose poked through. A hockey puck had flown up and hit the man squarely in the nose, shattering his skull. The unfortunate soul was suing the team and the arena, and my dad was defending the arena.

I arrived just as my father was beginning his closing argument. He began by telling the jury how violent a sport hockey is. How a reasonable person would not put his nose through chicken wire when such a fast-paced sport was unfolding only a few feet away. The argument was fairly predictable and logical.

Then it happened. My father ran across the courtroom and slammed his body into the jury box, fell to the floor, and rolled around in his suit, still continuing the oratory while on his back. He got up from the floor, calmly walked back to the part of the courtroom opposite the jury box, revved up, and slammed into it again. Three or four times he did this, and each time, the little old ladies in the front row of the jury box jumped back in their seats in fear. Each time, my father dusted himself off and resumed his closing argument. His voice was very calm, as if his flying around the room were perfectly normal.

His point, of course, was that hockey was a violent sport and sane people would recoil when bodies were smashing into the boards directly in front of them. He put that jury in the front row of the Cleveland Arena. It was insane theater. He won the case.

I sat there stunned, watching him roll around on the ground. I remember thinking my dad was very cool. Weird, but definitely cool.

I often wondered why my father spent his entire career defending insurance companies. I'm not putting him down, but he was a brilliant man with a great combination of street smarts and intellectualism. I always thought he was destined for greater things than protecting the world from insurance fraud. If he was a joiner, he could have become one of Cleveland's civic leaders. And if he did not have such a poor opinion of politicians, he might have been elected judge. If he had been any kind of risk taker, he might have written that great American novel he always talked about. But instead he defended insurance companies, and even though the cases were the big ones—shit and death were usually involved—he still found himself wedded to the whims of the insurance bureaucrats.

I broached the subject with him soon after I came back to Cleveland in June. At the time, he was still in fairly good shape, and anxious to talk about a whole host of subjects with me. When we went through a few of his topics, he was full of life, joking and joyously recounting tales of his youth at St. Thomas, telling the same old stories I had heard dozens of times before. But when I asked him "why insurance defense law?" he brooded. He just couldn't hide the sadness that quietly leaked out of him.

At first he talked of how the law changed over the years, of how the personal injury business had become rife with lawyers who had no sense of justice. He talked of how he and the other plaintiffs' lawyers of his era could settle cases based upon what they considered fair amounts. It was a private club they had, lawyers who knew and trusted one another, even if they were on opposite sides of a case. The new lawyers, he told me, had no sense of history, and they saw their practice as a job, not a profession. That he retired precisely at age sixty-five shocked many people because in his prime he claimed he would practice law well into his seventies. He left, he told me, because it was no longer fun.

But I had heard this all before. So I pushed him, trying to find out why a man with his gifts had given up so easily. His answer was obvious, but through the years I had somehow missed it. "When your mother died," he said sadly, "I stopped caring anymore. I decided being a hotshot lawyer wasn't very important."

We rarely talked of my mother's death. Even more than twenty years later, it was still a raw wound. But because of my father's stoicism and aloofness, I assumed he had come to grips with it over the years. He never did. It was the defining event in his life.

My mother, Karen Weed, was born in 1932. Compared to my father's family, hers was well off. They lived in a house near Lake Erie about a mile west of the hospice where my father would spend his last days. Her father, Charles Hviid, was a native of Denmark who sailed on the tall ships at the turn of the century. He settled in Ohio and went on to run a successful insurance and real estate business. I guess insurance is in my blood. He changed his name to Weed because of the confusing spelling of his last name. My maternal grandmother was Mary Zupancic, a Slovenian whose father had worked in the Collinwood Railroad Yards. My mother had four brothers and sisters, though her youngest sister, Virginia, died of whooping cough in infancy.

Karen Weed and Richard McGraw made a strange pair. In his youth he was the street tough who liked to drink heavily and brawl in saloons. She was a refined woman, athletic and tall, who would go on mile-long swims in Lake Erie. He was a natural performer who would quote Shakespeare and James Joyce in everyday conversation. She was a nurse by training who was practical and conservative.

They had known each other in high school but didn't start dating until he was in college. My mother's father was wary of her dating an Irishman. He considered the Irish to be dirty, lazy drunks who had little to offer society. Against her family's wishes,

Karen married Richard in 1954, at Holy Cross Church, and the two planned to start a family.

I asked my father what attracted him to her. "I wanted to get into her pants," he joked. "Back then, there was no sex before marriage, and if you wanted to get some, you had to get married."

But then he turned serious. "She was the most beautiful woman. She was strong, and she cleaned up my act. Before I met her, I was cruising through life without much direction. She gave me a plan—for a career, for a family, for what we wanted to do. I loved her very much."

He graduated from law school, and like good Catholics, they started their family. Kathleen came in 1956, Brian in 1957. I arrived in 1959, followed by Sheila, Mark, and Mary Margaret. My mother worked as a nurse until the mid-sixties, when too many babies made work impossible. We were a classic baby boomer family, with a stay-at-home mom and a father that took the bus to work every morning. When we outgrew our house in Cleveland, we moved a mile down the road into suburban Euclid.

My mother was exceedingly strict. She believed very strongly in her role as taskmaster. She tried to be perfect and expected to make her kids perfect, too. There was a lot of pressure in our house. My father demanded that all of us get As in school, and my mother ruled the roost at home. She cooked three meals a day, had the wash on the line by 8 A.M., and cut our hair in the kitchen or in the backyard. My cousins used to tell me that their parents constantly compared them to the "perfect" McGraw kids, and they always came up lacking. I never felt we were perfect. We were as screwed-up as everyone else.

Like much of suburbia, our idyllic life was a facade. I remember my father and mother fighting a lot. He played the unruly husband who needed to be subdued. She was the uptight suburban housewife who needed diversions. But all in all, their marriage seemed to work.

My father told me that things were starting to unravel in the late sixties and early seventies. His drinking was becoming a problem, and instead of coming home at six o'clock every day, he'd stumble home at eight or nine. "I thought I was a hotshot lawyer and stayed downtown drinking many nights," he mused. "When I was in trial—and I was doing two a month back then—I wouldn't make it home until eleven. Your mother didn't like it."

Divorce was out of the question back then, so they tried to work through their problems. But in 1971 fate began to push them together and apart, both at the same time. My mother was experiencing back pain, and several doctors diagnosed it as merely muscle spasms. But in September a doctor found the real cause of her distress. She was diagnosed with Hodgkin's disease, a cancer of the lymphatic system, and my dad was told she wouldn't live past Christmas.

She was thirty-nine years old with six kids, ranging in age from four to fifteen. She was hospitalized for fifty-six days, and my father was forced to play househusband for the first time in his life. She was put on chemotherapy, and somehow, through pure will, she survived for three years, but it was three years of being in and out of the hospital, and she never shook the disease. She was a beautiful woman whose outward appearance became grotesque.

Hodgkin's is very much like AIDS in that it attacks the immune system. Patients with Hodgkin's will eventually die from the cancer itself, but many die from immunodeficiency, unable to fight off infection, especially from viruses. In my mother's case, she developed shingles—a form of herpes that inflames the nerve endings—on her legs and in her left eye. Her body fought the viral infection valiantly, escalating her core temperature to 106 degrees. The fever burned the retina in her eye and caused partial blindness. It even burned the eyelashes and eyebrow from her damaged eye, and the doctors permanently closed the eye for fear that it would get infected.

For three years my mother's body was ravaged. She lost her hair from the chemotherapy, and she became painfully self-conscious of her appearance; she was beautiful enough to work as a model, and now her face was horribly scarred. When we went to church on Sundays, she wore dark glasses. She stopped hugging her children, as she was embarrassed by how she looked. We tried to work through it as family, and my father decided it would be best if she stayed at home. I reacted by spending as much time out of the house as possible.

We took turns caring for her. Toward the end, the cancer had moved into her brain and she could not speak. Her left side was paralyzed and she had to be propped up in her bed. One day I found myself alone with her. I was probably a freshman in high school, and I had to drag her up the stairs to her bedroom. It took me a half hour to do it. When I got her into bed, I told her everything would be okay, but she only looked away. That week, my father hired a housekeeper to fix lunch for the younger kids and clean the house. My mother wept uncontrollably. Her reason for being was over; her job as a mother to six young children was done.

She died in November 1975. My father was so devastated that he recoiled into himself. As a family, we never talked about her death. It was too painful for him to bring up. It was one of my father's great faults: pain was to be internalized and not shared. My brothers and sisters suffered through the years because we never came to grips with what happened. Our family had been ripped apart in a most painful and horrible manner. My father responded by getting drunk with his grade school friends after her funeral.

A few years after my mom's death, my father told me his friend Roger Saunders was coming over to the house. I asked him if this was the same guy who was at our house during the party after my mom's funeral. He looked at me and smacked me in the face, screaming at me as I ran out of the house. "That was not a party," he screamed. I had never seen him so angry.

For years after she died, I had recurring dreams that my mother was still alive and that my father was aware of it and tried to hide it from me. I still have them. My brother Brian told me he has had the same dreams.

In the next eighteen months my father's mother and his two brothers all died. He remarried two years after my mom's death—to Theresa Mora, whose husband had died about the same time as my mom. She had eight kids and we made the best of it. But there were always tensions in the house, and my father did his best to avoid them. Many of our neighbors and friends marveled at the circus atmosphere of my dad remarrying, the fourteen kids ranging in age from ten years to early twenties. We heard comments about *Yours, Mine and Ours* and *The Brady Bunch*. But mostly we muddled through, never quite a complete family anymore.

But the real problem for him was unresolved issues with my mother. Their marriage was strained shortly before she became ill, then they used all their resources to try to keep her alive. There was no time to reconcile their relationship. "After she died, I never thought of things as being that important," he told me. "She was a good woman who didn't deserve what she got. I don't think I ever felt the same way about life again."

I was surprised by his candor. He always put on a brave face when discussing my mother's death, resigned that he did the best he could under the most unfortunate of circumstances. But now in the self-examination of his own life, the past was beginning to haunt him. He knew he would see the love of his life soon. And he was worried.

# CHAPTER FOUR

# Not the Old Browns

Summer in Cleveland was uncomfortable. When I arrived in June, I was treated to temperature in the nineties and 70 percent humidity. The upstairs apartment I had rented in the Tremont neighborhood—a revitalized neighborhood near downtown that was once home to Eastern European steelworkers—was without air-conditioning. I put an old sofa on the upstairs porch and slept outside for two weeks. At night I could hear the horns blowing from the ore carriers navigating the Cuyahoga River about a mile away. The steel mills hummed loudly at night, and I could see the blue flames shooting thirty feet in the air above the rusty, hulking LTV Steel plant. There were a dozen or so old churches in this neighborhood, many with the onion domes of Eastern Orthodox sects that had served the new immigrants when they came to Cleveland a century before. Every day I was awakened to church bells at 8 A.M., ringing that was at once both annoying and joyous. They repeated at noon and 6 P.M. If you heard bells around 10 A.M., you knew there was a funeral down the street at St. John Cantius Church, a Polish church that had a bowling alley in the basement.

And that's what I liked about Cleveland: churches with bowling alleys, smokestacks and lake freighters, bells to welcome the new days and to mourn someone's passing, flames shooting in the air as seagulls circled, all while drinking a few beers on an old sofa on a creaky porch. If I leaned slightly out over the porch, I could see the city's skyline, lit proudly, and dominated by the spirelike Terminal Tower, built in 1930, when my father was born. When the Indians hit a home run over at Jacobs Field, I could see and hear the fireworks.

Cleveland had certainly changed since I had last lived there. I left in 1990 for a job with the *Fort Worth Star-Telegram* in Texas and had been back periodically for visits but had never spent extended periods of time. I had left before Jacobs Field and Gund Arena were built in a dilapidated section of downtown. I knew the area well, for I had walked to my job as a cabdriver right through the heart of the new sports palaces, past the Erie Street Cemetery, through the old Central Market, and down the Eagle Ramp to the cab garage. Now there were restaurants and bars catering to the sports crowd, and old warehouses being turned into apartments.

There was the I. M. Pei–designed Rock and Roll Hall of Fame down at the old Ninth Street Pier, with its triangular glass atrium and rather odd architecture. Next to the Hall of Fame was a science museum, and rising where ugly and smelly Municipal Stadium once stood was a brand-new stadium for the Browns, full of glass and shiny metal and bright orange seats. As I drove around town, I saw town houses being built in neighborhoods that used to be littered drug houses and after-hours drinking joints. The nationwide economic boom had brought relatively good times to some in Greater Cleveland, and while the high-tech industries stayed away for the most part, the city's manufacturing sector was doing as well as it had in twenty years.

But this new Cleveland had lost some of its old character. I missed the grittiness of downtown, the old department stores replaced by shopping malls, old restaurants like Captain Franks on the Ninth Street Pier—a dive that had a very strange crowd after midnight—squeezed out by development. In their place were cookie-cutter bars and restaurants pushing burgers and wings to the suburbanites who came downtown to watch their games. I went to an Indians game in June, and waiters—using palm pilots and wireless credit card machines—brought us our drinks in fancy new club seats. The West Side Market was still filled with stands selling Slovenian blood sausage and fully dressed goats, but now the tenants also included gourmet coffee stands and fresh pastas. Down in the Flats, an entertainment district that was once home to boat docks and sailor bars, there were now chain restaurants like Spaghetti Warehouse and Landry's Seafood. There was even a Hooter's down there.

Every few years the *New York Times* travel section would send a writer to Cleveland and talk about the city's alleged comeback. They would write in glowing terms about the city's fine orchestra, the new restaurants and bars in the Flats, and the gleaming new sports stadiums. But the unstated point of these articles was that Cleveland wasn't a hole anymore, that it was just like anyplace else. But I missed the Cleveland that teetered on the edge of despair. I liked the fact that the city had an edge to it, that we constantly had to defend ourselves against the cultural elite of the East Coast. I liked that you could hear a polka band playing on East 185th Street. I liked the Flats when it was a half dozen broken-down bars alongside a river that smelled like kerosene. I liked the fact that Browns fans pissed on the floor in the bleacher bathrooms.

I decided to move into the Tremont neighborhood because it seemed to be a combination of the old city and the new. Bordered by the Cuyahoga River and two interstates, Tremont was almost a village unto itself, cut off from the rest of the city by bridges. The houses were boxy old duplexes, most built in the late 1800s for the Polish and Russian and Hungarian workers that came to this country for factory jobs. From the 1960s through the 1980s the area fell into disrepair; the European ethnic groups fled to the suburbs, replaced by poor hillbillies from West Virginia and Puerto Ricans. When the property values hit bottom, artists moved in, and for a time in the early nineties, Tremont was a bona fide and thriving artist colony. But as in all trendy neighborhood transitions, the artists made Tremont too trendy, rents rose, and a gentrified cast reclaimed the old houses. These were lawyers and accountants and such, younger white-collar workers who wanted to spend a few years living close to downtown before they made their inevitable move to the suburbs.

Still, I found Tremont to be hardly an urban oasis. The neighborhood still had a volatile mix to it, as no one had told many of the poorer residents that they were being pushed out. My neighbor next door was a West Virginia hillbilly who collected cans and welded things in his front yard. Not anything I could identify, mind you, but welding just the same. Next door to him was a college professor who played classical music at night. Down the street were the Valley View Estates, a public housing project that was among the worst in the city. Every night about seven during the summer months, the brothers from the project would parade past my house to buy their forty-ouncers at the little bodega on the corner. Just past the bodega was an art gallery that seemed to specialize in homoerotica.

Town houses in Tremont were selling for $200,000, next door to dilapidated houses that might rent for $500 a month. The real estate market was white-hot in Tremont, despite the fact that the steel mills left a coating of dirt on your car every night and the Ohio EPA had warned people not to grow vegetables or let their pets out in the yard. On the weekends, trendies and dandies would descend upon Tremont to hang out in bars like the Tree House and Edison's, places full of young accountants and lawyers who had serious looks on their faces and jet-black wardrobes. The top restaurant in Cleveland—Lola—was just down the street from my house. Valet parking kept the beautiful people from coming in contact with the black folks and their Colt 45 bottles. Lola's signature dish was lobster-stuffed pierogi.

But there was still some of the old tradition left. Sokolowski's, a Polish cafeteria in Tremont that served cabbage rolls and sausage and fried walleye pike, was packed every day for lunch. Their pierogi were filled with mashed potatoes as they should be, topped with onions and sour cream. Bill Clinton ate there when he came to Cleveland. Can't get a much better endorsement than that.

Tremont was a microcosm of what was right and wrong with Cleveland. The old churches were beautiful, older houses were being restored, and younger white-collar workers were being kept living in the city, at least temporarily. Restaurants and bars brought suburbanites in on the weekends. But the poverty in Tremont was something you could not ignore. Bums would ride up and down the streets collecting cans, the kids at the Valley View Estates had no summer jobs, and no prospects, either. Car thefts and street robberies were not uncommon.

Statistics can lie, but they can also be used as a benchmark for the truth. In the city of Cleveland itself, the average household income was $23,654. The national average in 1998 was $38,885. Seventy percent of the pupils in the Cleveland School District qualified for free or reduced lunches based on household income below the poverty level. Nationally the poverty rate for children was around 20 percent. Ninth graders in Cleveland ranked 605th of 606 Ohio school districts in passing a basic proficiency test.

The only district that fared worse was the East Cleveland School District.

More than 66 percent of children born to women living in the city of Cleveland were born out of wedlock. The city ranked near the bottom of fifty cities in prenatal care and low-weight babies. In a story about the poor rankings in birth statistics, the *Cleveland Plain Dealer* led its story with a very telling sentence: "The city of Cleveland is one of the worst places to be born in the country."

But for a sports fan in the 1990s, Cleveland might have been the best place to be born. While the city of Cleveland was having trouble finding money for prenatal care or school funding, there was plenty of money for sports facilities. County taxpayers will have shelled out more than $225 million from 1990 to 2005 for Jacobs Field, new home of the Indians, and for Gund Arena, home of the NBA Cavaliers. In the next ten years, $150 million will have been paid for the new Browns Stadium. Bond interest payments had totaled more than $53 million by the end of 1999.

For the Browns themselves, the expansion fee totaled $530 million, the cost of which was paid by personal seat licenses, high ticket prices, and five-dollar beers. The stadium was originally pegged at $220 million, but cost overruns were shooting that up to almost $350 million. All told, Clevelanders were paying more than $1.5 billion for their sports teams and the new palaces they played in.

And in addition to having taxpayers foot the bill for these sports facilities, the teams were mostly exampt from paying any property taxes, most of which would have gone to the Cleveland public schools. The Browns were gaining a $2-million-a-year school tax break; the Indians and Cavaliers were being let off the hook for $8 million. Over the thirty-year leases for the teams, the school district could have enough money to pay for six thousand yearly salaries for teachers.

I'm not a weak-kneed liberal who believes that spending on schools automatically increases achievement. Nor do I think spending initiatives will automatically clean up crime or improve the quality of life in a city like Cleveland. But the very act of taxing hardworking people for their booze and cigarettes so billionaire owners and millionaire players can make their money is clearly wrong. And exempting them from paying their fair share for the public education of the city's poorest kids borders on criminal. What it does show is the hold that pro sports—particularly the Browns—have on this town. And how desperately Clevelanders wanted to be thought of as a big-league city.

In June I went down to my mailbox one day and found an interesting piece of junk mail. It was a credit card application from MBNA bank, offering me the exclusive right to own an official Browns Visa card. "The Browns are here, and you can be one of the Browns first draft picks with a Cleveland Browns Platinum Plus or preferred Visa credit card," the application gushed. I would "experience the roar of the crowd" upon having said card, and with the fraud protection, I would have "defense you can count on." And if there was any question of my loyalty to the team, the promotional blurb told me, "Now you can show you're a true Browns fan every time you make a purchase." And I thought I could be a fan merely by cheering for them on Sunday.

Then came this little kicker: "Plus, after qualifying use of your Browns Visa card, you will be sent a Cleveland Browns Commemorative Football with facsimile autographs of the team's new owners, Al Lerner and Carmen Policy!"

They actually put an exclamation point after Policy's name.

This is what it had come to. If I wanted to be a real Browns fan, I could take my credit card balances, transfer them to Al Lerner's MBNA bank card, and pay him 13.99 percent interest on that money. And for this privilege, Lerner was going to give me a ball (valued at thirty dollars, according to the brochure) with his and Policy's autographs. Pro sports' newest heroes, a credit card lender and a former corporate lawyer.

The departure of Art Modell from Cleveland has been chewed on for many years. It has a Kennedy assassination quality to it: Clevelanders and Browns fans around the country can tell you exactly where they were in 1995 when Modell announced he was moving the team to Baltimore. I was in Nacogdoches, Texas, writing a travel piece about the best barbecue joints in the place. I was sitting on my bed in the Holiday Inn eating a bowl of Frito pie, a native Texas dish where chili and onions and peppers are served over corn chips. It was Sunday morning. This was my breakfast.

What they were reporting on the NFL pregame shows was enough to give anyone indigestion, with or without Frito pie. I had heard rumors from my friends in the Cleveland media that Modell would move if he didn't get the stadium deal. But moving the Browns was unthinkable. There was the fact that Modell could sell 70,000 seats for every game whether they won or not. Then there was the tradition. You didn't just throw away fifty years of bond between a team and its fans. But more important,

I didn't think Modell would ever move the team because the Cleveland Browns defined who he was. He was regarded as an icon in Cleveland, sitting on the boards of many corporations and charities. Art Modell was a big deal in Cleveland, something he couldn't be anywhere else.

The media like to point out that the move was a result of the city not coming up with money to build Modell a new stadium. That is part of the story. True, the city of Cleveland had invested millions of tax dollars in the Gateway Project for new facilities for the Cavaliers and the Indians, as well as monies for the Rock and Roll Hall of Fame and the new science museum on the lakefront. Art came to the city and wanted his fair share, originally a renovation of the old stadium that was budgeted for $175 million.

But Modell's problems were far more desperate. He had intermingled many business interests, including the Browns, a downtown hotel, and management of the stadium, and this conglomerate of his interests, although not losing money per se, was not making much of a profit. Around this time, Modell also began having serious health problems. He was in his seventies, had just suffered a heart attack, and had to use a cane because of leg problems. His major problem, as he thought of his own death, was the lack of liquidity. His team was worth perhaps $200 million back in 1995, but his cash flow was negligible. His greatest wish was to leave the team to his stepson, David. But when Art died, David would have to sell the team to pay estate taxes.

The deal with Baltimore put cash in his pocket, and gave him new stadium revenues to keep it that way. Looking back on it now, it is hard to blame Modell for his decision. He could have stayed in Cleveland and kept his head above water, eventually using his leverage to get a new stadium deal. But his health was foremost on his mind, and the only way he could be assured that the team would stay in his family after his death was by leaving everything he had worked for in Cleveland and flee to Baltimore.

I had occasion to sit down and talk to Modell in 1994 while working on a piece for *U.S. News* about Dallas Cowboys owner Jerry Jones. Jones was the new breed of owner in the NFL, but in many respects, he was very much like Art Modell. Both had fired legendary coaches (Jones had canned Tom Landry when he took over the Cowboys), both had won championships their third year in the league, and both had moved into leadership positions with respect to the league's negotiations of national TV contracts. For all of their differences, Jones and Modell were the same guy; it's just that Art was older and had been pushed out of the way by new-breed owners like Jones.

Jones told me that he had planned to make his own licensing deals for the Cowboys, which the NFL regarded as a violation of their rules at the time. The NFL had achieved solid growth from the sixties through the nineties based on one simple premise: the league's teams were considered branch offices of one business, and they were to share in the revenues equally. This afforded competitive balance and kept teams in small markets like Green Bay and Cleveland on equal footing with those in New York and Chicago. Jones wanted to tweak this business plan by giving each team some autonomy so that they could make extra money if they marketed themselves efficiently to their fans. The NFL owners, particularly Modell, hated Jones's way of thinking. Modell was like the owner of a McDonald's situated at a busy intersection. He made money by just flinging the doors open every day, whether he ran his business efficiently or not. He was also propped up by the other franchise owners. Under the NFL way of doing business, guys like Modell didn't have to worry about marketing or hustling, or even winning, for that matter. The huge TV contract paid the players' salaries and office expenses; the tickets sold were gravy.

What Jones and the new-breed owners had done to guys like Modell was force them into a tricky position. Jones had started offering free agents huge signing bonuses to entice them to play for the Cowboys. The only way to pay for those bonuses was to be incredibly wealthy from other business ventures, or have lucrative luxury suites, local advertising contracts, and sponsorship deals—all of which were kept by each team. Modell was neither wealthy nor did he likely have the business expertise to maximize his local profit source. He was falling behind in a league he helped build.

I wanted to get Modell's views on Jones, and I flew to Cleveland to speak with him. His PR people had told him I was a Browns fan, and Art knew he would have a captive audience. He asked if we could sit in the stadium to talk, and he hobbled with me from his office to some seats behind where home plate used to be. I liked the man instantly; he was like a wisecracking old uncle who told the same stories, but always told them with enthusiasm. Modell was from Brooklyn, a street-smart former pool hall hustler who never graduated from high school. But he was a smart guy, who correctly predicted the confluence of TV and sports well before either industry held any great sway over the American public. He swore every other sentence and laughed easily. He reminded me a bit of my dad.

I asked him what he thought of Jones. "He's a cheap Arkansas used-car salesman, and I wouldn't trust him enough to buy a car from him." So much for the sterile NFL-speak.

Modell made his point over and over again, that the strength of the NFL was in its ability to share revenues, that a guy like

Jones trying to cut his own deals would undermine the whole league. "We're fat-cat Republicans that run a business based on socialism," he said. It was one of his favorite lines.

I asked him about the problems the NFL had with Al Davis moving the Raiders between Los Angeles and Oakland. "If the league cannot provide credibility for its fans, the whole league will suffer," he said. "If we continue to move franchises around the country, the fans will leave us, the TV networks won't get the markets they want, and the advertisers will eventually get up and leave. The only credibility we have with the fans is stability. The fans have to know the Browns play in Cleveland, the Giants play in New York, and the Packers play in Green Bay. When franchises move, they undermine the entire league. They undermine everything we have built."

The sun was shining on that Sunday afternoon, and the grass was greener than I had ever seen in old Municipal Stadium. They were setting up risers at the bleacher end of the stadium for the 1994 team picture. I told Modell that I was one of those guys in the bleachers who took their shirts off in the cold weather. I told him how some of his cops had hit me in the ribs with their billy clubs while I was hanging from the goalposts after the Browns had clinched a Central Division crown. He laughed. "So that was you, huh?"

Later he excitedly showed me the model of his plans for renovating the stadium. He thought the city would come up with most of the funds for the renovations. He was optimistic that the deal could get done.

I asked him what had become of John Morrow.

"Center on the '64 team, right? Why do you ask?"

"Oh, he was my favorite player."

"Pretty strange for a kid to have a center as a favorite player. What about Jim Brown or Leroy Kelly or Frank Ryan?"

"My brother got to be Jim Brown."

We schmoozed and talked for another half hour. About the Browns' glory days and how he thought the current team had a good chance for the play-offs. He was right. The 1994 team finished 11–5 and beat the New England Patriots in the first round of the play-offs before losing to the Steelers at Three Rivers Stadium. It was the last play-off appearance for the Browns.

A year later Modell was making his plans to leave. Al Lerner, then a minority owner of the team, would help Modell secure his deal with Baltimore and even take Modell and his family to Baltimore on his corporate jet. Fans in Cleveland would tear apart the stadium, advertisers would cancel their contracts with the team, and talk radio hosts would ask Browns fans to cut up their MBNA credit cards and mail them to Lerner. In a strange and ironic twist, Lerner would own the new Browns three years later and be feted in a downtown parade.

As for Modell, his plans never worked out in Baltimore. In 1997 he was having money troubles again and had to borrow $185 million to keep the franchise afloat. When his debt to operating profit ratio fell below league standards, the NFL forced him to get a minority investor. At the end of 1999 Modell sold a 49 percent interest in the team—valued at $275 million—to Baltimore businessman Stephen J. Biscotti. Biscotti retains the right to purchase the rest of the team in 2004, a right he will certainly pursue.

The upshot of all this? Modell moved the team so that he could pass the franchise on to his son. Within five years he had screwed up that plan. And the city of Cleveland was forced to go without football for three years, build a new stadium costing more than $300 million, and pay a then-record $530 million for an expansion franchise. If anyone back in 1994 had shown any foresight, the city could have kept the Browns for $175 million. It could have been so much more simple.

Al Lerner reminds me of the Montgomery Burns character on *The Simpsons*. Carmen Policy might as well be Burns's sidekick, Smithers. Burns, you may recall, is the owner of the Springfield nuclear power plant who is always investing in schemes that will allow him to gain more money from the citizens of Springfield, other than their massive utility bills. I could just picture Lerner and Policy after they had secured the new Browns franchise: "Well, Carmen, after we get the city to build us a new stadium and abate our taxes, and after we charge the fans licenses to buy season tickets, we'll sell them beer for five dollars and charge twenty dollars for parking. Then we'll get them all to transfer their credit card debts."

Perhaps I am being unfair. Lerner, like Modell, was born in Brooklyn and was a self-made man. A former furniture salesman, he began investing and got into the banking business, eventually buying a controlling interest in Maryland-based MBNA. MBNA quickly became one of the largest credit card issuers in the country, number three behind Citibank and Bank One. The company had $5.2 billion in revenue in 1998.

Much of MBNA's growth had to do with affinity cards—Visa cards and MasterCards that are tied to universities, sports teams, even *Star Trek* fanatics. Lerner saw a gold mine in these affinity cards and set up a deal with the NFL in 1995—around the time Modell was moving the Browns—to become the official affinity card for NFL teams. In five years MBNA grew from issuing roughly 100,000 NFL cards to more than 1 million as of 1999.

Lerner had lived in Cleveland for thirty-five years but was relatively unknown in his adopted city until he put Modell on that jet to Baltimore. And he repeatedly told the media he was not interested in owning the new Browns. But as serious bidders were weeded out, Lerner, who had courted former 49ers president Carmen Policy and former Browns quarterback Bernie Kosar to be included in his bid, decided to use his huge financial resources to gain the new team. His bid of $530 million was the most ever paid for a pro sports franchise at the time.

But it was the inclusion of Policy that sealed the deal for Lerner. Policy was a former Youngstown lawyer who had worked earlier in his legal career for powerful Youngstown businessman Edward DeBartolo, Sr. DeBartolo had built hundreds of shopping malls around the country in the sixties and seventies and was the wealthiest man in Youngstown.

As is customary for a successful lawyer in private practice in Youngstown, Policy found himself defending various clients involved in organized crime. The turf in Youngstown was constantly being fought over by the mob elements in Cleveland and Pittsburgh, and consequently there were a number of money-laundering, murder, and loan-sharking cases. In 1978 Policy defended Ronnie "the Crab" Carabbia in connection with blowing up Cleveland gangster Danny Greene. Despite Policy's efforts, Carabbia was convicted and sentenced to life in prison. Another longtime client from the era was Youngstown racketeer Joey Naples, who, according to federal agents, was responsible for at least seven executions, including that of Charles Carabbia, Ronnie's brother.

This is not to imply that Policy was merely a stooge for the mob. Any lawyer practicing criminal law at the time in Youngstown would have had his fair share of mob clients, and Policy was no exception. What Policy's experience as a criminal lawyer does show, however, is his unusual knack for escapability—his ability to swim with the sharks and remain unscathed.

Through his work with DeBartolo, Policy was able to transform himself from big time criminal defense lawyer to sports executive and eventually a part owner of the Browns. When DeBartolo bought the San Francisco 49ers in 1977, he installed his thirty-year-old playboy son, Eddie Junior, as chairman of the team. Eddie Junior hadn't inherited his father's work ethic and preferred to play in Las Vegas rather than learn about the family business. Still, Junior spent lavishly on his new toy, buying boats for coaches and Rolex watches as party favors. Originally Policy was sent to California by DeBartolo Senior to negotiate Coach Bill Walsh's new contract. But many believe that the elder DeBartolo wanted Policy to keep an eye on his son for him.

Policy began handling legal matters for the 49ers, and within four years he was installed as the team's vice-president and general counsel. By the mid-eighties Eddie Junior had tired of attending NFL meetings and sent Policy in his place. By 1991 Policy had been installed as president of the 49ers and assumed day-to-day operations of the team. One of his lasting legacies in the NFL was figuring out a loophole in the league's new salary cap, which was implemented to keep free spenders like Eddie Junior from spending more money on their team's payroll than their rivals could. Policy discovered that bonuses on player contracts, paid up front, could be prorated over the life of the contract. Thus, if a player signed a three-year $12-million contract with a $6-million bonus, the player would be paid $10 million in his first year, but only $6 million would be counted against the cap. The difference—$4 million—was important; a team could use that extra money to sign another player or all of its draft picks.

But like most accounting maneuvers, the real numbers eventually catch up with you. The problems in San Francisco began in 1997. Eddie Junior was accused of paying $400,000 in bribes to former Louisiana governor Edwin Edwards for his help in gaining a casino license in the state, and was asked to step down from the 49ers. Policy originally thought Eddie Junior's departure would give him greater control of the team, but Eddie's sister, Denise DeBartolo York, who ran her now deceased father's empire, took over and installed her husband, John York, as president.

Policy must have been able to see the writing on the wall, and some of that was his own doing. His use of the salary cap, signing star players like Steve Young and Jerry Rice with huge bonuses, was beginning to catch up with the team. By 1998 the 49ers were going to be tens of millions of dollars over the salary cap, and he began planning his escape route. That road ran right into Lerner, worth $4 billion, who needed an NFL insider like Policy to seal the deal. For his efforts, Policy was given 10 percent of the team and a salary of $1.5 million. Not bad for a former Youngstown criminal defense lawyer.

In an article in the *Cleveland Scene* in September 1999, writer Mike Tobin quoted an unnamed lawyer who offered this view of Carmen Policy: "If you walk into a room full of people, and you want to know who is the richest guy in the room, just watch who Carmen spends most of his time with. In the old days, the wealthiest and most powerful guy in [Youngstown] was Eddie D' Sr., and that's who he latched on to. Eddie D' Sr. is gone, Eddie Jr. is a washout, and now he's found Al Lerner."

As for the 49ers, they were forced to send players essentially free of charge to Cleveland—like Fidel Castro purging his island of criminals during the Mariel Boatlift—to get under the salary cap for the 1999 season. The 49ers finished 3-13, their worst record in decades, and faced the 2000 season a projected $24 million over the salary cap.

As for Policy, he promised that the Browns would be a different organization, one held to a higher standard and one that would contend almost immediately. He became the visible face of the organization that had done the impossible, bringing football back to Cleveland. And his autograph was used to peddle credit cards.

My first experience with the new Browns was instructive as to how this team would operate. Soon after the Lerner/Policy ownership group was announced in December 1999, I called the Browns public relations office and asked how I might get access to cover the team's first season. I was told to write a letter with my intentions. In my letter I told the new Browns flaks that I wanted to write a book about how Browns fans had supported the team through the years and how this new team would always be special. I was laying it on a little thick, but in reality those were my intentions. I overnighted the letter, with previous clips of my work and a letter from Doubleday, and waited a month. I called back and was told they didn't know who I was. I wrote another letter and waited another month. Finally I got a response:

Thank you for your correspondence to both Carmen Policy and myself regarding your book project with Doubleday. The interest in the Browns is at an all-time high and we feel your enthusiasm regarding the project!

The purpose of this leter is to inform you that the Cleveland Browns, in conjunction with "The Sporting News," will also be producing a book prior to the upcoming season. Due to our agreement with "The Sporting News," we will be unable to participate with you in the production of your work.

The letter was signed by Alex Martins, Vice President, Director of Communication & Public Affairs. Aside from the fact that they had no idea when my book was scheduled to be published, I was somewhat perplexed by the notion that the Browns had partnered up with the *Sporting News* in a profit-making venture. Wasn't the *Sporting News* supposed to be covering the new Browns for their readers?

I called the Browns and talked to Dan Arthur, who was director of Internet and publications for the new team.

"I just wanted to know why you guys don't want to help me out on this," I said.

"We already have the deal with the *Sporting News,*" Arthur responded.

"But I'm talking about publishing at the beginning of the second year, not the first. This book will not be in competition with your deal with the *Sporting News.*"

"We understand that, but we really don't want to cooperate with you because we don't have any leverage," Arthur said.

I knew what he was getting at, but I wanted to hear it out of his mouth.

"What do you mean by leverage?" I asked innocently.

"Well, if a beat writer from one of the newspapers or someone from a TV station reports something we don't like, we can go to their editors and have them reassigned. We can't do that with you."

I knew where this was going. Sports teams had long had great power over the media they covered. Beat writers and TV reporters were beholden to the PR people because they needed access. Without the access, the public wouldn't know how a player's groin pull was doing or how "focused" a player had become on his assignment on the field. The sports media constantly pulled punches: that's why you never heard what a cancer a player was in the clubhouse until after he was traded. And the media outlets knew that they couldn't afford to piss off the team or the fans. Newspapers and TV stations knew that sports coverage was among the top reasons the public came to them for information. A writer or TV sportscaster who caused problems would be frozen out.

Still, I had never heard a sports PR professional define the relationship in such blunt terms. As I saw it, what was happening here was that the new Browns must have known they were going to have the upper hand on the Cleveland media, and they weren't going to take their foot off the media's neck. The Browns knew that fan support was so strong that any media type who blasted the organization would be tattooed by the public. So the Browns knew they were going to have the upper hand, and they were going to make sure everyone in the media understood who was boss in this new organization.

"My intentions are hardly clandestine," I told him. "I just want to write an accurate view of how the team does in its first year. If you want leverage on that, you're not going to get it. But can't you guys just let me come in and observe?"

He said he would think about it. Six weeks later I was told I could have a generic press pass for practice and games, but without interviews with Policy, Lerner, or new General Manager Dwight Clark. And even though there were about a hundred seats in the press box for games, I would have no seat. The college newspaper the *Cleveland State Cauldron* got a seat, as did the free entertainment magazine *Cleveland Met*. I was permitted one free meal per game, however.

The Browns opened training camp at the end of July. I was soon brought into the mind-numbing routine that sportswriters must deal with when covering a team. The players began their practice about 9 A.M. For two hours they would hit blocking sleds, practice kick coverage, and toward the end of the session have a seven-on-seven drill.

From 11 A.M. until 11:45 the media are allowed into the locker room. On any given day there were perhaps thirty or forty media types, milling about and trying to get pearls of wisdom from players as they undressed. This aspect of the interview process was completely foreign to me. For the most part, players would walk around naked in front of the fully clothed sports media. It didn't matter that there were many female media members in the locker room. Some players—usually the married guys—would try to pull a towel around their waste when they walked to the showers. The younger—mostly single—players would parade around showing what they had, unconcerned about women in the locker room.

It was very strange seeing women—especially the TV reporters—trying to do their job in this environment. Most of the women in the media tended to be on the short side, while the players tended to be gargantuan. At times the scene would be almost comical. A short woman—like Mary Kay Cabot of the *Plain Dealer*—would be among a crowd of media types gathered around a player's locker. If she was in the front of this group, she would find herself taking notes while a large man's penis dangled at her chest. I guess it's a living.

Some of the old-timers told me a story involving John Elway of the Broncos. After the famous "Drive" in 1986, the media squeezed around Elway's locker to get his thoughts on the game. One radio sportscaster knelt in front of Elway's locker so that he could get his tape recorder closer to Elway. But as the crush of media pushed from behind, the poor fellow found his face up against Elway's dick. For the next five minutes he faithfully recorded Elway while the man's penis was pressed against his cheek. The Denver beat reporters had a field day with the incident, how a Cleveland reporter had to watch Elway beat the Browns and then suffer the indignity of having his dick in his face. Elway had a sense of humor about the incident; the next week he sent the radio reporter an autographed jockstrap.

And in this environment, with naked players being pursued by cameras and microphones, there is not much chance at substantive conversation. The electronic guys want a sound bite, and the print reporters need a quote to put in the third paragraph of their stories, as is the basic formula of the twenty-inch newspaper story. The media usually begin their questions with "Talk a little bit about" the pass you caught, the injury you suffered, the "scheme" the coaches have implemented, the great hit made in practice. The players respond with mostly unintelligible nonsense, which is dutifully recorded by the media. The key word of the modern pro athlete interview repertoire is "focus." As in, I focused on the pass I caught, I'll have to focus on rehabbing this injury, it takes focus to implement the coach's scheme, I really focused when I laid that guy out.

The other athlete interview crutch (besides "y'know") is to punctuate sentences with "and shit." As in, I was focused, y'know, out there, and shit. The media would routinely edit all the "and shit" out of their copy or their tapes, but "and shit" is perhaps the most common aspect of athletespeak. My father loved the role of "and shit" in the English language used by athletes. There was a racial element to his fascination with the language of mostly black athletes; he claimed that his years growing up in the ghetto and his job as a ditchdigger had made him an expert on black dialects and speech patterns. He was raised in a bigoted environment and referred to the various aspects of black speech as "jaboneyisms."

He and I would use "and shit" in our conversations on a regular basis. Sometimes we would have entire conversations with the "and shit" ending on our sentences.

"How is the morphine keeping the pain away for you?" I asked him one day.

"I feel like you guys probably did in college when you smoked bongs and watched TV all day. And shit."

"Are you ever confused because of the drugs? And shit."

"No more than my children. And shit."

"I guess if we're confused, we inherited that from you. And shit."

"How sharper than a serpent's tooth is an ungrateful child. And shit."

"So have the doctors given you any idea how long you have? And shit."

"I've got five if I hold it and fifteen if I jerk it. And shit."

As training camp unfolded during the summer, there was something strange happening. The Browns' practices had always been free and open to the public in the past, and usually filled the stands at their training camps at Hiram College and, later, Lakeland Community College. But the new Browns decided to make the fans park two miles away and pay five dollars for a "free" ticket. The fee was to offset the bus ride and to pay the parking lot operators, but many fans saw it as unfettered greed on the part of the new owners. The stands in the Browns training facility held 4,500 fans, but on most days only about 800 showed up.

And those that did show up were immediately pounced upon by the MBNA credit card folks. There were three kiosks around the field, and fans were offered a free T-shirt or hat if they applied for the card. As I walked around the field on that first day, I was asked to sign up for a Browns credit card eight different times.

I told them I wasn't interested. I mean, what did I need with a crummy T-shirt or Browns hat? I had an application at home where I could get a football with a facsimile of Al Lerner's and Carmen Policy's autographs. A thirty-dollar value. And shit.

# CHAPTER FIVE

# Take This Cup

This is the year I turn forty years old. I have always told myself that age is irrelevant, and the preoccupation with the inordinate importance of the decimalization of time is silly. How different is thirty-nine and forty, for chrissakes; life should not change as we move into a new decade. We are one day older and that should be it.

But for men, at least, moving into the cusp of middle age is a time for a certain soul-searching. When I turn forty in October, I will be closer to sixty than I am to twenty. I have a paunch now and a hard time running because of recent foot surgery. I am thirty pounds overweight, and no amount of exercise or diet seems to make a dent. I think I may need glasses soon, as hours before a computer screen have caused a permanent squint. My face is fatter and more wrinkled, my nose spreads out on my face, and my eyebrows are bushier and more wiry. I have the Irish curse of the permanent red face—something they now call rosacea—a condition that makes me look permanently out of breath, which I usually am.

I am looking more and more like my father. This is disconcerting, as the more I age, and the more I look at pictures of him in his fifties and sixties, the more I see my physical future. His future is behind him and it is not something I want to look at right now.

When my father told me he was dying, my first response was

to ask him what he wanted to do with his remaining time. This is how a man in his late thirties looks at death. We think of our lives as being woefully incomplete, and what we haven't done seems to take on far more importance than what we have accomplished. If I had six months to live, I would try to do something—anything—that might make my mark on the world. Try to finish that novel that's been rattling around in my head for ten years. Travel to places I had always dreamed about. Repair relationships I have ignored.

My brothers and I talked about possibly taking my father on a trip before he died, just the old man and his sons, maybe to Ireland or to Oktoberfest in Germany or to Italy, where he loved to tour the old cathedrals and art museums. We thought that during his last year on earth he would want to do things, do things with his children, do something unusual to make his mark. But he wanted none of this; in fact, he railed against doing anything out of the ordinary. As I think back now, I see that he wanted to spend his last days preparing to die. And those of us that wanted some grand final fling, some trumped-up feel-good event that would be more important for the living than the dying, well, he shot that down with his usual bravado. "There is nothing in my life that I need to do," he said during the summer months. "I have no regrets."

In my conversations with him, I saw how he had changed in his sixties. He had come to a point where he no longer feared death, not in the conventional sense of trying to bargain with God and gain a few years of life. He had begun to go easier on himself, forgiving himself for the relative misdemeanors of his youth and middle age. He had become comfortable with who he now was, an old man who had a decent life. There was no panic or any attempt to make his death anything special. He wanted to go out as he lived, with confidence and a certain grace, with the knowledge that he did his best, even when his best wasn't good enough. He had accepted the inevitable with a calm I could not understand.

I, on the other hand, saw him and became afraid of death. This is how men in their thirties view death. We view our lives in the prism of incompletion. Our kids are just starting to grow up, our marriages have become stale, our careers lead us to say, "Is that all there is?" When I looked at him fading away, I felt real panic. And this was a very selfish way for a man in his thirties to view death. I thought that doing something—encouraging him to try alternative treatments, trying to change his diet, keeping him on the chemotherapy—would give him some sort of chance, minuscule though it might be. But he knew what was inside of him. He felt the pressures in his abdomen, the pain of tumors growing inside his once healthy body. He wanted completion. And he needed a little help, though he would never admit it.

And that was my dilemma. I wanted to help him die, but I didn't know how to do it. In case you hadn't noticed by now, I have trouble dealing with problems head-on. Avoidance is a built-in defense mechanism I have relied upon throughout my life; if you ignore something, I have always thought, things might go away. In my youth I avoided problems with my speech; as an adult I have avoided problems in my marriage. In fact, I have been separated from my wife, Teresa, almost eight years now and still haven't figured out a good time to get a divorce.

Throughout my life, from the time I was about fifteen until now, I have avoided confronting my abuse of alcohol and drugs. Except for a few months here and there when I have been pressured to take the veil, I have been drunk or high almost daily for the past twenty years. Mostly, like most of my generation, I have avoided growing up. When my father's generation was in their twenties, they were married and building careers and serving in the military. In my case, when my friends and I were in our twenties, we were doing amyl nitrate in the bleachers during Browns games.

When my mother was sick, I made a conscious decision about two months before she died. I decided she was dead already and dealt with her illness that way. I didn't feel good about it, and perhaps my interaction with her during her final months was distant. But in my rationalization, that woman suffering in the upstairs bedroom was no longer my mother. My mother was a lively, beautiful woman who was so strong in the way she lived life I felt a permanent attachment to her. I decided that she had already gone, a decision I sometimes regret to this day. But it was the only way I could deal with her, and death, and how to go about living.

My father's reaction to my mom's death was one of reassessing his life. He realized that he hadn't paid enough attention to her or his family and changed the way he lived. And as he got older, he had achieved a certain comfort level with his life. He didn't give a shit about his work as a lawyer; what had once defined him had become superficial. He traveled the world in his later years, taking classes in Renaissance art in Italy and going to Oktoberfest in Germany. He had a passion for touring historic Catholic churches in Europe. Always a voracious reader, he was reading about a book a week in his retirement. He took an active interest in his children's lives, something that surprised most of us. I had always thought of myself in competition with him, but then I found out he was keeping a file of every story I had ever written, even the most spare and crappy little briefs I had written for *U.S. News*.

He had grown up a lot in his last five years. He became comfortable in his own skin for the first time. But just as I had regarded my mother during her last horrible months, I looked at him as if he were already dead. The last rites sealed it for me. Though he was somewhat responsive during the sacrament, he hadn't spoken or showed any signs of improvement for days. The nurses at the hospice told us that he had a few hours—maybe a few days—to live. In my mind he was already dead. And quite frankly, I thought that maybe he didn't need or want any help in his final hours. His stubbornness and independence were showing through. He didn't want any spectacle to be made of his death, nothing out of the ordinary. "Every person who has ever walked on this planet has died," he had told me. "Why should I think of myself as being anyone special?" No eulogies, no bagpipes, no mimes.

I didn't want to hang around his bedside waiting for that magic moment. Along with my basic problem of avoidance, I really didn't know what I could add to the equation. The nurses told me that patients in his condition are in a semiconscious state, that fragile place between life and death, but they can still hear. But I didn't know what more I could tell him. Say I loved him? Make small talk? Rehash old wounds? It all seemed too contrived and petty.

I also knew that he was the type of guy who didn't want a bunch of people surrounding him at this point in his life. He liked handling crises by himself; he got his power from that. I was beginning to think that he would probably sneak out after everyone had left the room. That would be his style. So after the last rites, I held his hand, told him I loved him, and wished him well. Not the send-off I had imagined, but at the time it was the best I could do.

One of my comfort levels when avoiding life's difficulties is engaging myself in mindless, repetitive activities. As a kid, when I was feeling as though the world had somehow wronged me, I would grab my basketball and go down to the park and shoot free throws. Sometimes I would skip stones for hours on the beach. When my father was fighting with my mother, he would grab me and we would toss the football around in the backyard in silence. Lately I would go to the driving range. Or watch VH1 *Behind the Music* marathons. Toss back ten beers in my brother's bar. Mindless and repetitive. Shallow, yet happy.

I was due to stay with him overnight on this Tuesday. I didn't relish the duty, because I was pretty sure he was going to die on my watch. I had a few hours to kill before I was due back at the hospice, so I did what I usually do. Avoidance. Mindless repetition. I went bowling.

*"Toma punueta."*

The booming voice belonged to Edwin, a Puerto Rican factory worker who had a tattoo of an eagle on his left calf and a string of cheesy gold chains around his neck. When Edwin shouted *"toma punueta,"* it was because he was throwing strikes. He told me it meant "jack off" or "you whore." He wasn't sure.

We were bowling against Edwin's team on this Tuesday night at Dickey Lanes, a quaint eight-lane bowling alley on West 25th Street in the middle of a hillbilly/Puerto Rican neighborhood. This was also the old porno district of Cleveland—before strip joints became glamorous and gilded like the ones down in the Flats. These places—the Peek-a-Boo Club, Teaser Show Bar, Buggsy's Speakeasy—were strip bars from the era when such establishments were not acceptable places to take clients for lunch.

They were full of sin and heavyset hillbilly women with stretch marks and bad teeth, tittie bars without all-you-can-eat buffets and lawyers doing deals. In the midst of this neighborhood, forgotten by urban renewal and the glitter of the downtown a few miles away, was the Dickey family business. In keeping with the pattern of businesses in the neighborhood, the sign outside the bowling alley was "Dickey Recreation."

Doctor Deadhead found the place about four years ago. In his mid-forties and as thin as he was in his twenties, Doctor Deadhead was a modern-day Cleveland Renaissance man. He painted signs for a living—not fancy signs that might adorn a business, but more practical signs like the ones that said "Stop" or "No Parking." He worked for the city of Cleveland in the sign painting department and made a good living. He was also an expert drywall hanger and a man who could tear apart a carburetor within ten minutes.

His red hair was thinning a bit, but Doctor Deadhead was in his prime in his area of expertise: he was a 180-average bowler, a darts player who could hit triple twenty on command, an eight-handicap golfer, and a horseshoe pitcher who wanted to join the pro tour. He was, in his words, "better than most at sports that involve beer drinking." His name, Doctor Deadhead, came from his frat house days at Cleveland State when he would stay up all night listening to Grateful Dead music until the keg was finished. And then, for him, it was usually time to tap the second keg.

He moved his bowling league team to Dickey Recreation when he became concerned that bowling was turning into "a pussy sport." The big bowling alleys out in Parma and Brook Park were having rock and roll bowling nights, complete with black lights and multicolored balls. For Doctor Deadhead, bowling was more spiritual, the type of activity that demanded the requisite concentration and skill, a man's game that was a part of the heritage of the city. Dickey's was the place that best exemplified that tradition: no automatic scoring systems, old Brunswick pinsetters that were always breaking down, hot dogs on the machine that had the spinning rollers, beers priced at $1.75. And the music on the jukebox reflected the blue-collar guys in our men's league: classic rock like Boston and Spanish salsa music.

We bowled every Tuesday at 5:30. Doctor had asked me to join up during the summer, and I told him I hadn't bowled since I was a teenager. "You're living in Cleveland this year, so you have to bowl," he told me. It sounded so simple. When in Cleveland you bowl, you drink beer, you hang out at Dickey Recreation. Bowling was like other bar games; we needed something to be mildly amused while we drank beer. Doctor pointed out to me that former Cleveland mayor Ralph Perk's wife would not go to the Nixon White House for a reception during the late sixties because it conflicted with her bowling night. "She was a broad who had her priorities straight," Doctor said.

I was not a very good bowler. I threw a straight ball, because for some reason I could not master the intricacies of the hook. This particular Tuesday was our second night of the league, a league that would last until spring. My first game during the previous week, I bowled a 94, but rebounded to fire a 154 in game three. I found I liked bowling, given my limited history in the sport. It was beautiful in its simplicity, yet in a profound way. Anyone can throw a ball and knock some pins down. But the best bowlers don't think. They get in a rhythm, where it is just the ball and the pins. Mindless repetitiveness. Insidiously vacuous. Happiness in a very shallow way. "I just think about pussy when I'm bowling," Doctor told me in the first week by way of advice.

Bowling also operated within the realm of the three-and-nine rule of life. Before three beers, my approach and arm swing were clunky. Between three and nine beers there was a fluidity to my stroke. After nine, I was in danger of throwing gutter balls and talking more than my usual nonsense.

*"Toma punueta."*

Edwin had another strike, his fifth in a row in game two, and we were in danger of losing another game. Edwin's team (some plumbing company was their sponsor) had beat us by forty-two pins in game one. They were up by sixty in this game, above and beyond the thirty-pin spot we were getting. Doctor was matching Edwin strike for strike, but the rest of us were falling flat. Lance was on our team, but he had little interest in bowling. He used it as an excuse to drink on Tuesdays, and his average clocked in at 135. Matt O'Connor, a chemical supply salesman with four young kids, was our fourth, but he had torn up his right shoulder playing touch football a year ago and was trying to relearn bowling left-handed. It was an admirable effort, but he had lost about twenty pins a game on his average, down to about 140.

Edwin came to the scoring table to pick up a card. During every game at Dickey Recreation, we had a deck of porno playing cards sitting on the table. If you bowled a strike, you got a card; the player with the best hand would win the pot. Thus, three blow jobs would beat two anal sex, three double-input would beat two cum-shots, and so on.

"Whatja get?" I asked Edwin.

"Another blow job," he answered. "I've got a full house, anal sex over head."

Doctor moved up for his turn. He had a fluid movement on his approach and always checked the lanes for their wax. He figured he would throw his ball about two boards from the right side, hook it about a foot and a half, and slide it right into the pocket. He slid hard on his left foot, swung his right foot out behind him, and hit the second board perfectly. The ball spun through the pocket and exploded, crushing the pins down without any cheap ricochets off the sides.

Doctor swung around and gave his strike call. "Fat girls need lovin', too," he shouted. Having a strike call in bowling was similar to having a good end zone celebration in pro football. The best were simple and reflected the individuality of their originator. Doctor's line came from a declaration he made at a frat party fifteen years ago. I had asked him why he always seemed to be dating fat girls and he came up with his now signature line. Fat girls need lovin', too. It had a certain simple ring to it. It was a good strike call. Not as good as *toma punueta*. But up there. Lance's was a simple "Eat me." Mine was a quiet call, based on Jim Bouton's book *Ball Four*. Coach Joe Schultz of the Seattle Pilots would tell his team, "First you pound the opponents, then you pound the Budweisers." My version of this, in bowling parlance, was "Pound that pocket, pound those Budweisers." Not especially clever, but it worked for me. I didn't have many chances to use it.

Lance and Doctor didn't get along too well. Lance was kind of a moocher, never buying too many beers, always late in his weekly ten-dollar payment for bowling. But Lance was an alpha male type, with good looks that lasted into his forties now; he looked like a combination of the character Eb from the TV series *Green Acres* and Elvis Presley. He said he worked as a consultant, but few of us had any idea what he consulted on. But he was legendary with the women, scamming and bullshitting women in their twenties. One girl told me Lance had asked her to pay his phone bill while in the midst of sex.

Doctor came to pick up his card. It was a triple-penetration shot. Gave him two in his hand. Still not enough to beat out Edwin.

Lance was up. First shot a weak effort, knocking just five pins down on the right side. His spare shot just grazed the pile, knocking down two more. A very weak seven.

"You big faggot," Doctor chided him.

"I can unequivocally say to you, Doctor, I am not a faggot," Lance said, sitting on the bench next to the scorers' table. "I am much more perverse than that. I'm into homo-necro-bestiality."

"That's a new one," I responded.

"I have sex with dead animals, but they have to be gay dead animals," he deadpanned.

"How can you tell?" O'Connor joined in. "I mean the gay part."

"All of God's creatures who are gay have the same features: weird lips and baggy eyes."

This was Lance's theory of being gay. He claimed he could spot a homosexual by the fact that his eyes had bags under them and his lips were often pursed—weird in his opinion. He had several other theories of gay behavior. If there was an unsolved, sensational murder, there was a gay subplot at its core. He also claimed it was impossible to be bisexual. "No such thing," he used to say. "If you've sucked on the pole, you can't lick the hole."

"Must be hard to find all those dead gay animals," I said.

"Yeah, I have a feeling some of the dead animals I've had sex with were actually heterosexual."

My turn. Threw a straight ball right down the middle. Seven-ten split. Second ball went right down the middle. Everyone threw up their arms signaling a field goal.

Lance laughed. "You suck, McGraw. You suck that big pole."

"I have been giving that some thought lately," I said. "I spend most of my time these days standing around half-naked black men who don't conjugate verbs very well. Does it make me gay if I stare at their dicks?"

It was something I had been thinking about, not the gay part, of course, but the weird place the sports media get put in when interviewing players in the locker room. You couldn't help but not look. At times it was like looking at a solar eclipse. If you stared too long, you'd blind yourself. But it was unavoidable. And uncomfortable.

"So who on the Browns has the biggest dick?" Doctor asked.

"You're worse than McGraw," Lance said.

"Actually, I haven't done any measuring per se, but I have noticed trends," I responded. "You'd expect the big guys, the three-hundred-pound offensive linemen, to have the biggest dicks, but the wiry guys, the defensive backs, seem to be bigger. I think it has to do with the size of the stomach. Guys with flat stomachs appear to have bigger dicks than those of us with paunches. When you have a flat stomach, you become all dick."

"I've always had a flat stomach," Doctor said.

"Cub Scouts need lovin', too," Lance opined.

And so the witty banter and repartee continued. Talk of dicks and hitting the pocket, car stereos and salsa music, fat women and beef jerky. I had missed this type of camaraderie down in Texas. Even though I had been there for almost ten years, I hadn't made very many really good friends. And my work with *U.S. News* had me talking to Ivy League policy wonks. Like anyone truly gave a shit what they had to say. In one issue of *U.S. News* the brain trust had us write about our hometowns as part of a package for an issue around the Thanksgiving holiday. I wrote about how I came to Cleveland and hung out at my brother's bar. The woman editing the piece at our office in Washington called me up and said she loved how it was written, but had one question. "What is a bowling machine?" she asked. I felt like kidnapping her and strapping her to a barstool next to Crowley.

So in a way, this bowling league was my attachment to the real Cleveland. Bigoted and sexist, immature and drunk, but hardworking and real. And bowling was the perfect place to find real Clevelanders. The guys in this bowling alley were real people, sign painters, the tool-and-die makers, the unemployed. We all got along well, because we were bowling and observing the three-and-nine rule of life.

We lost the second game but rebounded for the third, where Doctor bowled a 246. My series for three games was a respectable 447. Edwin continued to stay hot, winning the second pot and then taking the third with two pairs, three-inputs and blow jobs. *Toma punueta* to us all.

As I was changing my shoes, Doctor asked if I wanted to go shoot some darts at the Harbor Inn down in the Flats. "Sorry, Doc, but I'm staying with my dad tonight over at the hospice."

"How's he's doing?" he asked.

"He might go tonight," I told him.

"Come on in the bar and have a shot with us."

I agreed, if only to numb myself further. Doctor ordered four shots of Jim Beam, and we all held them up.

"To all of our fathers," O'Connor said.

"To the man who found me fucking in his basement," Lance joined in.

"To no pain when he goes," Doctor intoned.

"To shallow happiness," I said. "And shit."

. . .

I arrived at the hospice with a minor buzz going; I had only had about six beers and the shot of Beam, so I wasn't too looped. Pulling into the parking lot, though, brought me down in a hurry. There was a funeral home ambulance in the lot, and two goulish-looking guys were pulling out a stretcher and wheeling it into the building. The men pushing the stretcher were pale and thin, wore black work pants and white shirts, bore no facial expression, and didn't speak to each other. I arrived behind them at the desk just after they were given the room number of their pickup. I followed them.

They moved down the hallways quickly. I was hoping they would take a turn into one of the rooms in a different wing from my father, but they moved inexorably through the hospice, down one hall, then another. In some of the patients' rooms, TVs were blaring even as the patients slept, their heads mostly bald from endless chemotherapy. Most looked like Edvard Munch's *The Scream*. Very few had visitors.

The funeral home men continued through the visitors' lounge in the center of the complex and then moved down my father's hallway. I suddenly had the horrible feeling that they had come to pick my father up, that he had already expired. I stood at the end of the hallway and waited. They moved slowly down the hallway, like the angels of death that they were, and came to my father's door. The two men looked at the room number written on their note, and moved on, two doors down from my dad. I felt relief. But I also felt a sudden thud in my chest. I wondered what it would be like when those two guys came for my father.

It was about 9:30 at night. The door was cracked open a few inches, and it was dark inside. My sister Kathleen was sitting next to his bed, holding his hand. Kathleen was a professor of psychology at Ohio State University in Columbus and had moved back to Ohio a few years earlier from New York, where she had taught for about fifteen years at SUNY Stony Brook. She was the oldest child and had gone through more problems with my father than any of us. As the firstborn, she had felt his parental wrath first and more deeply. Her high school years coincided with my mom's illness, and she floated around for a few years after my mom's death without much direction. But she righted herself, took a job as a waitress, and paid her way through college. And through the years, she became a very successful academic, publishing numerous studies and becoming one of the leading experts in the field of political psychology.

I had watched her with him during the past few days. I was wondering if there were any residual problems from their relationship; she had separated herself from him for some years in much the same way I had. As she became more successful, by doing well in school and then in her career, she gravitated back to him. Kathleen and I, far more than did my other siblings, shared this experience with him. Was it him that forced us away, by being unreasonable in his expectations for us? Or did his expectations cause us to seek an identity outside of his shadow, the only way we could have succeeded?

I had asked my father this question, and he got a puzzled look on his face. I was thinking too much, he said. And I probably was. We look to our parents with so many strings attached and with such force of will that they know not their real importance to us. I would have liked to talk to my sister about this, but this is not what we did. We did not talk about things like that in our family, not because we weren't close, but because the old man had taught us not to become overly reflective on circumstances in which we had no earthly way of changing. For my father, focusing on such was just some form of mental masturbation.

I poked my head into the room, and my sister came outside. She gave me a rundown on his condition. Hadn't said anything since she was there in early afternoon, hadn't made a facial expression in two hours since his two-year-old grandson, Richard II, had given him a wet, messy kiss. He had eaten only a little ice cream, and she had given him ice chips when his mouth became dry.

"Are you going to be able to handle this?" she asked me, being the consummate older sister.

"I'll be okay," I answered.

"You have everyone's phone number, right?" she asked. This was a question that left the most important part unstated. The phone numbers were to be used when he died, to inform everyone that it had happened.

"Do you want me to call, like if he takes a turn for the worse?"

"No, he's already past that now. Just call when it happens."

We couldn't even say the words "die" or "dead." But we knew exactly what we were talking about. The nurses in the hospice didn't like to go out on a limb and prognosticate about when some patient would move on to that higher plane, but they had told us that he had gone on longer than anyone had expected. As everything in his body was shutting down, his heart remained strong. And they had increased the morphine so he at least appeared comfortable.

"I have to go now," Kathleen told me.

"Any advice?" I asked.

"Just be there for him," she said. "All he needs right now is a little help. He'll be okay. Just help him."

I appreciated her advice. Very older-sisterly of her. During the next few hours it would serve me well.

.   .   .

I sat down in the chair next to his bed and whispered that I was there for him the rest of the night. He opened his eyes slowly and looked at me, a deep and longing look that I had never seen before. He looked like he wanted to say something but couldn't. He looked frustrated and agitated. I also got the feeling that he was wrestling with something; that something was getting in the way of what he was doing. I didn't know what that was.

He closed his eyes again and his breathing became irregular. It was almost like the snoring from a sleep apnea patient, who will stop breathing for five or ten seconds and then start again. I sat there for what seemed like hours—it was only about ten minutes—listening to his every breath. Every time he stopped breathing I would stand over his bed and wait. His mouth and chest would suddenly jerk and his mouth would gape open again, the breath filling his lungs. He repeated this every ten or so breaths. I became very tense.

I left the room. If I spent all night listening to his breathing, I would go absolutely nuts. There was a big-screen TV in the visitors' lounge, and the Indians and the Angels were playing in a late night game from the West Coast. I recognized Jerome in the lounge watching the game. Jerome worked as an orderly at the hospice and was a regular at my brother's bar down the street. We made small talk about the game, but Jerome could sense my nervousness.

"How's he doing?" Jerome asked.

"Not very good. His breathing is irregular. It's tough to listen to."

"It gets that way toward the end."

"How do you guys work in this place, with all these people dying around you?" I didn't know if Jerome knew the answer, but I needed someone I could talk to.

"I guess you never get used to it," he answered. "But you realize how to handle it after a while. You just have to make them comfortable, do what they want."

"How do you know what they want?"

"Some of them want to be left alone, some of them need their hand held, some of them just need to feel wanted. What does your father want?"

"I don't know, Jerome. He seems to want to be left alone, but then I see him with his grandchildren or my sisters and he changes. I just don't know what he wants from me."

"You'll find out. Everyone does."

I made my way back to the room. I was shocked at what I saw. He was wide awake, breathing quietly and without strain, staring at the ceiling.

The nursing staff at the hospice was among the most amazing group of people I had ever met. They treated their patients with dignity; they asked them what they wanted, what they needed, how they could make them more comfortable. They had given me a pamphlet to read, which details the stages that terminally ill patients go through. Two months out, they tend to have less of an interest in television or newspapers. Later on they lose interest in most people. The booklet even mentioned something very strange that I noticed in my father's behavior: he would pick at his clothing as if he were trying to shed his skin. He had exhibited all of these stages as if by the book.

The last stage before dying was a burst of energy about a day or two before death. Patients were known to try to climb out of their beds, sit up and talk, usually about going home. Only in this case, going home was not about getting into their own beds at home; they were talking about the big "going home."

I stood over his bed and asked him if anything was wrong. His lips were pressed hard against each other, his eyes darting back and forth; it appeared that he was wrestling with something in his head. I had seen this look before when he was frustrated, not in control.

"Yes, I'm dying," he said softly.

"It's okay, Dad, it's the time we talked about. The hard part is over. This is something you have to do on your own."

He coughed a few times. His coughs were familiar to me now, just as parents know the cries of their children. Cries when they are hungry, cries when they want a toy, cries when they are really hurt. The roles were quickly becoming reversed here. I was listening for his cries, the same way he had listened to mine four decades ago.

He looked back up at me with his smirk. His hands were balled up in fists, and he looked at me as if I knew nothing of what I was talking about. He pursed his lips again and tried to get the words out.

"Danny, I'm scared shitless," he whispered.

Now I knew why I was there. This powerful and confident man had finally acknowledged he was afraid. I was afraid with him. But for the first time in our relationship, I felt I could really help him, not just provide some humor or entertainment, as was my usual role.

"I love you very much," I answered. "You've been a great father to me, and I admire you for what you have been through.

But this is the time you have to be strong. You're going to make it. You're going to do this. Just let things happen."

"Why do we have to do this?" he asked.

"Maybe this is what God wants for you. It's your time. You'll be seeing your mother and your brothers soon. You'll be seeing my mother."

This agitated him. I had struck a nerve. He was wrestling with some personal demons, and I began to feel that part of it had to do with my mother. Maybe he felt some guilt about their marriage, or maybe the way he responded to her death. But the fear in his eyes was very real.

"Are you afraid to see my mother?" I asked.

He turned his head to the wall. He tried to roll over on his side, but kept coming back to the middle of the bed, on his back.

"It's all right if you're afraid. Everyone is. But Karen will be glad to see you. It's going to be fine."

He smirked at me again. "Let's get out of here," he said, and began pulling his body up against the bed railing.

I held him back, and immediately thought of the only man I had ever seen die in front of me. It was in June 1997, and I was writing a cover story on the death penalty for *U.S. News*. As part of the story, I watched a man get executed in Huntsville, Texas, by lethal injection. The man's name was Kenneth B. Harris, and he was strapped to the gurney with arms extended as if on a crucifix. I was behind a glass window, no more than ten feet from him. Harris was a big burly man who had raped his neighbor and then drowned her in her own bathtub. I watched him die with little emotion. I saw no terror in his face. Just two quick gasps, and his eyes closed.

But I looked at my father and saw Harris's face clearly. And I was pushing my father back in his bed, sentencing him to death in a way. God, how I wished I could just pick him up and take him out of this place. We could go outside and toss around the football, head down to my brother's bar for a beer, sit and talk about Hunter Thompson and Milhous Nixon and Alger Hiss. I would give anything to get him out of that place he was in, that mind-set he was crawling through where fear lurked behind every thought. I would put myself in his place if I could.

He pushed me away. "In the name of Christ the King, in the name of Mary the Mother of God, Danny, please let me out of here."

I didn't know what to say. I muttered something about Jesus having his own plan, and how we had to follow the plan. It wasn't convincing because I wasn't very convinced. What did God have to do with any of this? Why did my father have to die when he had so much more to give? More to the point, why make this man suffer more? What was the point of all that? He was dying, and he was as ready as he could ever be. Just take him already. Jesus Christ, why prolong this?

"Christ will take this from you," I said. "The hard work is done. Christ will take care of you."

He turned his head toward me and gave a big smile. But his eyes were stern and serious, different from his pleadings a few minutes before.

"I am Christ," he said loudly. He closed his eyes and went to sleep.


I know how my dad would have preferred to spend his last days. He would have loved to be sitting in his recliner, with a few books at his side, a couple of magazines on his lap, and newspapers scattered around. He loved reading and the written word more than anyone I ever knew, including all the English professors and newsmag editors I had met through the years.

His tastes were an eclectic mix. He had subscribed to *Mad* magazine and the *Atlantic Monthly*; he loved James Joyce and Hemingway but was also a serious fan of Hunter Thompson. He called me up in an almost giddy voice in 1994 when he read Thompson's obituary of Richard Nixon in *Rolling Stone* (yes, he read *Rolling Stone* at times). He hated Nixon from the beginning, and I became an expert on the Alger Hiss affair when I was still in elementary school. He used to brag that he had five opportunities to vote for Nixon in his life (two for VP with Eisenhower, once in the race against Kennedy, and Nixon's two victories in 1968 and 1972) and was among the few Americans who never voted for the man.

"Listen to what he writes about Nixon," he told me of Thompson's piece. " 'Nixon will always be remembered as a classic case of a smart man shitting in his own nest. But he also shit in our nests, and that was the crime that history will burn on his memory like a brand.' That is the most perfect obituary I have ever read." He chuckled some more. "He got Nixon perfect. A shitter. And a shithead. And shit."

My dad was as comfortable discussing beat poetry or Tom Wolfe's *Electric Kool-Aid Acid Test*. He loved John Dos Passos and James T. Farrell and S. J. Perelman. In the past year I had been downloading articles from the *Onion*, a wickedly funny magazine written in deadpan Associated Press style. He loved the article about how Fox was considering a new show called *When Jews Attack,* which would rely on a hidden camera at a dry cleaner's.

He used to show me a passage from a book about the history

of the Renaissance. "Whatever his achievements," the passage began, "this 'Renaissance man' was always in motion and discontent, fretting at limits, longing to be a 'universal man'—bold in conception, decisive in deed, eloquent in speech, skilled in art, acquainted with literature and philosophy, at home with women in the palace and with soldiers in the camp." This is what he truly believed. This was the kind of man he was.

In July he found he could not read anymore. His hands were shaking so badly that he couldn't hold the book or magazine. His eyes were going as well, and I think he was losing the battle in his mind to keep trying. It was devastating for him, a man who had spent his entire life reading, deriving a good part of his identity from this pastime and then losing it quickly.

"What has been the hardest part about not being able to read?" I asked him.

He closed his eyes and began thinking of the words. And then off the top of his head he began reciting John Milton in a raspy voice:

> When I consider how my light is spent,
> Ere half my days, in this dark world and wide,
> And that one talent which is death to hide,
> Lodg'd with me useless, though my soul more bent
> To serve therewith my Maker, and present
> My true account, lest he returning chide,
> "Doth God exact day-labour, light denied?"
> I fondly ask. But Patience, to prevent
> That murmur, soon replies, "God doth not need
> Either man's work or his own gifts, who best
> Bear his mild yoke, they serve him best, his state

Is kingly. Thousands at his bidding speed

And post o'er land and ocean without rest:

They also serve who only stand and wait."

He paused, opened his eyes, and added his exclamation point. "And shit," he said.

Only my father would have committed a seventeenth-century poem to memory and melded it with the vernacular of the modern pro athlete. I had only a limited view of who Milton was. He was someone we were supposed to study in high school and college. I couldn't tell you anything he had written.

"Do you know what Milton was saying here?" he asked me.

"No idea," I said. "The only thing I know about Milton is that he was the subject the professor was teaching in the movie *Animal House*."

"Oh yes, the Donald Sutherland character. What was the motto of Faber College?"

"Knowledge Is Good," I answered. I might not know Milton, but I did know my Belushi.

"But I digress," he continued. "Milton had just gone blind when he wrote this, and he was speaking of talents lost, how his blindness had left him without the basic faculty he had used for his writing. But then he learns that God doesn't judge us by what we think are our greatest talents; those that serve him best do what God wants. And we still serve by waiting for him."

"Do you believe this?" I asked him.

"Oh, I think there is some truth in what he says. We get this overblown view of ourselves, how we are better and more special than anyone else. We think God loves us for these characteristics. But God doesn't care about what we think of ourselves. And whether we love God or not doesn't make any difference to God."

I hadn't ever heard him speak about such subjects before. Our discussion of God and religion had usually been limited to his telling me to go to church, and me whining about going.

"Are you mad at God for this illness?" I asked.

"Oh no, that would presume I am better than or equal to God. Just because we love God doesn't mean he has to love us back. No, wait. Just because he loves us, it doesn't mean that he has to make our lives easier. Our job is simple. We are just here to love God. The rest is out of our control."

"I feel the same way," I responded. "I don't worry about things that are beyond my control. That's why I never found religion appealing. People spend much too much time worrying about what is going to happen after they die, when, in fact, they have no idea, and whether they believe or not is not going to change the circumstances."

"That's easy for you to say," he answered. "Put yourself in my shoes."

"Well, do you know what is going to happen after you die? Are you sure about where you are going?"

"No, not at all. But I have a pretty good idea. Do you remember in Joyce's *Portrait of the Artist as a Young Man* how Stephen Dedalus was questioning his Catholic faith? His friend asked him then if he had become a Protestant. Dedalus responded by saying that he had lost his faith, he hadn't lost his mind. What Dedalus was really doing was questioning his upbringing, questioning where he fit in the world. It's something we all do, especially at your age. But we get over that with time.

"Do I know for certain that heaven awaits me?" he added.

"No, not in the least. But ever since I was a kid at St. Thomas Aquinas, I have been taught these things. Nothing else I have ever learned has persuaded me that there is any better explanation. I guess I'll find out for sure very soon."

So my dad told me he was Christ. I didn't know what to make of it, though I had a feeling he was going over in his mind about how Jesus died. Jesus knew when he was dying, as did my father. He also prayed for his father to take the cup from him, to try to find a way to redeem without death. My dad was also trying to have the cup of death passed from him. I often wondered if it would be worse to know you are dying or to just get hit by some big ol' bus while crossing the street one day. I had seen that inmate getting executed, and he knew precisely the time he was getting his. My dad knew it as well. I think it is probably better to know. Not easier, but better.

I listened to his breathing for a few minutes. It began to sound more and more like a death rattle. I retreated to the Indians game on the large-screen TV, stayed there for about an inning, then went back in his room. He was staring at the ceiling again.

"Do you want me to read to you?" I asked.

He shrugged his shoulders, and I took that as a yes. But there was nothing to read in his room beyond some magazines I had brought to pass the time. But then I remembered the chapel, the Art Modell Memorial Chapel, and thought that the Bible might be something my dad would listen to. He had always talked of the Bible as being literature rather than the divinely inspired word of God. We were, after all, Catholics, and the Bible was less important to us than it was to born-again Protestants.

I knew precisely what I would read. During my fifty one days in Waco covering David Koresh and his flock, I had read the Book of Revelation in my hotel room every night. Revelation is the best written and most fun book of the Bible, so I figured this might be good for him.

> *And I saw an angel come down from heaven, having the key of the bottomless pit and a great chain in his hand. And he laid hold on the dragon, that old serpent, which is the Devil, and Satan, and bound him a thousand years. . . .*

That was a good start, I thought. Plenty of imagery, som action to keep the plot moving, and proper sentence structure, syntax, and spelling. I kept going, through the lakes of fire and bottomless pits, the great white thrones and the dead standing before God. His eyes were still open and he was listening.

> *But the fearful, and unbelieving, and the abominable, and murderers, and whoremongers, and sorcerers, and idolators, and all liars, shall have their part in the lake which burneth with fire and brimstone; which is the second death.*

That part was a little weird. I was wondering if I should be reading passages talking about people being thrown into a lake of fire. But the more I did this, the more I enjoyed it. It was the first time I had read the Bible in years, and it was quite comforting in some ways. I kept on.

> *And the city had no need of the sun, neither of the moon, to shine in it; for the glory of God did lighten it, and the Lamb is the light thereof. And the nations of them which are saved*

*shall walk in the light of it: and the kings of the earth do bring their glory and honour into it.*

I had no idea what John was talking about, but this certainly did have a nice rhythm. Good clean sentences. More important, I was reading without stuttering. Reading aloud was one of the last vestiges of my stuttering. I found that my mind would race ahead and I would begin stammering as I found my place, but now I was calm and enjoying reading to my father.

*For without are dogs, and sorcerers, and whoremongers, and murderers, and idolators. . . .*

He lifted his hand up. "Enough of the whoremongers," he said. "Enough."

So much for our impromptu Bible study. It was about 6 A.M. He closed his eyes again and continued to wrestle with his demons. But I felt better about what we had been through. We had made it through the darkest hour and had come through the other side. I thought I had been of some help. Even with all the whoremongers and idolators.

My sister Sheila came at 9 A.M. She was a cardiac care nurse at the Ohio State University hospital and was the most calm of us all in dealing with death. She was only a teenager when my mother died, but she took care of her while I was turning my back to it all. She was the ultimate caregiver, and she knew what patients like my dad needed.

"How was he?" she asked outside his room.

"He got animated for a while, tried to climb out of his bed."

She laughed. "That's what they do when they get this far. I've had to put many of them back in their beds."

I went back in and held his hand. He looked up at me with a concerned expression.

"Sheila's here now," I told him. "I'll see you later. I have to get some sleep."

I kissed him on his forehead and went to leave. He held my hand for a second and looked into my eyes.

"Thanks," he whispered.

"Thanks for everything," I said.

As I drove home in rush-hour traffic, I carried that one word with me. After a lifetime of fighting and laughs, of admiration and heartache, of learning and relearning how to like each other, it boiled down to one simple emotion. Thanks. So simple. But such a difficult thing to convey. It was the last thing he would ever say to me.

# CHAPTER SIX

# August Is the Cruelest Month

In the late sixties my father would take us to Hiram College every summer for a day trip to the Browns training camp. Hiram was only about forty miles southeast of Cleveland, but in those days, before the freeways, the trip took more than an hour each way. My brother and I looked forward to going every year, because we didn't go to games at Municipal Stadium, and this was our only chance to see the Browns in person.

Hiram is a college town set among the hills of eastern Ohio, one of those picture-postcard little crossroads towns dominated by church steeples, oak trees, and a small school campus, complete with intersecting paths between old stone classroom buildings. Paul Brown had chosen Hiram as his training camp site because of the isolation; even though it was only forty miles from Cleveland, the town was dry and the nearest place for players to buy beer was a ten-minute drive down the road. There wasn't even a restaurant in Hiram, only a ratty little snack bar that served burgers and hot dogs.

Hiram seemed otherworldly to us. It was truly in the middle of nowhere, and we would carefully watch the road signs to see how close we were. There was a huge anticipation about going out to Hiram for the day, for this was where we could see our heroes in person. No one cared much about autographs in those days, and we didn't go there to have some guy sign a scrap of paper. My father was dead set against autographs. "Anytime you ask anyone for an autograph," he used to say, "you diminish yourself in some way."

The part I remember most about going to Hiram was the huge hill that we had to walk down to get to the football field. There were concrete stairs zigzagging their way down the hill, and from the top, you could see the beautiful green field a couple hundred feet below. Legend has it that the players feared that hill almost as much as the Browns' rough practices. After two-a-days in the searing and humid summer heat, the players would have to climb that hundred-foot hill to get back to their dorms. Many of the players suffered painful leg cramps climbing that hill. And when they got to their dorm rooms, there was no air-conditioning, no TV, no place to go out and watch a movie.

My brother and I would stand up close to the chain-link fence and see guys like Leroy Kelly and Bill Nelsen and Gene Hickerson and Lou Groza. I just remember everything being big, the players larger than life, me poking my face against the fence to get the best possible view. My dad would usually sit up in the stands by himself—he was unimpressed by watching football practice—while Brian and I would run around the field like the crazies we were.

We knew all of their numbers by heart. I even got to see old number 56 out there, my man John Morrow. By noon we would have a hot dog or a burger at the little snack shop, then we might stay for an hour of the afternoon workout. On the long ride home in the old Rambler he drove, my dad would explain and discuss with us why the Browns were going to be good that year. He explained how important the offensive line was to the whole team, that watching the line of scrimmage was the key to any football game. We asked him questions about whether Leroy Kelly could replace Jim Brown, whether Bill Nelsen's knees would hold up, and the big question: whether they could win the championship that year. He always assured us that this might be the year, that we were always a break or two away from winning it all. We hung on his every word. We became excited about the season.

In June 1999 Hiram College hosted an annual event called Browns Homecoming Weekend. About 120 former players showed up, greats like Groza and Dante Lavelli, but also regular players like Paul Wiggin, Don Cockroft, and Greg Pruitt. I thought it might be fun to visit such an obscure place from my childhood, so I drove down, taking the interstate most of the way this time. The campus still looked familiar, even though I hadn't been there in perhaps thirty years. The hill was still tough to climb, the football field still a luscious green, the oak trees still tall and proud. But there were no players on the field; the place was overrun with Browns fans And I soon realized this weekend wasn't about connecting with old players; it was an autograph show.

These Browns fans who had come to Hiram that weekend were what I would call the professional fans. Not professionals in the sense that they made money at it, but professional in the sense that they had nothing else in their lives. They came in vans painted bright orange and brown, wore their officially licensed jerseys and T-shirts, their orange-painted hard hats, and faces painted in the team colors. I didn't see many kids around. Most were my age and they were fat. They clutched their dog bones and they barked.

The Dawg Pound act was getting old for most people; it was a group mind-set that didn't leave much room for individuality. It is the difference between organized mayhem and mayhem just for the hell of it. The whole thing started in 1985 when Browns cornerbacks Hanford Dixon and Frank Minnifield started calling the defensive line dogs, and their job was to chase the cat—the quarterback. Soon the Browns defense was barking at each other, and the fans in the bleachers, drunk but still able to follow simple directions, barked along with them. Soon enough, the fans were dressing as dogs, eating dog food from the can, flinging dog biscuits at opposing teams, and pissing in the urinals while balancing on one leg.

And for a while it was fun. In 1989 the noise and the mayhem grew so out of control down at the bleacher end of the field that the referees let the Broncos start their offensive series at the other end of the field. There was some guy who called himself Deer Dawg who for some unknown reason waved freshly hacked-off deer legs at the opponents. When Mark Jackson caught Elway's pass at the end of the Drive, he said that the ground crunched under his feet from all the dog biscuits in the end zone.

But in the time since the Dawg Pound's heyday, the rest of the sporting world had caught up with Cleveland. Every NFL stadium in the country now had a cadre of face painters and men who would shed their shirts in freezing weather, network coverage would show the silly fans and their silly hats, and every team had its share of lunatic screamers. These antics didn't necessarily start with the Cleveland bleacher fans, but the copycat intensity was wracheted up around the league when the Dawg Pound became infamous.

My dad would call the antics in the Dawg Pound "igno," his shorthand version of "ignoramuses." He blamed the hillbillies from outlying towns far from Cleveland. "These igno hillbillies have nothing else to do," he would say. "They act like people from Pittsburgh, for chrissakes."

I didn't agree with his assessment. I knew plenty of people who hung out in the Dawg Pound, and they were not ignos or hill-billies (or igno hillbillies, for that matter). But this whole matter of dressing up like dogs for fifteen years had run its course as far as I was concerned. I've always thought that when everyone is doing one thing, the best course of action is to run in the other direction. I think the Browns fans needed to move on to something new. Guys with their bellies painted had now come to be the standard for NFL fan support. Cleveland fans needed to find a new outlet for their emotions.

But the Dawg Pound was not moving on. When the city of Cleveland pressured the NFL to give the city a new team after Modell took the team with him, the NFL agreed that the new stadium would provide for the "replication of the bleacher area known as the Dawg Pound." I could just see those lawyers in the NFL office wrangling over the proper wording to describe and define an agreement aimed at people that ate Kal Kan and puked in their boots.

At Hiram the professional dogs were strutting around campus. Dressing as a dog in your twenties may be quaint and even a bit humorous. Dressing as a dog in your forties, barking and throwing dog biscuits, comes off as a little pathetic. As Dean Vernon Wormer told Flounder in the movie *Animal House,* "Fat, drunk and stupid is no way to go through life."

And as I walked around, I realized this homecoming event was little more than a glorified autograph show. What is it about sports fans that they have to get some spare athlete to sign a piece of paper whenever they spot one? Autograph tables were set up for the likes of 1990 strength coach Gary Wroblewski and Fest Cotton, who played defensive tackle in 1972. And the fans had to wait in line two hours or more to get these autographs. Most of them were carrying around posters and framed pictures, and I could tell that a lot of these guys were regulars on the memorabilia circuit. Most of these autographs would likely be sold to a sports bar for a few hundred bucks.

It's not that I begrudge people for collecting autographs or making a few bucks. It's just that everything about these new Browns seemed regimented and scripted: Browns fans had to wear the authentic licensed garb, bark when ordered to speak, with an official MBNA Browns credit card in their wallet. In fact, the Browns officially wanted the dogs in the bleachers to still dress in their garb, but to heel upon command. "Bark but don't bite" was the team's new slogan.

I saw a former Brown named Allen Aldridge sitting at one table, and I couldn't place him. There were thirty people lined up for his autograph.

I walked up to Aldridge and asked when he played. Defensive lineman from the 1974 season, he answered.

"No offense," I began, "but why are you here for this?"

"They asked me if I wanted to come, and I thought it would be good for the fans," he answered.

"Do you think any fans know who you are?" I asked.

"Probably not."

"Any earthly idea why anyone would want your autograph?"

"Not really," he answered.

I decided to leave Mr. Aldridge alone. This new Browns thing was going to take some getting used to. The modern sports landscape had changed drastically in recent years, with the most importance being placed on autographs, licensed merchandise, and hero maintenance. I was being sucked along into the morass.

As I left Hiram, a young girl with a clipboard stopped me. She offered me a free Browns T-shirt if I would fill out the form. It was an application for an MBNA Browns Visa card.

In recent years, sports teams have seen training camp as a money-maker rather than simply as a way to prepare the team for the coming year. In baseball, teams have been playing Florida and Arizona cities against each other to come up with packages that will include free lodging and meals and guaranteed ticket revenue. In the NFL, teams share network TV money and ticket sales, but they are able to keep local media rights and marketing deals. Having a training camp close to town and having the local media covering the team inexpensively make places like Hiram obsolete. The thinking is that fewer fans will show up in a place like Hiram, and fewer fans make the signs of the "business partners" ringing the field less valuable. And the Browns have been very good about lining up business partners, gaining $30 million in local marketing and media deals.

The new Browns training camp was in Berea, Ohio. Modell had the taxpayers of the city of Berea build the $13-million facility for him before he left. It was close to the airport, about twelve miles from downtown Cleveland, with four nicely manicured football fields on which to practice. Though close to restaurants and shopping and freeways, the facility has no character. No big trees. No hills. Just a chain-link fence and lots of security guards. But the training camp isn't about character, or a comfortable place for fans to watch their team. This facility was built for the serious business of preparing a football team for the coming season. And for maximizing revenue. And serious these new Browns were about both.

The Browns had decided to hire Lew Merletti as their head of security. A former Green Beret in Vietnam, Merletti was working as director of the U.S. Secret Service when the Browns called. He protected the lives of Presidents Ford, Carter, Reagan, Bush, and Clinton. His new job was to remake the new stadium into

what team president Carmen Policy called "a fan-friendly, family-friendly experience." Merletti was an odd choice to head up
stadium security. He once had to come up with a security plan to
protect President Bush from terrorists during a drug summit in
Colombia. Now he was in charge of making sure no one pissed
on the floor of the bleacher bathrooms.

An article in the *Plain Dealer* by Sally Gardocki, a quasi-jour-
nalist and wife of Browns punter Chris Gardocki, gushed that
Merletti was "protector of our country, protector of the president, protector of the Browns."

She might have added "protector of the grass." There were
about fifty guards ringing the field during every practice, and they
seemed to be overly concerned with the new grass that had been
installed on the practice fields. The team spent a lot of money on
that grass, and the guards had been instructed to keep everyone
off it with the same zeal that Merletti might have had in taking a
bullet for the president. On the first day of practice, I found
myself standing against the rope line, with about an inch of my
size 14 feet touching the grass. Three guards came up to me and
demanded that I remove the offending toes from the grass. This
happened six times on the first day. Almost as many times as I had
been approached to sign up for a new Browns credit card.

I began thinking to myself that if these guys are this crazy about
the grass on their practice field, imagine what they will be like in
the new $300-million stadium down at the lakefront. Everyone
realizes now that the old stadium had gotten out of hand in recent
years, with the whole lore of the Dawg Pound based more on
drunkenness than any great fan loyalty, as some would have us
believe. But I was beginning to think that maybe these new
Browns with all their zeal of making everything "first-class" had
missed something important. The bond between the team and

the city had been sacred. And it was based on the old notion of pro sports: one that was devoid of marketing deals and licensed merchandise. It was hard to put your finger on, but many people I had spoken with wanted nothing to do with these new Browns. They were too slick. They had taken too many classes in generic sports management. They knew how to maximize local media profits. But I felt they knew nothing of the history here.

And it was funny how this team approached its new business. While the team was going to great lengths to make sure the bleachers would be fun for the entire family, with dozens of security guards to make sure it stayed that way, the league decided to make the Dawg Pound an official licensed NFL property. I felt proud. All those years of puking and fighting and dope smoking had paid off. We were now an official logo.

It may sound like I disliked these new Browns, but in fact I was getting very excited about this new season. I wasn't gushing like all the TV news babes who had just come into town from markets like Des Moines and Grand Rapids, but I liked our chances this year. I based my assessment of the Browns on what I considered my solid football pedigree. After all, I had played peewee football in Northeast Little League—quarterback and outside linebacker, I might add. I had played intramural football at Loyola University of Chicago and caught twenty-two touchdowns there one season. And I had watched football every Sunday afternoon and Monday night for as long as I could remember.

I thought this team would do well for a number of reasons. To start with, the Browns were coming into the league with a clean slate; that is, they weren't hampered by bad contracts and draft choices. Before any team took the field in 1999, it had to juggle the NFL's complicated salary cap rule and try to figure out who should be cut loose and who should be signed, based primarily on getting these players' contracts under the salary cap. The Browns certainly were paying attention to money issues, but they were starting without one cent guaranteed to an unproductive player. This ability to build a team without suffering from the sins of the past was thought to be a huge advantage.

They chose to use much of their money to sign players on the offensive and defensive lines. The Browns spent $64 million in long-term contracts on center Dave Wohlabaugh and tackles Orlando Brown and Lomas Brown. Guard Jim Pyne, another solid offensive lineman, was added in the expansion draft. These were all proven players and were expected to be a strength of the team.

On the defensive front they signed run-stoppers John Jurkovic, who had played on a Super Bowl team with Green Bay, and Jerry Ball, a former Brown who was thought to have a few good years left. At the defensive ends they had Derrick Alexander and Roy Barker, from the Vikings and the 49ers respectively, both of whom had decent sack totals in 1998. Linebackers Jamir Miller and John Thierry were both considered good enough to start on just about every team in the NFL.

Both lines were to be strengths on this team. The defensive backs—with veterans Corey Fuller, Antonio Langham, and Marquez Pope—were also considered to be better than the backs on most teams. On offense they were thin at skill positions—only running back Terry Kirby and wide receiver Leslie Shepherd had any real experience—but the thought was the rookie draft would shore up those problem areas. The Browns expected rookie receivers Darrin Chevarini and Kevin Johnson and running back Madre Hill to contribute.

And at quarterback the thinking was to allow veteran Ty Detmer to play while rookie Tim Couch developed. Detmer was a former starter in the league with the Eagles and the 49ers, and his biggest asset was that he wouldn't screw up. The thinking among the Browns brain trust was that the defense would keep them in games, and the offensive line would be able to avoid giving up sacks while controlling the ball on the ground. With any kind of luck, this team would win ugly, a lot of 17–13 games where defense would rule.

And looking over the Browns schedule, it wasn't far-fetched to see this team going 8–8. Only three games were against play-off teams from the previous year, two with division foe Jacksonville and one against New England. Pittsburgh was thought to be a team on the downside, and the Browns played them twice. Ditto for the Baltimore Ravens and the Cincinnati Bengals, teams that had sucked pretty bad for years. Tennessee, which they also faced twice, was seen as a .500 team at best. It wasn't unreasonable to think that the Browns could get four or five victories just from games against these teams in the AFC Central. The rest of the schedule—the New Orleans Saints, the Carolina Panthers, the St. Louis Rams, the Indianapolis Colts, and the San Diego Chargers—all had had losing records the previous year. There was no reason to think that the Browns couldn't squeeze three or four wins in these games.

Another intangible that was felt to have a positive impact on the Browns was the return to Ohio of linebacker and football legend Chris Spielman. Spielman had prepped at Massillon High School and then went on to star at Ohio State, the same lineage

Paul Brown had moved through before he joined the Browns. Spielman had starred with Detroit and Buffalo—made four Pro Bowls in those years—and was known as a throwback player. Spielman was the type who would stick his nose in the middle of the pile; he had a fiery intensity that would rub off on these new players. In short, Spielman was going to be the leader of this team.

He came with a lot of baggage, however. In 1997 he broke his neck halfway through the season. In 1998 his wife, Stefanie, was diagnosed with breast cancer, and Chris decided to sit out the entire season to take care of her. When her cancer went into remission, Spielman decided at age thirty-four that he would come home to the Buckeye State to help birth this new team.

The juicy story line was picked up by Cleveland fans. Spielman's number 54 jersey quickly became the top seller, and at training camp the stands were full of kids and adults wearing Spielman gear. This was a player the fans of Cleveland could embrace. He was one of their own. He grunted rather than spoke to the news media. He seemed to have a permanent cut on the bridge of his nose. He was a family man who sacrificed for his wife. He was the perfect, blue-collar, lunch-bucket player this town craved.

All of these factors led me to believe this team was going to be pretty good. Boy was I ever wrong.

To test my theories, I called up a scout I knew who had been working in the NFL for the past twenty years. He had watched the Browns through the expansion and rookie drafts and knew most of the personnel on the team. We spoke about halfway through training camp, and he agreed to talk to me as long as I didn't use his name. We'll call him Dave.

"Is eight and eight possible?" I asked.

"If they win four games, they'll be lucky," Dave answered. "There is a reason all these teams in the NFL let all these guys go to Cleveland. They all have serious downsides."

"What's the major problem?"

"No team speed. None whatsoever. Their defensive linemen are all slow. Aside from Jamir Miller, their linebackers don't have anything, either. The only way teams win on defense these days is with sideline-to-sideline pursuit."

"But what about Jurkovic and Ball? They can stop the run on first and second down, and that's going to force a lot of teams into third-and-long."

"You've got to be kidding. If either one of those guys is playing much this year, the Browns will really stink. Jurkovic hasn't been the same since he broke his leg, and Ball hasn't done anything in two years. Those two guys just stand there in the middle. Every team is going to run wide on the Browns."

"Any pass rush?" I asked.

"None."

"What about Detmer? He seems to be decent."

"Can't throw long, and can't hit the fifteen-yard-out pattern. He can dink it around on the short patterns, but he really has no one to throw it to."

"What about the defensive backs? They seem pretty strong."

"Antonio Langham is done. He hasn't done anything in about four years. Can't see him turning it around suddenly. Let's see, who else is there? Oh yeah, Corey Fuller is a head case. The Vikings were glad to get rid of him. He's not a good guy to have in the locker room. Always complaining."

"What about Marquez Pope?"

"At this stage of his career, he might be able to play nickelback on some teams. But he's lost a step. Solid guy, though. He'll be good for the younger players."

"Speaking of good influences, Spielman is going to make a difference, isn't he?"

"I hear he's done. He's lost his legs in the two years off. He might be able to stuff the run on first down. But I hear the Browns are worried about his play. They can't cut him because of the reaction of the fans, but they don't want to play him either."

"Christ, Dave, is there anything they can do? Really. It sounds like they suck in every facet of the game."

"The offensive line could be okay. The problem is that the offensive lines in the NFL take a few years to gel, and this group will have to become good in a hurry. If the line steps up, they might be able to control the ball. But they don't have anyone who can run the ball. And no one to throw the ball to."

"Should Couch be starting?"

"If Couch starts playing anytime before the sixth game of the season, it's a sign that the team has given up. Playing rookie quarterbacks can do more harm than good. The game is so much faster than in college. It takes at least a year to get your feet underneath you. Couch could be good eventually, but now isn't the time to throw him to the wolves."

"What about the other rookies? Anybody stand out?"

"You can't tell anything about rookies until they play for an extended period of time in the regular season. Call me back in three years."

And that was that. Spielman can't run, Detmer's a stiff, Carey Fuller a head case. The man brought my high down in a hurry. But he couldn't be right, could he? Everyone I talked to, in the media and among the fans, thought this was going to be different from other expansion teams. This was supposed to be the most successful expansion team of all time. Carmen Policy had told us so. We had waited for three years and suffered the indignity of the move to Baltimore. Certainly we wouldn't have to suffer through a rotten season as well.

We all should have known better. This was Cleveland. We were Browns fans. Why should we have expected anything to be different?

Throughout their short life as the new Browns, the team's management always talked about going "first-class," hiring the best people, treating this football business almost like a Fortune 500 company. Policy and Lerner had decided that by having the best facilities and the best people, and offering the most money, they would be able to attract the best players. It was a plan you couldn't argue with.

The major problem the team faced was the compressed time in which to organize the franchise. From the time that Lerner and Policy were named owners of the team until the opening game against Pittsburgh in September was a scant eleven months. When Jacksonville and Carolina came into the league, five years earlier, the two teams had more than two years. The reason for the delay in awarding a franchise was that the NFL couldn't decide if Cleveland was going to get an existing franchise that would move to the city, or an expansion team. But basically the NFL screwed Cleveland over by adhering to this compressed timetable. The major problem was hiring coaches. After hiring head coach Chris Palmer, the studious former offensive coordinator with the Jacksonville Jaguars who reminded many of Blanton Collier, Palmer tried to hire assistants. For the most part, he had to settle for his second and third choices because most assistant coaches were already locked up by their teams for the coming year. So not only did Palmer have to implement a complicated playbook in a very short time, he had to do it with assistants who weren't first-rate.

But the lack of a first-rate coaching staff did not keep these new Browns from offering the best amenities to the unproven players. Upon arriving at training camp, the players could give an intern a grocery list or clothes to drop off at the dry cleaner's. At the stadium, uniformed valet parking attendants would take their cars from inside the stadium and park them outside. If the players didn't want to be bothered with fans, they didn't have to.

Merletti implemented a system whereby each player had an 800 number that was put on the player's key chain, and five security officers staffed the line around the clock. Peter King of *Sports Illustrated* related a story about a few offensive linemen going out to dinner at a local steak house in August. In the middle of dinner, center Jim Bundren feels his legs cramping up. He makes it to a phone booth and calls the 800 number. Within four minutes a club security employee has Bundren in a team SUV and they are making their way to the Cleveland Clinic with a police escort. Precisely fifteen minutes after he noticed the cramping problem, Bundren has a saline-solution IV in his arm.

The Cleveland Clinic is a corporate partner of the Browns, so its interest in the athletes is understandable. But this partnership shows how out of whack the priorities of Cleveland had become with the new football team. Later in the year, Mount Sinai Hospital, a few miles from the Cleveland Clinic, closed its trauma center. This meant that gunshot and serious accident victims from the primarily poor East Side African American neighborhoods around the Cleveland Clinic would have to be transported for treatment about ten miles away to Metro General Hospital, on the West Side. The new trip is farther than Jim Bundren had to go to get his IV.

When Cleveland City Council asked the Cleveland Clinic if it could provide emergency room trauma service to make up for Mount Sinai's closing, the hospital said it was not cost-effective to provide such a service.

As July faded into August, I found myself not enjoying football very much. I would make it to the morning practice, sometimes toward the end, and sit in the shade watching the drills. Pro football training camp is mindless and repetitive, but not in the way I like. Modern sports franchises treat the media like caged dogs, letting us out occasionally to do our business and to run for a few minutes. Otherwise, you better stay in your place and not complain too much.

After the morning practice I would join the pack and go into the locker room. We had forty-five minutes to get the pearls of wisdom from the jocks, though most of them would hide in the training room or the showers to avoid what they considered media vultures. I couldn't quite understand their reluctance, because the Cleveland media were treating this team with kid gloves. I spent most of my time fading into the background, listening to the warmed-over clichés and making a mental note when I heard a verb conjugated correctly.

After the locker room gang bang I would drive out to my dad's house on the other side of town and spend an hour or so with him talking. Some days our conversations would be fun and enlightening; other days it seemed like we were rehashing the clichés of life. All of his verbs, however, were in the proper tense and person.

We had all the kids over for Father's Day, but he was having a very bad episode with nausea. We had set up card tables in his garage and had dinner with about twenty people. He came out when dinner was ready, ate a little bit, and then went back inside to be by himself. We watched a little baseball. He was very depressed.

I had asked him what he wanted for Father's Day earlier, and he said he didn't want anything. "You'll just have to come over here in a couple months and take it back," he told me. He didn't laugh when he told me that. On his sixty-ninth birthday, August 7, the family didn't do much of anything. Just more gifts that would have to be picked up later.

Though I don't know much about Milton, I thought of another author as the summer was coming to an end. In *The Waste Land* T. S. Eliot begins with the famous line that "April is the cruelest month," and I remember while studying the epic poem (in my case, it was probably the *Cliff's Notes*), it was explained to me what that line really meant. The setting was World War I, and Eliot was making the point that the joyousness of springtime hit the soldiers particularly hard. While life was being renewed around them, they faced death. The combination made them all the more depressed.

I was feeling the same way in August. There was a genuine and good buzz around town about the new Browns. People were planning their lives around the opening game on September 12 against hated Pittsburgh. It was going to be a glorious night for the town; we would be decked out for the national TV audience, chanting "Pittsburgh sucks" as we downed our beer; it would be just like the old days. And despite my cynicism for the business side of pro sports, all these credit card offers and civic hosannas to these new Browns, I was ready to embrace their new season. This was supposed to be fun. We, as a city, had done the impossible. We had sued the NFL, got our team back, kept the colors and the name and the records, built a new stadium, and assembled a new team. This had never been done before, and Cleveland was rightfully proud.

But in the midst of all this, I was feeling a little like those soldiers in France. The more I saw the joyousness of the town, the excitement of the team, everyone getting ready for the momentous event, the more depressed I felt. August in Cleveland was turning especially cruel, and I was drinking more than ever before. It was my way of dealing with the pain.

# CHAPTER SEVEN

# A Drinking Life

I don't remember my father being much of a drinker. The old stories were there, all right. He and his friends would recount their tales of going out to Geneva-on-the-Lake, a cottage resort with miniature golf and dance halls. There they would scam beers in the little resort saloons, find a way to crash in the state park or at someone's guest cottage, make out with young women by the shores of Lake Erie in the days when you could actually swim in it. I once saw a snapshot of him standing on a picnic table in a Geneva-on-the-Lake dance hall chugging two beers at the same time.

But I never saw him drink very much. He might have a Scotch on the rocks every so often after work. He was funny about that bottle of Scotch. He bought a bottle of Chivas Regal, and when that was empty, he bought some cheap Scotch and refilled the Chivas bottle. When company came over, he didn't want people to think he was serving cheap booze. But he was a cheapskate when it came to things like that. El Cheapo, he called himself.

I think he kept his drinking under wraps around his kids because of my mother. I don't remember ever seeing beer in our refrigerator when I was a kid. I'm sure he drank some at family weddings or christenings or funerals, but I was always off with the other kids and never really noticed. Aside from the episode after my mom's funeral, I don't recall ever seeing him drunk.

After my mom died and his kids were in college, he would drink beer more often. He said he enjoyed his children's college years, as he never had to buy beer; there was always some left over in the fridge. He said it was his way of recouping tuition money.

I never knew him to hang out in bars. He wasn't social in that way. As he got older, he would treat himself to a six-pack on Friday nights. He would drink his beer and read by himself, usually with some bad TV show like *Dynasty* or *Dallas* as background noise. His passion for great works of literature was only perhaps rivaled by his love of bad TV shows.

In one of our earlier conversations after I came back to Cleveland, I asked him if he had any regrets in life. He thought for a few seconds, stared off into space, and then shook his head. "I guess the only thing I regret is that I spent too much time hanging out in saloons," he said. "At the time, we think that there are a great many wonderful things happening there. But in the end, all of it is a waste of time. The stories are all the same, the people get to be the same after a while, and everyone feels witty and important. It's life's great illusion."

"But I don't remember you spending much time in saloons or being drunk," I answered.

"I never let you kids see that at home. Your mother was strict about that. And I think I had gotten most of that out of my system by then. Drinking is a young man's sport anyway. As we get older, we lose our wits more easily. There's nothing worse than a witless old drunk."

"How old is too old?"

"You are," he said, looking right through me. "I hear things about you, and you better watch out. I came very close to ruining my life several times with booze. Don't let it happen. You have too much talent to waste it."

"Pete Hamill wrote that the art of writing is the art of remembering," I said. "He quit drinking because he thought that his drinking was getting in the way of his remembering. I'm beginning to understand what he meant."

"So why are you spending all of your time in saloons?" he asked.

The question was left dangling in the air. I had no answer for him. No earthly fucking idea.

In 1796 Moses Cleaveland and his party of surveyors and explorers landed at the mouth of the Cuyahoga River. Cleaveland and his party were Connecticut Yankees, and their arrival was part of a land speculation deal. The state of Connecticut had been given 3 million acres in Ohio as payment for fighting in the War of Independence, and Cleaveland and his investors bought the land for forty cents an acre. When they arrived, Cleaveland was put off by the swamplike mess and the stink of the Cuyahoga, and left after a few months. It was the first Cleveland joke: the founder of the town hated it so much he got out as quick as he could. They did name the town after him, however, even though he never returned. (The "a" was dropped early on when a newspaper editor shortened the name of the town so it would fit in a headline.)

One of the few men who stayed was Major Lorenzo Carter. One of the first orders of business for Carter was to set up a still and sell whiskey to the Indians who lived across the river. Soon Carter had a tavern and hotel, and his little outpost served as the courthouse, jail, and trading post. This Carter fellow was a wild sort, according to lore, outdrinking the local Indians and coming out unscathed when the nightly boozing turned into fighting.

Carter served as the village's unofficial mayor, police chief, bartender, and bouncer. He was a sort of Judge Roy Bean of the Midwest.

In 1812 an Indian named John O'Mic was arrested for murdering a couple of fur trappers. He was brought to Carter's bar to be held, and the good major lashed him to some old beams in the attic while he awaited trial. During the next few weeks while the town waited for the traveling judge to arrive, O'Mic would taunt the drunks in Carter's bar from above, claiming that he would die with honor from the end of the rope. He would show the white man what real courage was. Presumably the drunks were amused by O'Mic's assertions of bravery, and bets were probably made as to whether O'Mic would be as brave as he let on.

They erected some gallows on Public Square, and on the fateful day in June, O'Mic was brought to meet his maker at the end of the rope. But as the rope was put over his head, O'Mic panicked and dove for one of the corner posts of the gallows. He hung on as the deputies tried to pull him away. Finally Major Carter was summoned, and after a long discussion with O'Mic, the prisoner agreed to gladly die at the end of the rope if Carter brought him a half pint of whiskey. The whiskey was produced, and O'Mic chugged it straight down. But when they tried to hang him the second time, O'Mic gave a repeat performance of his reluctance to participate in his own hanging. Major Carter climbed the stairs again, and O'Mic pointed to another half pint bottle of whiskey. After further negotiations, Carter decided to let O'Mic have the remainder of the bottle. O'Mic downed it and became a model prisoner. Seconds later, feeling no pain, O'Mic was swinging in a wide arc from the rope, filled with whiskey and death.

Just as his body stopped swinging, a thunderstorm blew in off the lake and scattered the crowd. O'Mic's body just hung there by itself in the cold rain, while the townsfolk found shelter.

The moral of this story: (1) without its bars, Cleveland can be very much a stinking and smelly swamp of a place to live, (2) it is easier to face death with a pint of whiskey in your belly than without, and (3) the weather here really sucks.

I tend to fall into bad habits when I visit Cleveland. For some reason this town turns me into something I am not, or more accurately, something I used to be. Down in Texas, I am Dan McGraw, senior editor for *U.S. News & World Report,* a very sober title for a very sober-sounding magazine. In Cleveland I become "Danny McGraw," former cabdriver and bartender, a guy who in some weird stretch of luck, became a writer for some magazine. "Dan" is the successful writer; "Danny" is the confused and stuttering drunk who never leaves the bar.

I don't know why life works out this way. But I am always nervous and looking over my shoulder when I'm in Cleveland, never sure of myself, always looking for diversions. It's probably a case of self-fulfilling prophesy going on here: I become what other people think I am. I become what I think my father thinks of me. And I know it's not fair to him for me to think that way. He had become extremely proud of me in the last few years, following my career and being as supportive as possible. But in the back of my mind I wondered why he wasn't proud of me before. I think I was the same guy. I never treated anyone poorly. I tried my best, even though I had little success. But to gain my father's affection through the years, I felt I had to be worth something in a tangible way. What if I had stayed a cabdriver or a bartender?

Would my life have less worth? And that's what I think of when I am in Cleveland. I think of failure. I think how horrible life used to be. And the more I think about those things, the more I drink. After all, there is no better mindless repetition than pounding down twelve beers at a sitting. And perhaps no better example of shallow happiness.

I remember the fights with him. I failed to clean my room one day, and he threw my clothes out of the upstairs window onto the front lawn. During dinner one night, I made some smart-ass remark to him, and he threw a baked potato at me and hit me in the head. One time he hit me in the head with a cast-iron skillet. When my grades were Bs, they should have been As, and when I got As, it was expected, and besides, school was supposed to be easy for us. It was for him, wasn't it?

My father was the source of great teasing in our family, teasing that bordered on savagery. There was a time when he had a client named Rontony Daniels, and my father was duly impressed by such a hillbilly name. He started calling me Rontony as a joke and then shortened it to Tony. Soon he had all my brothers and sisters calling me Tony, and then the kids in the neighborhood joined in. This may seem to be a trivial matter, but when your father decides to change your name in the fifth grade, it becomes serious. My friend Ken Dorsch still calls me Tony to this day. He thinks it's funny.

When my wife, Teresa, and I sat down with him to tell him we were getting married, he made a face and said to me in front of her, "Are you crazy?" And when he asked Teresa where her family was from, and she replied West Virginia, he said in a mocking tone, "And how many cars are up on blocks in your family's front yard?" Welcome to the family. Get used to more where that came from.

I don't mean to come off as whiny. But my father could be a real pain to live with. And as I became a teenager, with my mom suffering from her debilitating illness, I removed myself from the family. I found solace in drugs and alcohol. It's been with me ever since. But it's with me more in Cleveland, because that's all I know how to do here.

I remember the first time my friends and I got drunk. We were in the sixth grade at Holy Cross School and we planned for several weeks for a Friday night of drinking. Dorsch stole a bottle of vodka from his mother's stash, Tom Monroe took a few bottles of his father's homemade wine, and John Stack took a case of Old Dutch from his father's garage. A half dozen of us drank our booze down at the beach around a bonfire, and then we did what male sixth graders do. We played basketball at Monroe's house, which had spotlights in the driveway. I look at my fourth-grade daughter, Meredith, and am amazed at how young we were and how loaded we got that night.

I started smoking pot in my freshman year in high school. My father sent us to the Jesuit high school, St. Ignatius, an all-male school with the best academic reputation in the city. Ignatius was in the middle of a marginal Puerto Rican neighborhood, and we soon found that the little markets in the neighborhood would sell us as much beer as we wanted, even before we started shaving. We smoked pot at lunch, and when they would herd us off to mass at St. Pat's down the street, we would scatter in the alleys to get high while mass was going on. The priests decided that smoking dope while spiritual matters were going on was not the Jesuit way, and they devised a plan where we would have to get tickets at the church, later to be given to our homeroom teacher as proof that we had indeed attended church. But we were smart teenagers, the smartest in the city according to our test scores, and we found a way to accommodate the new rules. We came to the church, got our tickets at the door, then snuck up the stairs and got high in the choir loft while the priests said the mass below: Life was great in the old days, but your generation is totally screwed up. Let's stand for the creed. And pass the doobie.

I did some research a few years ago about teenage drug use and found that the high school class of 1977, my graduating year, had the highest incidence of marijuana use in history, and the mark hasn't been bettered since. I brought this up at my twentieth high school reunion and we were indeed proud. Something to hang our hats on. By the way, in the official history of St. Ignatius, the period when I graduated is referred to as "the troubled years."

My classmate Brendan O'Leary (God rest his soul) had a grandmother who lived close to school in some projects for old people, and we used to go over to her apartment at lunch to drink beer. She was a tough, old Irish broad and had no problem with us drinking or smoking there. I can still hear her saying in her thick Irish brogue, "Times must be tough for you boys. I haven't seen men share a cigarette like that since the Depression."

I went to college at Loyola of Chicago (another Jesuit institution) and spent the money my father gave me for books on booze and drugs. I started using LSD quite regularly and experimented with anything I could find. My dormmates used to concoct various combinations of downs and speed and pot and acid and see what these would do to me if I took them all at once. I was glad to oblige. One night I smoked heroin in a bowling alley. I was kicked out of school when I got in a drunken fight in the cafeteria on St. Patrick's Day.

I went back to Cleveland and moved into my father's house. Soon thereafter, completely drunk from a night at the Euclid Tavern, I wrecked his car at three in the morning by hitting a tree on Liberty Boulevard, not far from the ball diamond where my father played baseball as a kid. By the time the cops had finished with me and the car towed, I walked in the house just in time for Saturday breakfast, covered with blood and suffering a concussion. I don't remember my father being overly upset. Not picking up your room would cause him to go into a rage; wrecking the car at three in the morning while completely loaded would merely elicit a stern look.

I moved downtown into the Backhouse, and the real partying started. I worked at a fancy restaurant as a waiter, always had a hundred bucks in my pocket, and would start the night of drinking every day after work. I rarely got to bed before six in the morning and got kicked out of school again. One night I was sick with the flu, lying in my upstairs bedroom sleeping. Lance had several cocaine dealers at the house after the bars closed. They started playing around with a gun and someone shot a round into the ceiling. The bullet passed six inches from the edge of my bed and exited the house through the ceiling.

I almost overdosed one day when a friend said he wanted to repay me for a term paper I had written for him. He pulled out a bag of coke and shoveled out a heaping teaspoon. He told me to open my mouth and poured the coke in. He then told me to let it melt slowly, not to swallow it all at once, for if I did my heart would stop. I did what I was told, but within a half hour I began convulsing on the floor, and the eyes rolled back in my head. My friend poured buckets of cold water on me. Somehow I survived.

During my first newspaper job, at the *Lake County News-Herald*, I would go out at lunch and have five or six beers before heading back to the paper and writing the day's news. Mistakes began finding their way into my copy. I was writing an obituary one night after an afternoon out at the bar. Our obituary style was fairly boilerplate, as it is at most newspapers, and the part about visitation hours was to read, "Friends may call from 2 to 4 and 7 to 9 P.M." at a particular funeral home. The obit I wrote came out this way: "Friends may ball from 2 to 4 and 7 to 9 P.M." The spell check, of course, did not catch the error, and neither did any of the editors. I fielded a call from a crying widow about the embarrassment I caused. I thought it all to be very funny.

Sensing I was about to be fired from the paper, I started looking for a new job and ended up in Fort Worth, Texas. I still drank quite a bit in Texas, but I was married now and tried to hide it from my wife. I would make excuses to leave the house at night, usually saying I had to go to the post office to mail some materials, and would buy a six-pack of tallboys and drink them while driving around for an hour. My wife eventually had enough of my lying and drinking and moved out.

Left alone and working as a freelance writer in Texas, I concentrated on my work. I still drank quite a bit, but never until I had finished my writing. I stayed home most nights with my daughter and would sit and read while watching TV, drinking a six-pack of beer before bed. In many ways I was becoming like my father. In his youth he was as wild as I was, but the times dictated a different type of intoxicant. But I knew what he was saying about spending all that time in saloons. It was a waste of time. I knew that, and had changed the way I lived.

And that's what scared me coming back to Cleveland. Among the Irish, alcohol is the great equalizer. It is the conduit that allows the professional to stand shoulder-to-shoulder with the factory worker. No man is allowed to get too high and mighty, and no drunk is considered to be too low-life. Alcohol drives everyone into the safe middle ground, where one's ambition defers to the crowd. And there is no better equalizer, no better way of fitting in, than to be fucked-up with the rest.

In my life I drank in celebration, I drank when I was depressed, I drank when I was bored. When my mom died, I recoiled into myself, comforting myself with getting outside my head. After writing a story, the only way to get the careening sentences out of your head was to wipe the inside of your brainpan clean with alcohol. And in Cleveland, drinking seemed to be the natural state of affairs. This was a town that could wear on you if you let it, too many ignos and hillbillies and days that needed diversion. And there might not be any greater diversion than facing death. John O'Mic proved that.

So here I was, my dad lying in a bed barely conscious, his legs and arms like matchsticks, his abdomen distended like a Biafran child, and what was I to do? I did what I knew best and felt most comfortable doing. I drank.

There is a misconception around the country about why Cleveland has the Rock and Roll Hall of Fame. There are certainly other cities more deserving—Memphis, San Francisco, New Orleans, Chicago, Detroit—but none of those cities did what Cleveland did. Cleveland embodied the alienation and dark ruminations of adolescence that rock music spoke to. We lived the life, and we lived the lyrics. When Bruce Springsteen sang "It's a town full of losers, I'm pulling out of here to win," we pretty much knew what he was talking about.

The official version of how Cleveland got the Hall of Fame is that DJ Alan Freed coined the term "rock and roll" during the early fifties and was the first to put on rock concerts, his celebrated "Moondog" balls. This is all very true. But it has little to do with why the Hall of Fame is located next to the new Browns Stadium in downtown Cleveland.

In the 1970s Cleveland was in the pits. The jobs were running out of town, and the people were leaving with them. But a funny thing happened to all of those baby boomer kids just coming of age in the midst of all those Cleveland jokes and Rust Belt doldrums. We partied more than our parents ever did. And a big part of this citywide drinking binge was going to rock concerts. In larger cities, with a citizenry fully employed and a host of entertainment options available, rock concerts didn't hold the importance they did here. It's like football in Los Angeles these days. No one cares about having an NFL team because there is so much else in L.A. that can occupy your time. In Cleveland during the seventies, there was nothing that could occupy your time. People didn't have jobs and they had few prospects. Rock and roll was a great diversion.

In the 1970s Clevelanders bought more albums per capita than any other market in the country. Radio station WMMS became famous around the country for breaking out new artists, like Bruce Springsteen and David Bowie. What was happening was that the record companies began to view Cleveland as an ideal test market, a city that was neither hip nor completely hick, either. For the powers in the music business Cleveland was important, as rock music in the seventies wasn't selling very well in other markets. So they sent their acts here, usually a few times on each tour, because they would always get a sellout in Cleveland.

WMMS began a promotional campaign that called Cleveland

the Rock and Roll Capital of the World. The campaign was self-serving and without any truth to it. Cleveland was never important to any musical genres, nor did we have any homegrown bands of note—the O'Jays, Michael Stanley Band, and the Raspberries come to mind, but that was about it. What we were best at was watching bands when they came to town. Clevelanders were very good at being spectators. And the music industry liked that about us.

The "Rock-and-Roll Capital" schlock did have some lasting effects on the city. In the seventies and eighties, clubs like the Agora and Peabody's Downunder began booking national acts and drawing people downtown. On Fridays after work, they began throwing "parties in the park" downtown for office workers, with beer trucks and bands and secretaries and young guys on the make mixing it up. Our parents were confused by their children's socializing downtown. That was the place you ran away from when work was over. That was where all the black people were.

All of this rock music and drinking helped build up the Flats, which in turn made it cool to live downtown. And with more people downtown, new stadiums and skyscrapers started to be built, and writers from out of town started writing stories about the "Cleveland comeback." It was very much economic development built on beer drinking and head-banging music.

The record companies never wanted to put the hall in Cleveland, but a promotional push by WMMS forced the music moguls to choose this Midwest city with virtually no musical heritage. The message from Cleveland was clear: we bought all of your albums when business wasn't very good, so you owe us one. The record industry decided to blackmail the city, demanding all sorts of public money and private donations to get the hall built. As Cleveland was in its usual mode of feeling inferior and desperate, it did everything the music guys wanted and built the damn thing.

And now attendance at the rock hall is declining, and the promoters are trying to figure out how to keep the hall from becoming a financial drain. The rock stars and the music industry snub the Hall of Fame, holding their induction ceremonies in New York. Imagine if the greats of the NFL decided not to show up every year at the Pro Football Hall of Fame in Canton. Would the Hall of Fame in Canton mean anything? Of course not.

So Cleveland has this glass monstrosity on the lakefront, and it is becoming apparent that it will be a white elephant one day. The music scene in Cleveland is now geared toward classic rock, and original bands have a tough time finding bars that will let them play. And the music industry thinks of Cleveland as some country cousin they want nothing to do with. Still, every so often, some rock star cleans out his closet and sends a pair of old tennis shoes and a jumpsuit off to Cleveland, where the civic leaders find a very expensive glass case to display it in . . .

My brother's bar was now becoming my second home. The Time-Out Grille was only about a mile from the hospice, and it became a way station for me. It was a place that was always alive, full of inimitable and inane conversations and the din of twenty TVs. I could always find someone I knew in the place, cousins and friends from grade school, a neighbor I hadn't seen in twenty years. And it was a great place to kill time.

The days were falling into an uncomfortable routine. Go to the hospice and sit by my father's bed. Do that until I couldn't stand it anymore. Run down to my brother's bar for dinner. Blast down about five beers. Back to the hospice for another bedside vigil. Back to the Time-Out around ten. Drink there until 1 A.M. Back to the hospice for one last look. Back to my brother's bar for last call. A six-pack to go in case I needed any more before bed when I got home.

My experience with him that night had lifted my soul and scared me at the same time. Having your dad tell you he is scared shitless can do that to a man. I also hated to think that he was struggling with seeing my mother. I tried telling him it wasn't something to worry about. But I wasn't the one lying in that bed. And I wondered what all that morphine was doing to him. They had jacked up the dosage level as time went on, and having had experiences with morphine in my life, I knew he was probably having some heavy-duty hallucinations.

It was now Thursday, and my father had been lying in that bed for four days. The nurses at the hospice were surprised that he lasted as long as he did. His vital signs were slowly deteriorating, but he had no history of heart disease, and the heart was the last organ to shut down. He was staying alive because he had a strong heart. I always suspected he did.

I made my way to my brother's bar that night. The regular crowd was there, and I took my seat as usual next to Crowley. For some reason, I felt more comfortable talking to Crowley than to anyone else at the bar. He was an old drunk, but a friendly sort. He had been a drinking pal of my Uncle Jack's back when Jack was really hitting the sauce, and through the years, Crowley had been a regular at just about every bar on 185th Street. When my brother bought the bar, he got Crowley in the deal, no different from the glassware on the beer taps and the jukebox. Crowley lived in the apartment above the bar, and my brother put him to work in exchange for his drinks. He had a small Social Security income, and my brother cashed his checks for him. He had been separated from his wife for more than twenty years, but being good Catholics, they never divorced. He had a couple of kids and grandkids and saw them on holidays.

Crowley had found a place where he fit perfectly, something men spend lifetimes searching for. He had access to booze and had a job—he was the only one in the bar who knew how to work the complex satellite TV system. He was old and weathered; drinking had definitely taken its toll on his body. His face was wrinkled and red, his nose the big Irish type, complete with a few broken blood vessels. He always wore a baseball cap, hiding the baldness on top of his head, but he compensated by growing his gray hair long in the back. The more he drank, the more irascible he became, yelling at the bartenders and poking fun at the customers. They would usually cut him off about eleven every night and shoo him out the door. Going home consisted of two left turns: one out the front door and the next into the side entrance to his apartment.

There had been some do-gooders through the years who had thought that Crowley might be better off if he gave up the booze. But the consensus around the bar was that Crowley would probably die if he ever stopped drinking. You don't do that kind of hard drinking for thirty years and just shut off the tap. And besides, this was the life he chose, and for the most part, he wasn't hurting anyone but himself.

"Get Danny one, Sheila," Crowley rasped. This was his usual greeting to me. Not Hi how are ya, or What's new Dannyboy, but Get this man a drink.

"I hear he's not doing very well," he said to me.

"Yeah, well, there's nothing more any of us can do about it," I answered. "I just wish he would get it over with already."

That sounded harsh and I regretted saying it as soon as it came out of my mouth. Crowley looked at me with his funny little grin and took a blast of his Canadian whisky.

"I mean, I don't want him to die," I explained. "I really don't. But he's just lying there, waiting for it to come, and I just feel so sorry for him."

"I saw a lot of guys die in Korea," Crowley said. "You lose a little bit of yourself when you see a man die. It's something that you never get back. It comes out of here." He pointed to his heart.

"How did you handle the war?" I asked him. "How did you keep your composure while watching those guys die?"

"You change yourself. You develop some insanity. It protects you from seeing what is truly in front of you. Over there we called it the Asian stare. It was the look we all had on our faces when we knew we only had six months to go. Your only thought was getting out of there alive.

"But it's nothing special," he continued. "This bad shit happens to everyone. I was one of the lucky ones. I made it out alive. But I still think about those guys every day."

I bummed a Marlboro Light from him. I had now added smoking to my bad Cleveland habits. I had smoked in my twenties, and quit for more than ten years. But now, every time I had a beer, I craved a smoke. And given the amount of beer I was drinking, the smoking was becoming a full-blown habit.

"Are you mad at your dad?" he asked.

Now, there was a question out of left field. But Crowley knew. He could tell I was agitated and nervous, sorting things out in my head while I drank with him.

"I guess what makes me mad is how he never took care of himself," I replied. "I mean after his first colon cancer surgery, I came over to his house one day and he was eating pork chops and mashed potatoes cooked in the pork grease. I got so mad. I told him that that was the absolutely worst thing a colon cancer patient could be eating. He told me to fuck off."

"So you're saying his cause of death is pork chops?" He paused for a second and let out a loud laugh, followed by a minute of hacking.

"I guess I'm just trying to figure out what to do. You feel so helpless. I keep telling myself that he had a good life and that we had mended our fences, and now is his time. But it doesn't make it any easier."

"Your dad was a good man," Crowley replied. "I didn't know him that well, but I know his kids. And all you kids are good people. A man has to be a good guy if he raised good kids like your family. As much as I fight with your brother Mark, I know he is a good man. I like your brother Brian. Your sisters have all been nice every time I've met them.

"Everyone in your family has treated me with respect. They could have looked down on me because I'm just an old drunk. But no one ever has. And I know you guys all got that from your father. I know you got it from him, because that was how he was."

I guess I knew that about my dad. But somehow in the midst of all this shit and death, I had forgotten some things about him. He always told us not to be impressed by celebrity or money. If he was at a wedding reception, you would usually find him talking to one of the busboys. When he was still accepting visitors at his house, a few lawyers he worked with came by, but every single secretary who had worked with him made a point to see him.

He never used his position to run roughshod over people. He was a champion of the virtues he learned as a kid in that Irish neighborhood he grew up in. Don't show you're better than anyone else, even if you are. Treat everyone decently. Don't be impressed with yourself. Take care of your family.

I was glad I talked to Crowley. Sometimes wisdom comes from the oddest places. Sometimes from an old drunk at the bar. From a man who has nothing to prove.

I went back to the hospice. The lights were dark in the room. Just a sliver of light made its way from the hallway into the room. My sisters Mary Margaret and Kathleen were in the room, sitting in chairs next to his bed. Mary Margaret was holding his hand, sobbing softly. My baby sister was having a hard time with his death. She was the last to move out of the house and had become very close to him in the past few years, living close by and taking him out to run errands. She brought her new baby, Maura, to see him often. And because she was so young when my mom died, she and my father had developed a special bond.

Mary Margaret gave up her seat so I could sit next to him. His eyes were stuck back in his head, and the gasping for air was making every breath a struggle. I held his hand, but there was no pressure back. I leaned over and told him I was there for him, and kissed him on his forehead. It was funny: I had never remembered kissing my father in my whole life, but now in the past few days I had kissed him half a dozen times. He didn't react to my voice or my kiss. His hand was limp.

I sat and sobbed for a few minutes, not knowing why, not knowing if this was real emotion or just a crying jag from the beer. I stayed there for about fifteen minutes, praying to whatever god there was to take this suffering from him. With every gasp, I thought it might be his last. I remembered that guy down in Huntsville, how he gave two last gasps before the poison jerked his heart to a stop. I really didn't know if one of these gasps might be the end. I couldn't stand it anymore.

My brothers Brian and Mark were out on his patio. The mood was decidedly different. Mark had brought a couple of twelve-packs over from the bar, and my brothers were telling stories about my dad. Some might think it callous to be drinking beer while the old man was lying a few feet away on his deathbed, but in our family it was oddly appropriate. I grabbed a cold one and sat down with them. The three of us had become closer than ever this summer, and I could trust them now.

"Remember when he destroyed that Ping-Pong table?" Brian asked. We all started laughing. The story was epic in our family. My dad had bought a Ping-Pong table for our basement rec room, and we played with it for about two months before getting bored. During the next year or so, the ping-pong table became a place where we put our junk, and the cheap aluminum legs became bent. My father decided he was going to fix it, and he was not terribly gifted when it came to tools and handyman skills. At some point he snapped in his frustration and began flailing at the table with his hammer. In a matter of minutes the fiberboard tabletop was smashed to bits, pieces of aluminum flying around the room.

"I remember getting hit with a piece of wood in the head," I said.

"I remember running out of the house scared," Brian said. "But when I got outside, I never laughed so hard in my life."

"Remember when he saw you with that beer bong, Mark?" I

asked. A beer bong is a large funnel with a piece of plastic hose taped to it. The way it worked was that the beer drinker would pour three or more beers into the funnel and suck the contents out through the smaller end. My dad was curious about the apparatus and asked Mark to show him how it worked. Mark grabbed three beers from the fridge, poured them into the funnel, and sucked them down in about fifteen seconds.

"He told me he had been drinking for thirty years and never saw anything like it," Mark said. "You guys didn't know how to impress him. I knew what would make him proud of me."

I told them about our conversations from the night I spent with him. I told him about my theory that he was afraid to see our mother and that this might be one of the reasons he was hanging on so long. One of the social workers told me this was a common occurrence, that terminally ill patients have some things to work out before they die. She agreed that he might be working through those things now.

"He had a tough time back then," Brian said. "A lot of people saw him as being this life of the party, but there was a certain sadness in his life. He kept that buried in him."

"Do you ever wish he had handled things differently?" I asked Brian. "I mean about the grieving process."

"I don't know. Think of where he was in his life. He was forty-three years old, and he had six kids. He was probably just trying to make it through each day. I'm that age now. I don't know what I'd do if Mary died and I had to raise my kids by myself. And I only have three.

"It's easy for us to make judgments on that time, but you have to put yourself in his place. He had watched her deteriorate for so long that her death itself was probably a relief for him. I can't imagine what he must have been going through."

"He did his best. That's all you can ask for," added Mark.

I decided to go. It was about midnight, and Mark was going to take the night shift. I went in the room to say good-bye. I didn't plan on coming back. I figured it was the last time I was going to see him. It was very anticlimactic.

But I did come back. I couldn't really stay away. I needed to see how this whole thing played out.

I was driving home past my brother's bar and decided to stop in for a nightcap. I saw Mike Marcic at the bar and sat down next to him.

"How's Papastein?" he asked. "Papastein" was the name my younger brothers and his friends had for the old man. I had no idea where it came from—maybe these guys were making some attempt at German philosophy—but my dad liked the moniker and referred to himself as Papastein at times.

"Just about checked-out," I told him.

Marcic sold furniture for a living. His nickname was "Massive Head." As a kid, his head was abnormally big for his body, and though his body eventually caught up, the name stuck. And I thought I had a bad nickname in "Tony."

"It's just too bad. He was a great guy."

Marcic then told me about how he and my father had bonded during a trip to the Bahamas a few years earlier. My brother Mark arranged a yearly trip to the Bahamas for his bar bowling league. It was always a wild drunken affair, and my father decided to go with the group one year. Marcic said he sat next to my dad by the pool every day, drinking beer together, while my dad told him stories about his childhood and his life as a lawyer. My father loved a captive audience like this, a kid who hadn't heard his stories before. It was typical of my father to befriend some kid he had little in common with.

"I laughed so hard one day," Marcic said. "He kept telling stories about circus geeks, and would go into great detail about the proper way to bite off the head of a chicken. He was almost scientific about it. That's what I'll remember about your dad. Circus geeks."

"What about the hot tub?" I asked.

"Yeah, he kept asking me about the hot tub. Said he wouldn't go in the hot tub again until it was drained and disinfected."

The incident in question involved Marcic and some young woman he met on the trip. After a night of drinking, they repaired to the hot tub. Because they each had a roommate on the trip, the two of them decided to take care of business right there in the hot tub by the pool. My father apparently wandered by during the episode and spent the next few days asking Marcic very pointed questions about his liaison.

"He was funny about it," Marcic said. "He was asking me if I used the bubbles to my advantage and he told me I had a moronic look on my face. Then he told me about a similar experience he had in a pool when he was younger. I felt embarrassed by the whole thing because we were really drunk. But your father had so much fun with it that I had to laugh."

"Yeah, he loved to tell the hot tub story. You got more studly every time he told it."

"I really wish I could see him before he dies," Marcic said.

I thought about this for a minute. For the past few days, my stepmother had been limiting the people who could see him, and rightly so. There were so many relatives, so many lives he touched, old neighbors and friends, coworkers and childhood friends, that the hospice was becoming overrun with people. I knew there was no way my stepmother would want someone like Marcic to go see him. But she was home in bed, and I thought why not? Why shouldn't a guy who had circus geeks and hot tub sex in common with my old man be allowed to see him?

"Let's go," I told him.

We made our way over to the hospice, and I warned Marcic about how my dad looked; that he was gaunt and probably weighed only 150 pounds (he was about 220 before this latest bout), that his legs were bluish black and he was having trouble breathing. "Can you handle that?" I asked.

Marcic nodded.

We approached the room by way of the patio. My sisters had left, and Brian and Mark were still having a few beers in the cool night air, checking in on him every few minutes.

"Massive Head, what are you doing here?" Brian asked.

"Just came to pay my respects to Papastein," Marcic said.

We led him inside, through the partially opened French doors. The four of us stood over his bed; he was still gasping for air, but he seemed more peaceful than before. A look of horror came over Marcic's face. He hadn't seen my dad in about a year and wasn't prepared for the sight. I guess we had gotten used to how he looked over time, but for someone who hadn't seen him in a while, the gruesome sight of a man in the throes of death can be unsettling.

"Just go up to him and hold his hand and tell him who you are," I told Marcic.

Marcic approached the bed slowly, took my dad's hand, and moved his mouth closer to my dad's ear. "Hey, Papastein," he started. "It's Mike Marcic. Remember me? I was the guy who fucked that girl in the hot tub down in the Bahamas."

We all cracked up. We were at various stages of drunkenness, but the whole scene was just too weird. Of all the things to say to a man on his deathbed.

But then something very strange happened. My dad gripped Marcic's hand, turned his face to him, and let loose with his trademark smirk.

A few seconds later it turned into a grin. There was definitely some shallow happiness going on here. And then he closed his eyes and the grin stayed on his face. We all looked at each other like we had seen a miracle. I wondered what my dad was thinking. He was probably picturing Marcic fucking that girl in the hot tub. What a way to go out.

We went back outside and Marcic started bawling. He was really torn up seeing my father that way. But we consoled him, telling Marcic that it was the first time my father had smiled in days. Marcic started laughing through his tears, and I gave him a beer. We toasted to my father and Massive Head and his hot tub escapades. And shit.

I decided to go in the room by myself. The smile was now gone from his face, and the two of us sat in the silent darkness. I decided that this was going to be it for me. It was late, two in the morning now, and I was exhausted. I didn't want to come back. I decided to say my piece.

"Dad, it's Danny," I started. "I love you very much and you've taught me a lot. I'm very proud of you, how you've handled this, but now is the time. It's okay to die."

I don't know if it was all the beer, but I raised my voice so I was almost shouting at him.

"My mother is going to welcome you. Don't worry about her. You're going to see everyone and it's going to be great. Don't worry about any of your kids. You've done a great job with us.

Crowley told me so tonight. You know Crowley, the guy who cleans up at Mark's bar. He said you were a great guy. Everyone says the same thing."

I was starting to ramble.

"But Jesus Christ, Dad, there comes a time when you just have to do what you have to do. No one will think any less of you if you just let go. You've been so brave, but you're not proving anything to anyone by keeping this going any longer. It's okay. Mark's going to spend the night, and he'll take care of you. Don't be afraid. You've done the hard part."

I started crying. "I'm going to miss you terribly, but we had a few good months. Just remember how much I love you and how I always admired you. That's it. I'm going now. I'll see you on the other side."

I got up, kissed him on the forehead. "Tell my mom I said hi. Tell her I miss her. Bye."

And with that I left. I walked outside, had one more beer with my brothers and Marcic, and drove home. I sat out on my porch, listened to the ore freighters on the river, and watched the blue flames shoot from the steel mills. Everything in Tremont was quiet and peaceful. I felt a little hollow, but I was happy that I had said what I had to say. This thing with my father, our life together, was over as far as I was concerned. Time to move on.

I was sleeping on the couch in my living room when the phone rang at about eight the next morning. I didn't bother to answer. I knew what the message was going to be. I waited a few moments and then listened to the message from Mark on my answering service.

My dad had died about six in the morning. Mark had fallen asleep in the room about four, and my dad checked out soon after that. It was just like him to do it that way, wait until no one was around and then sneak off on his own. His last moment of consciousness was smiling at Mike Marcic about the hot tub. Maybe that's what he was thinking about when he died. Good for him.

I stared at the ceiling for a few minutes. Life would be different from now on. I felt an odd mixture of relief and trepidation. I was glad for him, happy that he was finally able to get through this hard part of his life. But I also felt lost. Almost everything I did, every decision I ever made, I would think of how he would react and what he would think of me. It was a blessing and a curse to be so connected to a parent like that. I didn't know what to think anymore. I rolled over and went back to sleep.

# CHAPTER EIGHT

# We're Together Right or Wrong

In the lexicon of demographers, my father's age group is known as the Silent Generation. They were the group sandwiched between the overachieving GIs from World War II and the self-absorbed baby boomers of the 1960s. Officially, he belonged to the group born between 1925 and 1942 (who chooses these dates anyway?)—too young for the Great Depression or World War II, too old to be part of the drugs and free love of the sixties. Novelist Frank Conroy said of the Silent Generation: "We had no leaders, no program, no sense of our own power, and no culture exclusively our own."

I was born in 1959, and those same demographers lump me into the baby boomer generation. I never quite understood being a part of the boomers; I was too young for Vietnam and the sixties, too old for Generation X and the technology boom that came along later. Those of us born in the late fifties and early sixties have little in common with those born directly before or after; we are a demographic sliver that belongs to neither. I came of age with punk rock music and drug use that was for kicks rather than enlightenment. Like my father's generation, we come to the table lacking any clear identity, no wars to fight, no philosophical battles to hang our hats upon. Conroy might have been speaking about my own age group in his assessment of a lack of leaders, culture, or power.

There are similarities between the two groups. My father came of age during the sexually repressive era of the fifties; my generation came of age during the beginning and hysteria of AIDS. My father's generation had Eisenhower, we had Reagan. His generation had to choose between the music of Frank Sinatra or something new called rock and roll. When I was in college, there was a battle between the punks and disco. My father missed World War II and Korea; my age group never had to register for the draft.

There was a huge cultural difference between our two groups, however. And this may have had to do with growing up in Cleveland more than just being part of different eras. My father's generation was born into a culture, and they fought hard to get rid of it. Their parents were generally born in the old country, and to them this was a stigma they needed to rid themselves of. If they had no culture, as Conroy writes, it was of their own choosing; in my generation's case, our lack of culture was the direct result of our parents' decision to get rid of it.

We like to think of ourselves as better than our parents, able to learn from their mistakes and move along with our lives with a certain amount of accumulated knowledge that will push us along further than they were able to go. And our parents generally have the same ideals; their goals are to create better lives for their kids, platforms to propel their kids into better homes and better schools and better jobs. In my father's generation, this upward mobility was real and objective. Their parents came of age in the time when help-wanted signs in Cleveland said that "Irish Need Not Apply"; their enemies were the oppressive Wasp upper crust above them and the black men pushing them from below. The Jews were both envied for their book smarts and reviled for being the neighborhood landlords. In many ways, their success was to be judged not only from doing better than their parents but also from rising above the other ethnic groups that lived nearby.

My father had a sense of who he was, rooted very much in being Irish and Roman Catholic and having something to prove. And in post–World War II Cleveland, he and his neighborhood friends did just that. In the space of one generation they had gone to college, moved to the suburbs, given up much of their "Irishness," and melded into a thriving industrial city. They had become near equals with the Wasp establishment, had gained control of political institutions, and had moved from iron ore unloads to lawyers and doctors and bankers. In some ways, they succeeded far too well.

My generation did not have the clear enemies of my father's, or the clear sense of purpose. My family grew up in the nondescript suburb of Euclid, in a nice house down by the lake. A college education was an expectation, not some far-flung dream. We didn't compete against the Wasps or the Jews or the blacks or the other ethnic groups; hell, we didn't even know who they were. There were a lot of Irish families in Holy Cross Parish, but many were the watered-down variety, like my own ethnic mix of Irish, Slovenian, and Danish. Being Irish was something we did on St. Patrick's Day, when we would skip school and get drunk down at Public Square while watching the parade. There we would make fun of the "professional Irish," all those fat old men dressed from head to toe in green who would be drunk and home in bed by seven at night.

For those in my generation, there wasn't such a clear plan as my father's generation had. We couldn't rely on economic gains or moving up the social ladder as proof that we had been successful. In the sixties the older baby boomers at least could claim some moral or philosophical higher ground as a way to differentiate themselves from their parents. For my brothers and sisters and friends—those of us born in the late fifties and sixties—being different or better than our parents was more obtuse. We thought we might be more sensitive parents, show more emotion to our kids, not be so consumed with work. Maybe we would be better at showing our emotions than this generation of silent, confident—but standoffish—men, who had raised all of us.

I always thought of myself as very different from my father's generation. They had bought into the white flight, the prospect that moving away to the suburbs might make life better for everyone. Work every day, own your piece of dirt, and retire to Florida: that was the plan for life. Raise your kids, send them to college, punch that time clock and wait for the reward. I had never bought into any of that. When life became that predictable, I ran the other way. It wasn't that his generation had done all these things; it was that they had gone along with the flow so passively. At least that's what I thought when I was younger.

I remember when I was about ten years old and our family was discussing a local murder at the dining room table. Euclid Municipal Judge Robert Steele was accused of hiring a hit man to kill his wife (he was eventually convicted), and my dad knew him pretty well. Part of the evidence early on in the investigation was that Judge Steele had been heard telling people he disliked his wife so much he could kill her. I told my dad that this was significant information. My dad laughed it off, saying all men had expressed such sentiment at some time in their marriage. I countered that my generation would never dream of saying such a horrible thing. My dad looked at me seriously for a moment, reached for a baked potato in the dish in front of him, and threw a strike right into the side of my head.

I remember that incident now because I myself have thought those things when I am angry at my wife. Every man I know has thought those things about his wife. It is part of marriage, not a part of a generation. Most of my friends now live in houses in the suburbs, save for their kids' college, and invest in 401(k) plans for their retirement. This is also not part of a generation; it's just how life works.

In the next two decades, baby boomers and people of my age group are going to bury their parents. As we bury them, we are going to think of their legacy and the effect of that legacy in us. They gave us education, they gave us a comfortable lifestyle, and they gave us a set of values. And they are going to transfer a huge amount of money our way. But even though we are richer moneywise than our parents, I wonder if we have done better than them. I suspect that ours is the first generation in many where we are not substantially better off than our parents. This is not to overstate their accomplishments, nor to disparage my generation. It just is.

As I think about my father, I realize I have become him. Not in every aspect, of course, but in many important ones. I am not a joiner, I am mostly analytical and unemotional, and I am not easily impressed by celebrity or money. I am cynical yet optimistic; I share my father's penchant for being a consistent contradiction. I love the written word, and I like to tell stories. I like to be the center of attention. I can be a curmudgeon when I want to and I generally like it. Increasingly, reading a good book while drinking beer and watching *Baywatch* is considered a good night. I sometimes think that it might be fun to have a big house in the suburbs. After years of fighting against him, I have become him.

So we have become our parents. What of it? It is not such a bad thing. But who do we become when we plant them in the ground? Do we continue to be influenced by their memory, by their legacy, becoming more like them? Or is there some freedom in their deaths, something that allows us to be someone else, people we always wanted to be?

I don't know the answer to these questions. But I very much want to find out.

I have a good laugh now when I hear that someone "died in their sleep." Unless you have a heart attack or brain aneurysm or are sleepwalking in front of a fucking bus, you don't die in your sleep. The whole phrase is hilarious. That's what some people might say about my father, that he died in his sleep. Died in his fucking sleep. How funny.

For more than six months I watched my father die. He died a little bit every day in that time, slowly losing some functions, slowly losing the optimism, slowly losing the ability to care much about the daily goings-on in life that seem to consume those of us that are not facing death. I asked him once if he would prefer to know exactly when he was going to die, or if it would be better to not know. "I think it's better to know," he told me. "There are a lot of things you have to do to get ready to die. Not so much the things you think about. The spiritual stuff has been easier for me than I thought. The hard part is to make sure everyone is as ready as you are. That's been the hard part for me."

When I eventually woke up the day he died, I thought much about how he had tried to prepare me and my family members for his death. He had joked to me that when he died I would be an orphan, and how being the attention-grabbing sort (as he was), I could use this to my advantage. He said it would be a great way to get free drinks in the bar. The combination of my vocation as a journalist—and all the free drinks my profession gloms in our role as truth-seekers—and orphanhood might make me the champion free drink getter of all time. I told him I would do my best.

And I laughed to myself while thinking of being an orphan. But it takes two to be an orphan, and my thoughts turned more to my mother than my father. I wondered how he was doing seeing her in the afterlife. I wondered how much life would have been different had she lived. It was weird, because my father's death didn't seem to bother me that much. I had been there with him, had felt death, had looked him in the eye when he was scared, and joked with him when he was feeling on top of the world. When my mother died, I was a sullen teenager, and my father tried to keep all the bad parts away from his kids. And as I thought about his death, I wanted to cry, but there was no one to cry with. I wished she was there with me.

I had a nasty hangover, something that was becoming more and more common with every day I spent in Cleveland. I looked in the mirror in the bathroom and noticed my eyebrows. I had inherited the bushy and wiry eyebrows of my father, a bit like Andy Rooney's but without his evil stare. The strange thing about inheriting my father's eyebrows was that they reacted the same way his did. When my father had a hangover, his eyebrows hung lazily over his eyelids. When he was excited, they seemed to jump off his face. He never allowed them to be trimmed by a barber; like Samson, he saw them as his source of power.

On this morning, my own eyebrows were hanging limp over my eyes, in need of regeneration from a most eventful night. So in the interest of eyebrow maintenance, I grabbed a beer from the fridge and sat out on my drinking porch. Being midmorning on a Friday, and being that my neighborhood was mostly filled with artists and welfare cases, there was not much activity on the street. But the rhythm of the city was going on full blast in the noises of Cleveland; I could hear the horns from the ore carriers begging the bridges to rise as they went by; gears of the trucks were grinding as they brought their loads out of the Flats: the beer truck was unloading at the market on the corner. A young woman was hauling three crying kids down the street to pick up some milk at the market. And I heard the bells at St. John Cantius down the street; some other family was burying a loved one.

And then I remembered that I had some work to do. My father had prepared us all for some chores to do after he died. As a lawyer, my brother Brian was tapped to handle his will and his legal affairs. My sister Kathleen was to help my stepmother with the funeral arrangements. My two other sisters were to call relatives. My brother Mark was to make sure the drinks were flowing. And my job, as the writer in the family, was to write his obituary.

He had broached the subject with me when I first moved back to Cleveland in June. We had been making small talk about books or sports or some such when out of the blue he looked at me in a very serious way.

"I've decided you're going to write my obituary," he said without emotion.

"Jeez, Dad, that's kind of creepy, you know, talking about stuff like that." I wasn't so much against the idea of writing his obit; it was just that I knew how newspapers worked, and I knew that any attempt to write something that fit his life and personality would be beaten out of my copy. That's what newspaper copy editors do: they beat the enthusiasm out of any writer until their copy reads just like anyone else's. I knew it would be a thankless job.

"I'm giving everyone a job to do," he continued. "Your talent is writing, so you get to do this." He then opened up a folder with a stack of papers. He showed me the list of pallbearers he had chosen, his appropriations of funds for a party after his funeral, and his "no eulogies, no bagpipes, no mimes" edict.

"Well," I stammered, "newspapers have a certain style they want to use, so we'll have to talk sometime about your work history and military service and all that. Plus, newspapers are very big on clubs and organizations, so we'll have to come up with a list of those things."

"That's no problem," he said. "I have notes."

And with that, he pulled two pages out of his folder with handwritten notes about his life. I thought he was very organized that way; it was admirable to distill one's life into two pages. He had listed the dates of his air force service, the dates of his two marriages, and his work history. I pictured him working on this in his La-Z-Boy chair, watching *Jerry Springer* or something else equally absurd, going over his life in a way that would fit into Associated Press newspaper style.

He put on his glasses and started going over it point by point. "In this law firm," he started, "I don't want you mentioning this guy's name, even though he was a name partner. He was a prick and I don't want him in my obituary. And leave out this law firm entirely. They were all a bunch of assholes and I am sorry I worked with them. The *Plain Dealer* won't know any better, so leave them out."

"I take it that you're going to be getting back at people from the grave."

"Why not? It's my obituary. Let them write their own."

I could tell he had put some thought into this and was having some fun with it. His smirk was going full-bore now, knowing that he was going to have something to say even after he was gone. I decided to play along.

"Well, I know they are going to want some clubs and organizations," I replied. "What have you got there?"

"I've got that covered. Write that he belonged to only two organizations in his life and he was born into both of them: the Roman Catholic Church and the Democratic Party."

"That's good, Dad. Everyone will get a good laugh from that."

"I thought so. I'm just trying to give you some good material. It will make your job easier."

My reporter's instincts were taking over now. "What about some personal stuff?" I asked. "You know, like hobbies or descriptions of you?"

"Put in there that I was a raconteur."

"A raconteur?"

"Yes, a raconteur. It means someone who is adept at telling anecdotes. Oh yeah, and put in there that I was a world traveler. And that I appreciated fine art and literature."

He was clearly enjoying this too much. I had lost my uneasiness over the conversation. He was using this as an exercise to become more comfortable with his death, and he was dragging me along with him. What a great way to perform the self-examination of your life. Get out a legal pad and take some notes.

"Anything else?" I asked.

"Yeah, say I had a wit like Mike Royko."

"Maybe we could put in there that you had the humility of Gandhi. Or the writing ability of John Dos Passos. Or the perseverance of the little Dutch boy who had his finger in the dike."

"No dykes," he said, laughing. "No guys with weird lips or baggy eyes, either."

"You realize, of course, that you'll be at the whim of the day's news events. If some guy who was the president of LTV Steel or some famous athlete dies on the same day, you might be bumped off the page. I hope, for my sake, you die on a slow news day."

"I'm serious about this," he continued. "Don't screw this up. You're the only one who can handle this. More people are going to remember me from this obituary than anything else. I just want people to know who I was."

"Oh, I'll be able to write up something telling who you were," I assured him. "I just don't know if the *Plain Dealer* is ready for an obit like that."

Now, a good conscientious son would have gone home at that point and started writing up the first draft of this all-important obituary and worked steadily during the coming weeks to refine and edit the piece so that a masterpiece was in the waiting when the time came. But if anything, I am a procrastinator and avoider, so I gave little thought to my little task during the succeeding months. But as I sat there on that morning, first beer of the day in hand, I remembered the little task my dad had left with me.

It was about then the phone rang.

"You're writing the obituary, right?" It was my brother Brian. He was acting big-brotherly, but also wanted to make sure I wasn't too drunk or too goofy to complete the task. "Have you written anything yet?"

"No."

"When do you plan on doing this?" he asked.

"I thought today might be a good day for obituary writing. Maybe next week, if I get around to it."

"Don't be an asshole. Call the funeral home and get the number of the *PD*'s obit editor."

"Don't worry about it. I'll get it done. I am a professional, after all."

"Professional what?"

"You'll find out when I die. I'm going to write my own obituary when I get done with this one. I have notes, you know."

With that he hung up. Similar conversation followed with other brothers and sisters, all wondering whether I had done any work on this project yet. I'd been busy, I told them. Watching football practice, drinking beer, bowling—all of life's essential components. And besides, I told them, the *PD* is not going to run this tomorrow. The calling hours were going to be on Sunday and Monday, with the funeral on Tuesday, so there wasn't much chance the *PD* would run this until Sunday morning. At least that was my educated guess as a former newspaperman.

I talked to the obit editor, Richard Peery. He said I could write the obit, but that he needed it that afternoon for the Saturday paper. And I needed to get him a picture of my father. And the sooner the better if we wanted this to get good play. He also told me I couldn't get my byline on the piece because of union rules, but that he would print my obituary of my father "if it is any good."

Well, so much for pressure. Deadline writing had never been like this. I guess I was becoming a tourist at my own tragedy.

And it came very easily to me. I grabbed a beer, went into my little writing room—a large kitchen pantry with a window that looked out on a brick wall—and cranked out a decent little obit for my dad. This is what I sent to the *Plain Dealer*:

*Richard James McGraw, a prominent retired trial lawyer and father of 14 children, died Friday from complications of* colon cancer at the Hospice of the Western Reserve in Cleveland. He was 69.

McGraw was known for his aggressive style of trying legal cases, and in more than 40 years as an attorney, he lost only a handful of cases. His love of literature produced lyrical closing arguments, full of pomp and fury and old-fashioned oratory, often laced with references to Shakespeare, Thomas Wolfe or Ernest Hemingway. "When Dick McGraw was trying a case, law firms would send their young lawyers to the courtroom to watch his performance," said James V. Moroney, McGraw's son-in-law and Assistant U.S. Attorney in Cleveland. "No one could try a case better. He was among the last of his kind, the kind of lawyer who was respected by everyone in the legal community, including those who tried cases against him."

Born in 1930 in Cleveland, McGraw grew up in the heavily Irish St. Thomas Aquinas neighborhood on Cleveland's East Side. His father died when he was just 11, and McGraw worked a variety of jobs—soda jerk, scorecard salesman at Cleveland Indians games, ditchdigger for a utility company—to pay his own way through high school, college, and eventually law school. He graduated from Cathedral Latin High School in 1948, then received a degree in history from Western Reserve University. He received an academic scholarship to Western Reserve University Law School, graduating in 1954.

A United States Air Force veteran, McGraw married the former Karen Weed in 1955, and together they had six children. After his wife's death in 1975, McGraw remarried in 1977 to Theresa McCarthy Mora, whose husband Leonard had died around the same time as McGraw's spouse. Theresa Mora had eight children of her own, creating a new family of

14 children. "My first instinct was to run," McGraw used to joke when he learned his bride-to-be had eight children. Ironically, McGraw met Theresa Mora while trying a case, as she was seated on the jury. In that case, McGraw won a verdict for $500,000, which he estimated was about the cost of his children's college tuition bills.

The family lived in Euclid until all the children were grown. In the past four years, Richard and Theresa McGraw lived in Willoughby Hills.

McGraw's legal career began as a litigator with the Cleveland Transit System in 1961, and he was a name partner in the firm Hesser, McGraw & Armstrong during the 1970s and 1980s. In recent years he worked with the firm of Mansour, Gavin, Gerlack & Manos, before retiring in 1995. In his retirement he traveled the world, and spent much of his time reading and studying art. He will be remembered as a raconteur, a man with an acerbic wit, a world-class storyteller in the great Irish tradition, and a loving father and husband.

He belonged to only two organizations in his life and he was born into both of them: the Roman Catholic Church and the Democratic Party. His wit was often compared to that of newspaper columnist Mike Royko.

Survivors are his wife, Theresa; his sister, Helen of Wickliffe; sons Brian of Cleveland; Leonard of Mayfield Heights; Daniel of Fort Worth, Texas; Mark of Lyndhurst; Michael of Cleveland; Jeffrey of Chicago; daughters Sharon of San Diego, California; Susan of Strongsville; Kathleen of Columbus; Sheila of Lyndhurst; Sandra of San Jose, California; Sheila of Columbus; Theresa of Kennewick, Washington; and Mary Margaret of Euclid; 29 grandchildren, and numerous nieces and nephews.

*Services will be held at 9:30 A.M. Tuesday, at St. Felicitas Church, 140 Richmond Road, Euclid.*

*Arrangements are being handled by the Mullally Funeral Home of South Euclid. Donations are requested in Richard McGraw's name to the Hospice of the Western Reserve.*

It took me about an hour. Three beers' worth of writing. I felt it wasn't bad, given the restrictions of space and the newspaper style of obits. I was tempted to put in there that "friends may ball from 2–4 and 7–9 P.M.," but I thought that might be a tad disrespectful. My dad would have enjoyed it, though. After all, his last vision before death was that of drunken sex in a hot tub.

I had warned everyone in my family that the *PD* would run all or part or none at all. And, as usual, they did their best to edit all the fun out of it. They slapped a most absurd headline on the piece, "Richard McGraw, Set Example for Lawyers"—a headline that would have made my father gag. They also cut out the part about his being a raconteur and being born into the two organizations. As writer Pete Hamill once observed, "newspapers will break your fucking heart every time." They always do, and they always will.

But what choice do we have? When I worked as a waiter, Demetrius the busboy had his own ghetto logic about how to make it through life's ups and downs. "You gotta stick and move, brother, stick and move," Demetrius would say. I think he was applying this bit of wisdom to his love life, but I took greater meaning. Make your point and then get out of the way. Lob a bomb and then run for cover. Don't ever hang around long enough for the consequences.

And that's all I wanted to do with my father's death: stick and move, brother. But life doesn't work that way, especially when it involves your own personal tragedy. You can stick and move all you want, but eventually you have to face the consequences. And no better way to face the consequences of death than to look at a corpse at the funeral home. Especially when the corpse looks a lot like you, eyebrows and all.

I hate to say this, but I felt a certain amount of release when I learned my dad had finally died. Not release in the sense that I was glad he died or wouldn't miss him. I was already missing him terribly. But for the first time in my life, I felt I didn't have to prove anything to anybody. I thought about it in terms of physics. My father was like a huge celestial body that was always pulling me with his gravitational field. My usual response was to push away. And even when we had achieved some equilibrium, his power still affected my orbit. The good part of this new equation is that I felt free to find my own orbit in the galaxy. The disturbing part is that I had no idea where the orbit would take me.

In every decision I had ever made in my life I had thought of him first. When I was homeless, I was ashamed, not because I was on the skids, but because of what he would think of me. When I got married, I worried about what he would think of my bride. Whenever I was published, I wondered if he was sitting at home with a red pen, correcting any awkward constructions. I worried needlessly about these things; the fact was that my father was either too self-centered to care all that much or too proud of me to be that critical.

But it was always in the back of my mind, and now that part of me was gone. It felt wonderful, on one hand. Maybe at the age of thirty-nine, I could finally become my own man. But if I wasn't proving myself to my father anymore, then to whom was I going to prove myself? Maybe it was time to look inward, to not give a shit what anyone else thinks, and to care a little bit about what I think. Shallow happiness on the run. Sticking and moving in my own orbit. Tapping the second keg while still alive.

As I have mentioned before, death means different things to different age groups. As a man approaching forty, I thought mostly of myself. You can't look upon the death of a parent at this age without putting yourself in his or her shoes. We think only in terms of what we have not done, of what we want to do, and of what other people might think of us. Maybe in twenty years I'll be able to face death like my father. But now I am only filled with fear. I realize I am very much afraid of death. I want to get hit by a bus. Preferably while sleepwalking.

The Irish seem to love wakes, and there is a bit of history to it. When the British occupied Ireland, they passed a law that prohibited the meeting of two or more Irish on the grounds that it would be considered a sign of uprising and treasonous. The exception made by the British was funerals. The Irish soon realized that their best chance to overthrow the crown was to do their plotting at funerals. And while they were at it, they decided that it would be a good time to throw a party and get loaded.

My father recalled going to a few Irish wakes when he was younger. The corpse would be laid out in the living room, with a group of "keeners"—women hired to cry in front of the casket—occupying the solemn area around the casket. There would be a bar in the kitchen and another in the basement, where a band would be playing. These affairs would last a few days, full of dancing and drinking and storytelling. Over the years, these full-blown Irish wakes had fallen into disfavor; most Irish thought they were classless and encouraged drunkenness too much. Instead, families now went to two-day wakes at funeral homes and went to bars to drink afterward. We had come a long way as a people.

My father did not want an Irish wake as such. He had contacted the funeral home himself and made the proper arrangements before he died. He had also instructed my brother to use his estate to pay for a reception after the burial. But he did not want any Irish greenhorn ceremony to send him on his way. He had always expressed a disdain for families that carried on too much when they faced a funeral. We were to show our strength as a family by carrying on with a certain detached dignity. Emotions were to be kept to a minimum.

But nothing quite prepares you for seeing your father up there in that casket. And as I made my way up to his corpse, holding hands with my daughter, Meredith, I noticed the funniest thing about him. They had embalmed him with that fucking smirk on his face. I could just see those funeral home guys pushing his smile down, only to have it bounce back up. There was something almost sinister about his facial expression. I had never seen a smiling corpse before.

I stood in my place in the receiving line, shaking the hands of more than one thousand people who had come to pay their respects to my dad. One by one, they would file past me, offering their condolences and telling me that I looked just like him. "He does look good, doesn't he?" I would respond. Or I would say, "Are you saying I look like I'm dead?" Some got the joke; others just looked at me with a very strange look.

All of which became very tiring after ten hours over two days. I hugged relatives I had rarely met, plastered a smile on my face that rivaled the guest of honor's, and tried to work the room like an Irish politician. And I was very grateful when Doctor Deadhead and Lance came in on the second day.

After they paid their respects, we went outside in the parking lot. I had some beer in a cooler in the trunk of my car and wanted some nonrelative to do some drinking with. They were quick to oblige.

"You know you look just like him," Lance said, laughing. He knew how I hated that line and was quick to stick it to me. I gave them both a Busch tallboy.

"Well, you look just like the guy in the next room," I answered.

"He must be good-looking, then," Lance said.

I thought it was quite appropriate how my friends and I viewed this funeral. The joking and the drinking were all part of the avoidance. But at the same time, it was an acknowledgment that bad things happen to all people. It was all part of the Cleveland drinking tradition: never put yourself above anyone else. And a good buzz equalizes the emotions.

"Did you know that your dad has a smile on his face?" Doctor Deadhead said.

"I did notice that," I answered. "I guess even when he is dead, his personality comes through. I've never seen a corpse like that, though."

"How's everybody handling things?" Lance said.

"Well, everybody seems to be okay. My stepmother has been pitching a fit over my brother's decision not to make my father's will public until he's in the ground. My stepmother is worried he might have left money to a mistress, and that's why my brother is holding the information back."

"Maybe that's why he's smiling," Deadhead said.

"Yeah, Dick McGraw probably had some young chickie on the side," Lance chimed in. "Did he go to a lot of strip joints? Maybe one of his secretaries."

"Please, boys, a little respect for the dead here," I said. "As far as I know, he never did that."

We drank some beer in the twilight. It was hot and muggy, and I desperately wanted to get out of my newly bought suit. It was like we were twenty again, just a couple of guys drinking cheap beer from the back of a car. After about an hour, I had to go back in.

"Do you get to hug any good-looking chicks who need comfort?" Lance asked.

"There have been a few. I do my best to comfort them."

"Are you going to be at bowling tomorrow?" Doctor asked.

"I doubt it," I said. "His funeral is tomorrow. What's the proper grieving period with respect to bowling, anyway?"

"I think it's a week," Doctor said. "And then you have to wear a black bowling shirt for a period of at least a week but not to exceed a month. I think that's in the PBA bylaws."

"Well, if that's the bowling rules, I will abide by them. Are you guys going to my brother's bar later? There should be a lot of people there."

"I've got to get up for work early," said Doctor.

"I've got a nurse's assistant to see," Lance said. "She's twenty-three. I've got my hands full."

"Stick and move, brother. Stick and move."

"Are you going to the Steelers game?" Doctor asked. The Browns were opening their season in about a month, a Sunday night game. It was looking like this would be one of the all-time Cleveland jakefests, football returning for real after nearly four years, the Steelers in town, and a night game to boot.

"Yeah, I'll be there. I've got a press pass. You guys got tickets?"

"In the Dawg Pound," Lance answered. "We're going to get drunk and vomit on Big Dawg."

"That sounds like a plan," I said. "Let's be the first ones to be thrown out of an official game. It should be easy. Pissing in the sink now is considered a felony. Cheering too loudly is considered a misdemeanor. Smuggling in a bottle of Jim Beam calls for public execution."

"And we're just the guys to do it," Lance said.

I bid them good-bye, ready to take my place in line for the last hour. Everyone complimented me on the obituary, and I quit explaining which parts had been taken out. And as I stood there shaking hands and hugging old ladies, I could feel my father watching me. I half expected him to jump out of that casket and preside over his own wake. That would be his style. But it was over. No joking or crying or serious introspection would bring him back. I was free now to do what I wanted. I just didn't know what I wanted to do.

My dad's funeral was a blur. We met at the funeral home and said our prayers before they closed the casket for the last time. I kissed him softly on his forehead and held my daughter close. She had flown up with her mother and was a great comfort. It's amazing how resilient a nine-year-old can be. When I cried, she stroked the back of my neck and told me it would be all right. She had spent most of the summer with me and had gotten to know her grandfather a bit. But she didn't have the emotional attachment to him; to her he was just an old man who sent her presents in the mail for her birthday and Christmas. She said that all he ever did was sit in his chair, read books, and fart.

At the funeral mass, the priest said that my father used to sit in the front row with his arms folded and a scowl on his face. This intimidated him, the priest told the congregation. Join the club, dear Reverend, he did that to everyone he knew. My brother Brian and stepsister Sharon had planned to say a few words at the mass, but the priest forgot about it. I thought it was appropriate. Remember, he wanted no eulogies, no bagpipes, and no mimes. He got his wish.

When we arrived at the cemetery, I was anxious. I hadn't been there since my mother's funeral, and I wanted to see her gravestone for the first time. He was going to buried next to her. But they covered the ground with that horrible Astroturf, and I couldn't see her grave. To this day, I haven't been back.

After much family squabbling, it was decided that the reception following the funeral would be held at some cheesy Italian party room instead of the equally cheesy East Side Irish American hall. There we enjoyed a buffet lunch for three hundred and an open bar. For the first time in many months, I wasn't really in the mood to drink. I just wanted to get away. There were just too many people, too many relatives, and too much roast beef and fried chicken.

But before I left, there was something I had to see. Back in the spring, my stepsister and her husband had video-recorded my father singing a song. There was some talk about playing it at the funeral mass, but it was decided that it would be a bit much to have Dick McGraw singing at his own funeral. But someone had the good idea to bring a TV and a VCR to the reception. I hadn't seen the tape and was curious as to what my father would be doing in front of the camera.

There was a crowd around the TV, friends and relatives with beers in hand, guys he had gone to second grade with, secretaries he had worked with. It was a strange group, people without much in common, except that they had been touched by my father at some point in their lives. The tape was being played and re-wound, then played again. It seemed to be almost as popular as the open bar.

My father gave a brief introduction to the song, saying he had learned it during his "pseudo hillbilly period" and had wowed some geriatric tour group in London a few years back by singing after dinner. And with that, in a very clear voice and in perfect tune, he sang what seemed to be an old country-western song:

> When you're all alone and blue
> No one to tell your troubles to
> Remember me
> I'm the one who loves you
>
> When the whole world turns you down
> And not a true friend can be found
> Remember me
> I'm the one who loves you
>
> In all kinds of weather
> I'll never change
> Through sunshine and sorrow
> I'll be the same
>
> We're together right or wrong
> Wherever you go I'll tag along

> Remember me
> I'm the one who loves you.

My daughter was holding my hand and crying. I asked her what was wrong. "Grandpa was so cool," she said between her tears. "I didn't know he was a cool grandpa."

Yes, I told her, he was a pretty cool grandpa. Much cooler than a lot of people knew. And I told her he was watching all of us from heaven now, and that he was happy. She stopped crying and we watched the tape a few more times. Now it was my turn to cry. Goddamn him anyway. He had to have known exactly what he was doing when he taped this. And just when I was trying to act so unemotional and very much the good and responsible son, he pulls this on me. Not only did he get to help write his own obituary, he got the last word at his own funeral. Just like him to be the center of attention.

I still pull out the tape every now and again. I later found out that the song was written by a man named Stuart Hamblen in the 1940s, for his Western swing band called the Beverly Hillbillies (how oddly appropriate, as my father was always a big fan of Jethro Bodine). But even though this genre was out of character for my father, he picked his swan song carefully. "Remember me. I'm the one who loves you." I guess there is no better message a parent can leave for a child. Perhaps when we think about what our parents leave to us, and how they make life better for us, well, maybe we miss the obvious. Maybe life is all about letting your kids know that you love them.

I always thought I knew that he loved me, but I was never quite sure. I knew now. He made sure of that.

# CHAPTER NINE

# Tapping the Second Keg

The first sign that the new Browns' team song might be a funeral dirge happened during a preseason football game against the Chicago Bears. While defending against a screen pass, linebacker Chris Spielman spun off a blocker and raced downfield to chase down a Bears receiver. As Spielman plodded downfield, Casey Wiegmann, a backup center, blindsided Spielman, and the new Browns linebacker crumpled to the ground as their helmets collided. As hits went, this was nothing out of the ordinary. Wide receivers going over the middle get helmet-to-helmet blasts frequently, the force exacerbated by the sheer speed of the participants. Stingers are the most common injuries, a shooting pain down one side of the body that follows the nerves from head to toe. Players get up and play again from stingers, but with the speed of modern pro football players, paralysis is possible and happens from time to time.

But the Spielman-Wiegmann hit looked as though it happened in slow motion. That's why it was so strange when Spielman didn't get up. He lay facedown in the grass for a few minutes, and later said he felt nothing for ten or twelve seconds. He was helped to the sideline by the Browns training staff and put into a waiting ambulance bound for the Cleveland Clinic.

A few days later Spielman officially retired. He had had some vertebrae fused in 1997 while playing with the Buffalo Bills, and even though no permanent injuries were found after the hit during the Bears game, the Browns front office thought it best for all concerned that Spielman quit the game he so loved. The nagging question was whether Spielman retired on his own or was pushed off the cliff by the Browns brass.

Spielman had had a tough training camp. Since he had been out of football for almost eighteen months, his legs were not what they used to be. He was slow in the drills, and during the preseason games he was unable to pursue sideline-to-sideline, a prerequisite for linebacking in the speed-hungry NFL. More important, the Browns had drafted a speedy linebacker from Virginia, Wali Rainer, who—though inexperienced—had much more of an upside than Spielman.

The day after the hit in the Bears game, Spielman told Coach Chris Palmer he intended to continue playing. The organization decided that if Spielman did decide to return to the team, they would suspend or release him. Spielman got the hint and announced he was through with football the next day. He refused to use the word "retire" during his press conference, instead saying that he "never quit anything in my life. Surrender is not in my vocabulary." I took his comments as athletespeak for being pushed out rather than quitting on his own.

Spielman then went on to talk about the relationship with his son, three-year-old Noah, and the time he was forced to spend away from his kids during the rigors of football season. "[Noah] said, `Well, you know, Daddy, if you don't come home, I'm going to go to the store and buy a new daddy.' To him, I'll be home in a little bit. And to my daughter, who had her first day of [kindergarten yesterday], I'll be home to her."

Of course, like all athletes, Spielman didn't go home to become a househusband. During the football season he was jetting out to Los Angeles on weekends to be a TV talking head for Fox Sports.

But the loss of Spielman for the Browns—and especially for the fans—was huge. The team had done a lousy job of connecting Browns history to the newly constituted team. Former players were routinely not even considered for front-office jobs—even the cushy "community relations" posts that often go to ex-jocks who do nothing more than make appearances at churches and schools. The attitude from Carmen Policy was that this was going to be a first-class organization and that the best and brightest would be hired to fill all of the front-office jobs. This left former Browns like Herman Fontenot and Eddie Johnson, who had worked tirelessly in bringing the Browns back, without any job with the new team.

What the Browns were saying was that, yes, the past is important, and yes, the fifty-year history of the franchise is storied, but this is a new team and we are going to run it like the new team that it is. The new era in pro sports placed a premium on efficiency; there was no room in this plan to become overemotional about the past. And from a business perspective, all this is well and good. It is better that fans buy into the new program—and all the licensed merchandise that goes along with it—than look to Otto Graham or Bernie Kosar.

And that's why Spielman's loss was so tragic for the new season. Other players on the roster—tackle Orlando Brown and defensive back Antonio Langham—had played for the old Browns. But Spielman was Ohio football personified. He had played at Massillon High School and Ohio State. Wheaties had put him on a cereal box while he was still in high school. Plus, he was a linebacker. He grunted rather than spoke in complete sentences. When I asked him for an interview in the locker room one afternoon during training camp, he grunted, pointed to the exit door, and said, "Over there, ten minutes." He had a cut over the bridge of his nose that never seemed to heal. He took care of his wife while she fought breast cancer.

And there was a racial component to Spielman's popularity in Cleveland. There is no way to avoid the racial undertones of life in this city. Everything orbits around who you are, what race you are, and what parish you're from. The city itself is a majority black, and the suburbs white. That is true in most cities, but in Cleveland the animosity toward blacks by the white ethnic groups that helped build the city was fierce. Blacks were the people that forced them to move out to the suburbs, and blacks were the people that caused property values to fall, and blacks were the ones that were responsible for crime, and blacks were the ones that took over Cleveland and made it worse. This was not just the view of the undereducated blue-collar crowd. I knew plenty of white-collar suburbanites with graduate degrees who felt this way.

Of course, there are varying degrees of truth to any of these statements, but the underlying current among whites was that the black population in the city of Cleveland proper was responsible for most of the region's ills. And a dirty little secret in pro sports is that white fans were becoming increasingly turned off by the high salaries and criminal mischief among players. White fans saw these problems as being black problems, rooted in race more than anything else. Over and over in bars around Cleveland I heard the same refrain: these athletes can't handle their money; they don't have the smarts to compete; you can take the boy out of the ghetto, but you can't take the ghetto out of the boy.

During the preseason it was very noticeable that blacks weren't a big part of the new Browns fan mix. The high prices for tickets and PSLs (personal seat licenses) assured that poor Clevelanders—black and white alike—weren't going to be able to afford to come to games. And with blacks making up a disproportionate share of the city's poor residents, they were the first group to be shut out. It was a problem that all of pro sports was facing: the increasingly corporate nature of the ticket-buying public was making stadiums and arenas whiter and whiter.

So when Spielman stepped aside, there was a loud groan, the latest chapter in the heart-wrenching Cleveland sports history. He was the lunch-bucket, blue-collar player from the past, a link to old glories. Fans bought his number 54 more than any other jersey; he was the stereotype that the fans wanted to see; they thought he was one of them. The only problem was the lunch-bucket, blue-collar image no longer existed. Million-dollar players no longer sold insurance or were reps for beer companies in the off-season. The average fan was the white upper-income variety from the suburbs. The notion that the players were just like us—the fans—was no longer true.

At some point, somewhere in the mid-nineties, the wave that pro sports was riding crested and started falling back. Sports figures were no longer role models, we were told, and sports pages began running jurisprudence sections. Discussions of salary caps and rights fees dominated sports talk radio. We no longer cared about discussing the merits of the prevent defense, but instead argued whether a $4-million signing bonus was justified. Instead of sports heroes, we became preoccupied with the guy who beat his pregnant girlfriend.

Chris Spielman was slated to become a sports hero in Cleveland. And it is symbolic that he never played a regular season game for the Browns. Sports heroes were dead, and had been for some time. Spielman was a throwback to a time that no longer existed. He was now just another ex-jock spewing ex-jockisms to a national TV audience. He had tapped his second keg.

. . .

It was the day we had all been waiting for, a glorious Sunday in Cleveland, September 12, 1999, three and a half years after Arthur B. had done his evil deed to us. Since the opening of training camp, Cleveland had been pointing to this day. It was to be our deliverance from the evils of pro sports; we were going to show the world that a community can fight city hall and win. No other city had done what Cleveland had. Other cities had lost teams, but none ever got them back. And the celebration was going to be huge. Drinking and cheering just like the old days. And the hated Steelers for our first opponent. Most fans thought the Browns could beat the Steelers. Such was the optimism. Such was the expectation.

We met at Doctor Deadhead's house on Sunday morning. His pet iguana was loose. The previous night, Doctor had arrived home about 3 A.M. and thought he fed the damn lizard. But he hadn't closed the top of the glass tank, and during the night the four-foot scaly critter had gotten loose. He told us it happened all the time, and if anyone felt a nip at their ankles, he said, just wave him over and he'd capture it. I didn't feel all that safe. It was only 10 A.M., and Doctor had already been drinking for a few hours. There is perhaps nothing more maddening in this world than watching a drunk man chase down a four-foot lizard.

Doctor's house was a rather spare affair, about fifteen miles southwest of downtown Cleveland. While 3,500-square-foot homes were going up around him, Doctor lived on a half acre in an old, run-down single-story structure, with rusting farm implements in the backyard and a gravel driveway with weeds growing down the center strip. The gray paint was peeling, the window screens ripped from their frames, an old sofa with duct tape repairs on the front porch.

It was a house without any female influence. Doctor had been married for six months in the early nineties, but marriage ended when his wife found him in bed with another woman during a New Year's Eve party. Doctor's explanation of the event was succinct. "She didn't want to put out on New Year's Eve," he told me, "so I found someone who would. No one is going to tell me I can't get laid on New Year's Eve."

During the eighties Doctor and I were famous for our pre-sporting event parties, with the best being opening days for the baseball and football seasons. These were always morning affairs, and we created our own version of brunch, Cleveland style. The menu was simple: a huge pot of chili that would be ladled over three-egg omelets; smoked sausage cooked on a grill and served with sauerkraut; stuffed cabbage rolls; Blood Marys made with beef broth, chunks of Cleveland Stadium mustard, and jalapeño peppers; a garbage can full of beer; and several bags of pot. We had always encouraged our guests to bring beer for the garbage can and meat for the chili pot; in fact, the two were almost interchangeable. It was common for guests to show up with a case of beer and some Hungarian Magyar smoked sausage, dumping both in the receptacles after they arrived. During one party for the Tribe's opening day, Doctor showed up at my house with a fully dressed snapping turtle and calmly dumped it in the pot as he strolled through the kitchen.

I showed up prepared for the opening of the new Browns season that night against the Steelers. I opened my trunk and looked at the contents: a twelve-pack of Genesee Cream Ale; a bottle of tequila; a forty-ounce of Old English 800; twenty smoked Slovenian sausages for the grill; Mexican chorizo for the chili pot; two dozen "smokies"—a homemade Cleveland version of the

Slim Jim—for snacking; and my golf clubs for hitting nine-irons into the woods behind Doctor's house. In my jacket pocket I carried the little bag of weed I had pinched from my father six weeks before.

I was a little wary of having the pot. I hadn't smoked marijuana much since I left Cleveland and wasn't really much of a pot smoker before that. I leaned toward drugs that had a bit more kick to them: coke, acid, Percodan, speed. But serious drug taking is a sport for the young; a man approaching forty cannot possibly keep up and looks foolish when slurring his words with eyes spinning in his head. Pot had always made me a little more goofy and sleepy than normal, and I figured I didn't need much help in those areas.

I had pulled out that little bag of pot a few times since my dad's death, staring at it late at night and wondering how my dad felt smoking pot for the first time in his life at age sixty-eight. He had been having a very difficult time with nausea and a lack of appetite. He had quit the chemotherapy, but the dry heaves continued. I suspected that the cancer had moved into his stomach and that nothing could be done to keep food down. But some family members suggested that he try "medical marijuana," and he sought my advice. I told him it might work, but that pot did different things to different people. I had even become nauseous while smoking pot in my youth, I told him. And I warned him that the effects might not be all that pleasurable.

He called about midnight in the middle of July and asked if I could get some pot and come over immediately. I told him I'd try, but said it might take a few days. I mean I had been in town only about two months, and I really was out of the loop drugwise. But I went down to a bar in my neighborhood, found a bartender I knew pretty well, and within a half hour had a quarter ounce of some greenish weed that didn't look like it was very good.

When I got to his house, he was still awake, sitting up in bed by himself (my stepmother had taken to sleeping in the guest room). He had a little puke bucket next to him on a bedside table and was in the midst of a dry-heave attack when I came to him. He looked desperate.

"Why did you call me?" I asked him when the episode had subsided.

"I figured you were the only one of my children who could get it quickly," he answered.

"I guess I'll take that as a compliment," I said.

And as I lay in the bed beside him, I rolled up a small joint. I hadn't rolled one in more than ten years, but I guess it's like riding a bicycle—the old habits come back with a certain clarity when the need arises. My father and I had never really talked about drug use; I assumed he knew about me, and he assumed I knew he knew. I didn't ask him too many questions about how he came to the decision to try pot at this stage of his life, nor did I try to joke about it with him. He was in desperate shape, the worst I had seen him yet, and I could tell he needed help.

I fired it up and passed it to him. He hands were shaking and he had trouble holding the joint, so I held it to his mouth for him. He took a hit and went into a coughing fit; his lungs couldn't handle it. So I took a hit and blew it in his face, kind of like the "shotguns" we used to give each other in high school. I felt like a bird feeding her young, dropping little pieces of worms in their mouths as they eagerly gobbled them up. Slowly he stopped his dry heaves and seemed more comfortable. We lay in the bed together in silence as he started to fall asleep.

"Remember when you found that bag of pot when I was a sophomore in high school, and you flushed it down the toilet?" I asked him.

He didn't say anything, but nodded.

"Pretty ironic, isn't it?" I said.

He nodded and closed his eyes. I thought it best to leave him alone. On the way home I listened to Johnny Cash's "Long Black Veil," about a man who chooses to be executed rather than tell police that he had been with his best friend's wife during the time of the murder. This theme of choosing to die seemed to be following me around. "Nobody knows, nobody sees, nobody knows but me," Johnny sang. And I realized then that my dad was holding a lot in; nobody really knew what he was going through but him.

I was pretty stoned when I got home. Ate half a frozen pizza, three smokies, an old half a sandwich from Papa Joe's, and drank three beers. I fell asleep watching Andy Griffith reruns on Nickelodeon.

The next day I bought my dad a little one-hit pipe that had a battery-operated motor, a device that could give him shotguns without any help. I warned him to take only a little bit at a time, but he had no experience and didn't know his dosage. Within days he was doing about three or four bowls a day. With the morphine and all the other drugs he was taking, his mind turned into oatmeal.

One afternoon I came over to his house and had a very strange conversation.

"You know, I can't trust you for anything," he said. "You are my daughter, aren't you?"

"No, Dad, it's Danny. I'm your son."

"Can you see what's happening? There's no good place to get pie. There was an old Slovenian woman that made pies, but she died a few years ago."

"Is there anything I can get you?"

"No one understands why I can't drive anymore. Why doesn't anyone understand that?"

It would have been funny if he wasn't so out of it. Medical marijuana had reduced him to a babbling idiot. He was so doped up he didn't even know who he was. He stopped a few days later and went back to the dry heaves. He told me the marijuana was among the worst experiences of his life. "I thought everyone was plotting against me," he said. "I was paranoid and couldn't sleep. It was awful."

Doctor's party was in full force when I asked a few people to join me for some of Dad's weed in the backyard. I only had a few hits myself, but I figured if I was going to watch the game that night, I might as well have some part of my father with me. A little babbling nonsense might serve me well, I reasoned. Doctor joined us outside, but by this time of the early afternoon, he was raving mad, complaining that we were running out of vodka for the Blood Marys and, being Sunday, we couldn't buy any more. His iguana was still loose.

Doctor got in my face. "I told you to pick up some vodka," he yelled, his eyes spinning around curiously in his head.

"I didn't get around to it yesterday, and this morning it was too late."

"Jesus, McGraw, are you so fucked-up you can't even do a simple thing like buying a bottle of vodka? All I asked you for was a simple bottle of vodka."

"There's still tequila left. Just use that."

He wasn't listening. "Have you bought a bowling ball yet?

Have you bought shoes yet? How can you expect to be a good bowler if you have rented shoes and an alley ball?"

He was raving now, doing a good job of segueing between drinking and bowling. That's what I liked about Doctor, the insane way he cared about drinking and bowling as if they were the most important parts of his life. He was a man of principle, this Doctor Deadhead, living in a world where his curious expectations were sacred. If you didn't put out, he'd move to someone else.

"I'm going to try to buy them this week," I said sheepishly.

"And you have to work on throwing a hook," he continued. "How the fuck can you improve if you are throwing a straight ball? You've got to commit to bowling if you are ever going to be any good. I know you think you are some hot-shit writer, but that doesn't matter to me. You have to commit to bowling. You have to commit to something."

I was a little stoned, almost drunk, and thought to myself that he did have a point. Committing to anything had never been my strong suit. But he was also a raving madman, and it is hard to take a man seriously with chili stains on his shirt and a missing iguana. As his mind raced, he had forgotten about the vodka. I took this as a good sign.

"I promise I'll get shoes and a ball this week," I told him. "Let's hit some nine-irons."

Doctor had some clubs in the backyard, leaning against the house, and we pulled out some range balls and started hitting. I hit some nice iron shots into the woods; Doctor chose to work on his three-wood. The shots ricocheted through the woods and disappeared across the property line into the neighborhood on the next street.

"I've come up with a new strike call," I told him as he sliced another three-wood. I had been thinking that my "Pound that pocket, pound those Budweisers" wasn't making it.

"Now you're taking bowling seriously," he said. "Lay it on me, brother."

I struck a pose as if I were cradling a ball in my hands, took three steps forward, and threw out my right leg as if I were shooting the ball down the alley. I pumped my fist as if I had made a strike, and looked Doctor in the eye.

"Lick me sow," I shouted.

I didn't know what it meant. My brother Brian's fraternity brothers down at Kenyon College used to say that during frat parties when they drank. At that moment in time, drunk and stoned and hitting golf balls into the woods, it made good sense.

He laughed. "I like that. That's good. Now you have to find a way to use it more in our league."

We went in the house and had another beer. The ABC affiliate was showing *Rocky III* and running a continuous crawl at the bottom of the screen counting down the time to the new Browns' kickoff. I spied Doctor's iguana smirking from underneath a pile of newspapers in the kitchen pantry. I decided not to tell him. He didn't need to be chasing around the iguana at this point. I also thought it would be fun for Doctor to be looking for his pet after a night of drinking down at the stadium.

"Do you know they don't put any beans in their chili in Texas?" I told Doctor.

"Fuck Texas," he said.

And somehow we made it down to the game. All over the radio, the media were telling us how lucky we were to have this new team and how there would be new rules in place at this new stadium. Cheering would be encouraged, but the old drunk-and-disorderly act that had become a ritual at the old stadium would not be tolerated. "Maybe I can be the first drunk thrown out of the new stadium," Doctor said.

We parked down in the Flats, making our way through the thousands of people tailgating down by the bars. Someone had used PVC pipe and duct tape to fashion a triple beer bong, making it possible to have a beer-chugging race. It was an ingenious invention. Two men would hold opposite ends of the pipe, while three lucky people would fill up the funnels attached to it. Doctor and I put three beers in each of our funnels of the triple beer bong and raced some fat guy wearing a Spielman jersey. Doctor won, of course, and I came in a close second. That fat guy puked on his jersey.

I had never seen so many people down in the Flats. The cops didn't care about open containers, and people were stumbling along Old River Road, falling off of curbs and walking into buildings. Strippers were standing outside the Circus, flashing their titties to drunken men and enticing them to come in so they could take their money. One guy pulled down his pants to flash the strippers.

About two hours before game time, I decided to make my way to the stadium. I wanted to stop in the press box, check out the scene there, get my free meal courtesy of the Browns, and then meet everyone in the bleachers. I stumbled up the hill to the stadium, which looked to be shimmering from so far away. The sun was low in the sky over the lake, and the Cleveland skyline looked magical, all lit up and reflecting the orange sunset. I pushed ahead through the crowd, avoided footballs being thrown and drunks stumbling in my path. Cheers were breaking out—"Pittsburgh sucks" and "Muck Fodell." Maybe we could get the old days back.

But as I wandered through this crowd, I could tell it was a bit different from the old days. They were trying too hard. They had fallen into the trap of face painting and tailgating and licensed gear, as if they were out of central casting for an NFL fan commercial. In the old days the game mattered, and all the pregame hype was just that. Tailgating was for some hick from Erie who was seeing his first game. Not that we didn't get loaded before games; we just didn't make a spectacle of it like this.

What had happened in Cleveland was that the football fans had been cleaved into two groups from the moving of the team to Baltimore. There were those that cared not at all and those that cared too much. There was little middle ground. My brother Brian, for example, said he could care less about these new Browns. He had been a dedicated fan in the past but bristled at all the media hype and the tax spending to get the team back. He had found other things to do on Sunday afternoons, taking his kids to the park or catching up on some work around the house. Mostly he perceived pro sports as a greedy undertaking, and he felt the people of Cleveland had been taken by a sports league that had no scruples.

The people who cared too much were out in the parking lots before the Steelers game. Sunday afternoons—and in this case, Sunday night—were about football, and it didn't matter what it took to get their team back. It was as if these people of Cleveland had to prove that they were worthy of gaining this franchise. It didn't matter that they had paid $300 million and counting for a new stadium; it didn't matter that they were paying an outrageous amount of money for tickets and PSLs. This crowd wanted to let the world know that the Browns were back and that the best fans in the NFL were back as well.

I made it up to the press box and got in line for my gratis meal. I caught Joe Maxse, a sportswriter from the *Plain Dealer* whom I had known since my bartending days, sitting at a table by himself. Maxse was kind of the black sheep of the *PD*'s sports department; they knew he had talent, but no one wanted to go out on a limb by giving him a good beat. Maxse drank a little too much, joked about his job even more, and this was too much for the sullen *PD* sports editors to take. He covered Cleveland State basketball and boxing.

I sat down with him and took a big bite of a sub sandwich and squirted mustard on my shirt.

"Having fun down in the Flats, were we?" Maxse said.

"Just doing research for my book." I pulled a Genesee Cream Ale out of my bag.

Maxse grabbed a plastic cup, poured my beer in it, and threw the empty away. "I don't think drinking is thought too highly of among this crowd," Maxse said. "How many have you had today?"

"Ten, twelve, maybe twenty. Just doing research for my book. I have to put myself in the average fan. You know, it's journalism, Joe. You remember that, don't you? And shit."

Maxse was laughing now. "You planning to watch the game here or out in the stands?"

"Remember when I saved you from those lesbians, Joe? They were beating you up and I saved you from them. You had a fucking bloody nose and everything. I thought they were going to kill you."

Maxse loved and hated the lesbian beating story. When he was sober, he wouldn't bring it up, but after a few beers he would tell the story himself. I was bartending one night at the 2300 Club, and two offensive linemen from the Cleveland Brewers—a ladies' professional tackle football team—had just left the bar during a snowstorm. Their car got caught in a snowdrift, and Maxse—walking up the street completely jakey—tried to help push them out. But he kept slipping under their wheels, and the more they pushed, the more stuck they got. Maxse then decided to throw some snowballs at them and they were not amused. They chased him into the 2300, where they proceeded to beat the shit out of him. I jumped over the bar and landed on the three of them. After calm was restored, Joe asked to use the phone to call his lawyer. He said he was suing on behalf of all heterosexual men who had been wronged by lesbian football players.

"Did you every file that suit, Joe?"

"You know, Dannyboy, let's get you out of here. You saved me once, and I'll save you this time. If you stay here, they'll take away your press pass."

Joe held my arm and we made our way down the hall to the press elevator. I almost bumped into Bernie Kosar and Otto Graham as we negotiated our way through the hallway. As we passed through, NFL Commissioner Paul Tagliabue was holding court among a group of awestruck sports media types. Someone asked Tags if he thought the Browns fans were the best in the league. He said they were. I tried to stop and ask a question. Maxse pushed me through.

"I just wanted to ask him if Art Modell ever blew him, Joe. The public has the right to know. I mean the people of Cleveland got it up the ass from those NFL guys. I just want to know if Modell had to give any special favors. Let me go back and ask him."

Maxse was pretty good at pushing me along. "Press conference is over, scoop," he said. "Let's get you downstairs."

As we got off the press elevator, Maxse asked if I knew where I was going. I pointed to the beer concession stand. He gave me his business card. "If you get in any trouble with the security cops, call me on my cell phone. I'll take care of you."

I thanked him and bought a five-dollar "souvenir" beer. It was a souvenir, I guess, because it came in a hard plastic cup that you could take home. As I stumbled through the lower concourse, I ran into a kiosk offering me a free T-shirt if I signed up for an official Browns MBNA credit card. I tried to fill out the application but spilled my beer all over it. Some things were not meant to be.

I remember parts of the game. They trotted out Cleveland native and comic Drew Carey for a pregame pep talk. There had been some talk about introducing the greatest Browns players in history before the game, but ESPN had nixed that idea. ABC/ESPN had paid the league more than $8 billion for the rights to NFL Sunday and Monday night games, and they were not going to let some Cleveland nostalgia get in the way of the hype. The TV people thought it might be unwieldy to televise all those introductions of former players. Instead, Carey raved something to the effect that Cleveland was no longer a joke and anyone who thought it was could shut up.

I went into the bathroom and saw security guards removing a man who had tried to urinate on the floor. A fan who had brought a banner into the game was told that the new stadium would have no banners. The only banners I noticed were from corporate sponsors, especially a certain credit card company affiliated with the new Browns owner. I tried to get into the bleachers but was told I would need a ticket. I gave the usher a "do you know who I am?" line, and he threatened to call the cops.

At the kickoff the flashbulbs popped and the crowd let out the loudest cheer I had ever heard. The first time the Browns got the ball, Detmer threw an interception. Pittsburgh ran the ball at will down the field, and Steelers quarterback Kordell Stewart ran around right end for a one-yard touchdown. The next time the Steelers got the ball, they kicked a field goal. The Browns kept going, three-and-out. By halftime the score was 20–0. Tim Couch came in for mop-up duty in the fourth quarter and had his first professional pass intercepted. By the end of the game, the score was 43–0. Few of the new deadhead fans were left in the stadium at this point.

It all happened so fast. Cleveland had been a city that was bursting with pride, a city that was proud of its accomplishments, and within a few minutes it was all over. This wasn't just a beating, this was a thorough ass-kicking. I didn't think Cleveland could find a new way to lose, but we found a way to add another game to our list of losses.

I had passed through the point of being drunk and was now well on my way to a hangover. At the end of the game I went back to the press box and grabbed the official stats. Maxse was nowhere to be found; he was probably in the locker room asking a bunch of naked men how they felt having the shit beat out of them before a national audience.

It was perhaps the worst night in the history of the franchise. The Browns' forty yards of total offense was a franchise low (breaking a record set in 1950), and their twenty-eight total offensive plays was also an all-time record for futility. It was the worst opening-day loss in team history and the worst shutout loss in team history. The Browns had a total of 9 yards rushing, and the Steelers outgained them in total yards, 460 to 40. The Steelers sat down their starters in the middle of the third quarter.

No one in the stands booed. They were in too much shock for that. The ultimate irony for this team and their fans was that the city had fought hard to keep the team colors and records. Little did they know that they would rewrite their record books on the very first night. And not in the way they wanted.

As the crowd filed out, there were no more chants of "Pittsburgh sucks." I made my way up West Sixth in the warehouse district and looked in a few bars to see if I knew anyone there. The bars were mostly empty and quiet; as much drinking that went on before the game, the fans in the stands were very much the corporate kind and they couldn't be caught out late on a Sunday night. I decided to catch a cab over to my neighborhood in Tremont, stopping in the Tree House bar around midnight for a few beers before calling it a night. Sitting at the end of the bar was Doctor Deadhead.

"I thought you might make it here," Doctor said. "What happened to you? We were waiting for you in the bleachers."

"The guards wouldn't let me up there without a ticket. I told them I just wanted to go up there for a few minutes. I tried to bigfoot them with my press pass, but they said if I didn't leave, they would call the Browns PR guys and have my press pass revoked."

I took a large sip of my beer. "So how'd you like the game, Doctor? Worst team you ever saw?"

"I got kicked out," he answered. "I jumped up at one point and spilled some beer on some bitch in front of me. She thought I took a piss on the back of her neck. She complained to the ushers, and pretty soon the cops were up there. Weirdest thing I ever saw. They were serious about it. I mean, have you ever heard of getting kicked out of a game because you spilled a beer?"

"Well, at least you achieved your goal," I said.

"Now get this," he continued. "They said if I ever get in any more trouble there, they are going to take away my season tickets and revoke my PSL. Can they do that?"

"I told you they were going to be Nazis out there. They can and probably will take away your PSL. They can do anything they want in this town—everything, that is, except beat the Steelers."

And so we sat at the postmortem, drinking beers until closing time and laughing about how bad the Browns were. It was odd, but losing felt comfortable to us; it was something we had always prepared for in Cleveland. Why should this night be any different? In Cleveland you realize early on in life that when the expectations are the highest, and the city is looking its best, heartache is just around the corner.

"Why can't we ever just win once in a while?" Doctor asked to no one in particular.

"Because we live in Cleveland, Doctor, because we live in Cleveland."

We didn't know it at the time, but the season had ended pretty much right after Drew Carey had made his pronouncements about the end of the Cleveland joke as an art form. That was the ultimate Cleveland joke. It was the quickest ending in the history of the franchise, another record. And for Browns fans in Cleveland and around the world, it was definitely time to tap that second keg.

# CHAPTER TEN

## *Getting Religion*

If you want to turn young Catholic kids against their faith, make them altar boys. Looking back now, I can pinpoint the time in my life when I began doubting almost everything I had learned about God and Jesus and the Holy Ghost and the Virgin Mary. After I became an altar boy, the wholly mysterious process of faith became utterly and completely unmysterious. I had, in effect, moved into the inner circle, pulling back the curtain so to speak, and when you see things like that from the inside out, you are never quite the same. Seeing a priest sober up before saying mass can do that to a young man, and you learn to wink at the power of God and the notion of salvation.

I remember being in the third grade and having the assignment to serve 7 A.M. weekday masses. There wasn't enough time to make it home for breakfast and back to school in time, so we grabbed our breakfast in the school yard: a fresh bag of hosts and a jug of altar wine. One Sunday a priest accidentally knocked over a container of freshly consecrated hosts—they were now officially the Son of God—and we moved into action to clean up his mess. The priest tried to hand us specially blessed little towels to pick up the hosts, but the four of us on the altar pushed them away. That would take too much time, and we probably wanted to get home to watch football. We scooped them up bare-handed like we were cleaning out leaves in the garage. The priest frowned at us, but he knew he could do nothing. We had all seen too much from him. The respect was lost.

My career as an altar boy ended in the fifth grade after a funeral mass. The deceased was named Elmer, and every time the priest prayed for "our dearly departed Elmer" we cracked up. We all pictured Elmer Fudd in that casket, and to fifth-grade boys, this was something you couldn't keep out of your mind. The more we tried to stop laughing, the more we laughed. Even when the widow was crying in the front pew, we still laughed. The five of us in the funeral mass crew were permanently dismissed, but no other punishment was exacted. I was mainly troubled by the fact that I would no longer get out of school when someone died.

This is not to sound callous. But the whole belief system of the Catholic Church never made much sense to me. We were taught that unbaptized babies—not to mention Jews, Protestants, or any other "non-Catholics," as we called them—could not make it to heaven. Going to mass on Sunday and not eating meat on Fridays seemed to be more important than doing good works. By high school I thought the whole thing was a load of crap. I was sent to detention one day because I refused to pray before my sophomore Latin class. My mother had died a few months before. Prayer seemed like a complete waste of time.

We grew up just down the street from Holy Cross Church, and the priests and nuns came over to our house all the time. I was never much impressed or fearful of them. To me they always seemed like they were mooching; our family always had to have a spread of food out for them, and we were expected to be on our best behavior. As crazy as it sounds, I actually considered joining the priesthood in grade school. It seemed like a cushy job with good benefits and free drinks.

My basic rejection of the Catholic faith came not from to so-called truths or lies that might be contained within. My attitude was, why bother? Why worry about what you have no control over? The existence of God was not predicated on whether or not I believed. As far as I was concerned, there was some evidence God might exist, and there was some evidence that he didn't. Who was I to say? I didn't think the whole thing was worth spending a lot of time wringing my hands over.

My father was always very disappointed in my attitude. We stopped getting into arguments over the years about doctrine and such, as we were so far apart on this stuff that any discussions would invariably disintegrate into shouting matches. We learned to avoid the subject, as there was little room for compromise. For him, there was nothing but belief in the Roman Catholic Church. It was not something you thought about; it was something you just did. Faith was to be accepted as just that. Just go to fucking church and the rest would take care of itself.

His death didn't change my views. I had been preached to all my life that we must bear our crosses, that suffering was the way to salvation. I doubted that any God of love would make such claims upon us. All I knew was that my father was taken from me at an age when he should have been healthy and enjoying himself. Selfishly I missed him terribly. Maybe he was in a better place, surely better than the place where he found himself at the end of his life. But I didn't kid myself trying to be happy about it. For the place I found myself in immediately after his death was not a better place. It was a dark and lonely and hurtful place, and I resented any belief system that said this was good for me in some way. I wasn't about to offer up this cross for some future salvation.

But I didn't worry about it too much, either. After all, why get all bent out of shape over something you have no control over? That's what shallow happiness is all about, isn't it?

. . .

The inner sanctum of professional sports is a lot like the Roman Catholic Church. As young sports fans, we are taught that professional athletes are heroes. They have a certain godlike quality, and you accept this on faith, based on the preaching of the sportswriters and the TV and radio yakkers. Reason would tell us that these athletes are just regular guys like the rest of us, but we want to believe so badly that we disregard the obvious. In the past there was a mystery about these guys. We didn't know everything about them, nor did we want to. We accepted their hero status on faith.

When you hang around pro athletes long enough, the first thing you lose is the awe you held as a youngster. It's not so much that the guys are running around acting like assholes all the time (though some do); it's just that you see them as the humans they are. Most are not particularly bright or well-spoken, and many are downright hostile and angry. Most regard the media as absolute poisonous creatures, and some are. But mostly, when you peek behind the curtain, you see that pro sports are a business, and if you had any hero worship left in your being, it is long gone after hanging out in the locker room for a few weeks.

For the most part, life in the NFL is so scripted that any spontaneity that a player may have is stamped out quickly. As in the movie *Bull Durham,* players are taught by the club and their agents to feed the media the usual "we play 'em one game at a time" lines and leave it at that. The sports media rarely push it beyond that, knowing if they anger a player they will lose access. So most of the time, players answer stupid questions with equally stupid answers, and both the players and the media pretend that something interesting is going on.

I can't blame the players much. Look what happened to Atlanta

Braves pitcher John Rocker when he opened up to *Sports Illustrated*. Rocker thought he was being hip and cool with his tirade against ethnic groups in New York. What he basically showed was that he was kind of an idiot. And he paid for it dearly.

So anytime spontaneity is broached in the locker room, players run the other way. After the Steelers game, I approached quarterback Tim Couch about an endorsement deal he had. In the new Browns Stadium I had noticed lighted signs with Couch's likeness on them advertising the Armada Fund, a stock mutual fund he was endorsing. I told Couch I had saved some money and wanted some advice on investing.

"Do you think I should invest in an overseas fund with the implied risk, or do you think I should play it safe with a blue-chip portfolio?" I asked.

"What?" said Couch.

"No, really, you're endorsing this fund, so I thought maybe you had some inside investment advice." I smiled at Couch while I asked, just to let him know this was supposed to be fun.

"I really don't know anything about that," Couch said in his Kentucky drawl.

"So, no personal recommendations?"

"You'll have to call my agent," he said. And with that he walked away. And he was serious about the agent thing.

You could have some fun with a few of the guys. I got veteran defensive tackles John Jurkovic and Jerry Ball to stand belly-to-belly one day to see who had the bigger gut (Ball won by about three cheeseburgers). Linebacker Jamir Miller was always friendly and we talked about his young kids often. Rookie wide receiver Kevin Johnson was always smiling and optimistic, and even though he had little substantive to say, he was more than friendly in his dealings with the press.

But the rest were either hostile or unresponsive. If you tried to talk to offensive tackle Orlando Brown—who called himself Zeus—in the back left corner of the locker room, he would glare at you if he wasn't in the mood to talk. Though the locker room was open to the media for just forty-five minutes each day, most players didn't even bother coming out of the training room to talk. Most of the regular media guys just chalked the unresponsiveness of the players to losing. A winning locker room is a happy locker room, but when a team loses, everyone walks around on pins and needles.

The grumbling in the Browns locker room began right after the Steelers game. Coach Chris Palmer and Carmen Policy decided to throw in the towel right then and there, announcing that Tim Couch would replace Ty Detmer and rookie Daylon McCutcheon would replace cornerback Antonio Langham. The veterans on the team thought that the club had quit on them too quickly, and after just one game. But the coaching staff could see that this team was far worse than they had imagined, and decided—rightfully so—that development of the younger players was in the best interest of the team long-term. Plus, more losing would mean higher and more draft picks the following season.

The Browns had signed eight veteran free agents to be on their inaugural team. Most were on one-year contract, and they saw the team as a way station to a better contract the following year. And like most mercenary free agent players in the NFL, the veterans were looking to put up some good numbers before moving on. But with the coaching staff replacing the veterans with rookies, the numbers couldn't be put up and their value on the market would go down.

The main problem was that Palmer could put in only about a third of the team's offense when Couch was quarterbacking. That meant they were predictable, and a predictable team can't move the ball. Especially when the players aren't all that good. So the complaints started early when Couch was named as starter. Tackle Lomas Brown, thirty-six-years old but no longer the All-Pro he was earlier in his career, began complaining that the offensive play calling wasn't up to his standards. It didn't matter that defensive ends were running by him like he was standing still. Wide receiver Leslie Shepherd complained that Couch wasn't throwing to him enough, even though he had dropped many passes when Couch did. Cornerback Corey Fuller professed that he did "not regret my decision" to sign with Cleveland, but added that "if I was a prophet I wouldn't be here." Not that I'm against careful contraction, but Fuller made no sense.

And as the losses piled up, the Browns became more and more guarded in what they said. First Tennessee beat them, 26–9, and the Browns made backup quarterback Neil O'Donnell look like Otto Graham. In Baltimore, in a grudge match against the hated Ravens, Art Modell was cackling in his luxury suite as his mediocre team won a game 17–10 behind spare quarterback Stony Case. New England beat the Browns 19–7 at home, in a game that wasn't as close as the score indicated.

It wasn't that the team had quit exactly, though no one would blame it if it did. It was just that this was a very bad team, a lot worse than what the front office had promised the fans in the pre-season. The team was uncompetitive, and worse yet, it was boring. It had below-average players, ran a boring brand of offense, and ran and hid when the media came to record pearls of wisdom. At least with other expansion teams—like the Mets of the early sixties—there were characters on the team. They were lovable losers. This team didn't seem to have an identity or character; they were losers but certainly not lovable.

Many of the veteran players knew they would be gone after a year and were playing like it. They should have realized they were in Cleveland, and learned to enjoy the losing. As athletes, they should have played to their strengths. In Cleveland that means losing. That's what we're good at.

I felt like calling up Uncle Johnny to see if there is a third keg in the pantheon of his theory of the afterlife. The Browns could sure use another one.

I've spoken to friends who have lost a parent, and they all seem to have the same story. A period of lethargy sets in, and you don't even know you are in the middle of it until you wake up on the couch for the third week in a row. I found myself not caring much about anything. I stopped going out to the Browns' practices after the New England loss. I told myself that it was because the team was boring and a bunch of losers, and why should I waste my time. But the reality of the situation was that I lacked the energy to do most anything.

A few weeks after my dad died, I would make up and plan my schedule for the day. Go out to training camp for the morning practice, go to the locker room for interviews, drive out to see my dad . . . Oh, yeah, he's not here anymore. Subconsciously I still thought he was around. It was the dull pain that an amputee feels soon after the limb is cut off. He can feel pain in the limb even though it's not attached. That was my dad: an unattached limb that had withered and died.

My brother Brian told me he felt the same lethargy. But he had his wife and kids around him, and he was forced to deal with people. My daughter was now in school down in Texas, and the depression of her not being around, combined with my dad no longer around, put me in a deep and mysterious funk. I shouldn't have thought it so strange: my two favorite people in the world were gone. So I found myself lying on the couch, drinking enough beer every night to help me fall asleep. And reality was setting in. I still had five months left in Cleveland, with no real job and no real purpose. I was beginning to resent being in my hometown.

But there were silver linings. I found myself looking forward to bowling on Tuesday nights. No one gave a shit about my lethargy or my deepening depression. No one ever asked how I felt. I just concentrated on the task at hand, rolling that ball toward the pins, trying to hit that pocket. Trying to get as many porno cards as possible. And lick me sow, y'all.

By the middle of the football season, I had raised my average to 140. I had climbed my way from the worst bowler in the league to about the fifth worst. Every week I kept an eye on Ed Junior, one of the worst bowlers in the league and my own created nemesis. If I beat Ed Junior on Tuesday, I considered the week a success.

Doctor Deadhead was dubious of my goals: "If all you think about is Ed Junior, you'll always be a shitty bowler. Never bowl against another bowler. You bowl against yourself. Just you and the pins. Nothing else should matter."

Doctor was a natural, of course. He would empty his mind of everything on bowling night, sort of a Zen Buddhism approach to kegling. Become the ball, be the ball, become the pins, be the pins. For him it worked: he had a 185 average and was fourth in the league. Our team was fourth out of six, but we were usually close on any given night.

One night in October I started the first game with three open frames. I was no longer sitting with the team on the plastic seats around the scorers' table. Between frames, Doctor came back to join me. He was one of the few people who could read me, and he knew something was wrong.

"Hey, why don't you get up by the scorers' table and grab the pencil for a few frames?" he said.

"I'm not very good at math."

"You're not very good at bowling, either, but that doesn't stop you."

It was my turn. The first ball slipped off my hand and into the gutter. The second ball clipped the right side of the pin triangle, and just five fell.

"You're thinking too much," Doctor said. He handed me a twenty and told me to go buy some beers. From the bar area I heard the telltale "Fat girls need lovin', too." I brought the beer out for the team and stood back behind the seating area. Doctor came back again.

"What's wrong with you, anyway? You started out okay, but the last few weeks you've sucked. What's the problem?"

"I don't know. I just don't really care about anything anymore. I miss my daughter a lot. And I guess I miss my dad, too. I haven't been leaving the house much."

"I didn't ask you what's wrong with your personal life, asshole. I meant what's wrong with your bowling? Do you think I really give a shit about your personal problems?" He had a sly smile on his face, and chugged the rest of his Labatt's Blue as he stared me in the eye.

"Oh, you meant my bowling," I said, finally laughing with him. "Technically I don't think I'm throwing my right leg far enough. And the wax in the lane we're playing on tonight is a little too fast for me. I think I have to throw a few more boards to the right."

"You wouldn't know the boards if they came up and hit you

in the ass," he said. "Just get up there and throw it right down the fucking middle. Don't think about anything. And then get up and do it again."

That's what I liked about Doctor Deadhead. He didn't give any bullshit and didn't permit it from his friends. So I followed his advice. Grabbed my ball and threw it right down the middle. Almost closed my eyes when I did it. And the ball stayed right down the middle, hitting the head ten pin square. I thought it was a sure seven-ten split. But for some reason the ball rolled through the pins and all of them fell. "Lick me sooooow," I said, pumping my fist.

Edwin looked up from across the lanes and smiled. "*Toma punueta,* you asshole."

"Puerto Rican girls need lovin', too," Doctor yelled.

I finished the game with three strikes and two spares. In the middle game I bowled a 213, the highest of my short-lived career. In the last game, I was outside the boundaries of the three-and-nine rule, but still bowled a 167. We won by thirty pins.

It may sound strange, but I needed that night. Sometimes you need a little success at something trivial to get you going again. I needed to beat Ed Junior, but I was finding that was too easy. What I really needed to do was beat myself, quit whining and complaining, and quit thinking all the time. A little shallow happiness goes a long way in life, especially when you're bowling.

After our game, Doctor and I went to my brother's bar and ate pizza. I beat Doctor two games to one on my brother's bar bowling machine. Doctor picked up a woman who was reputed to be a nymphomaniac. I stayed and talked philosophy with Crowley. It was a good night, best I'd had in a while.

. . .

I believe the worst day in the history of Cleveland sports was October 10, 1999. I say this as an expert on losing in Cleveland, someone who has personally experienced the Drive and the Fumble and Tony Horton losing his cookies. There have been other days that may have been more heartbreaking in an individual sense, but cumulatively, nothing can quite compare to the tenth of October. But even for Cleveland fans, this day offered new meaning to our city's tendency to new and glorious ways to lose professional sports games.

It was a Sunday, and the Browns were scheduled to play the Cincinnati Bengals that day at the new stadium. For the new Browns, the game was a crucial test to see how bad they really were. Like the Browns, the Bengals were 0–4, and the sports pundits around town were saying that this was the best chance—and perhaps only chance—for the team to win a game that year. As a sidelight, the Bengals were starting rookie quarterback Akili Smith. During the previous draft, the Browns had debated whether to draft Smith or Couch with their first pick, before settling on Couch. Smith and his agent, Leigh Steinberg, were pissed off at Carmen Policy because they felt Smith was used as leverage to sign Couch before the draft. Policy had reportedly struck a deal with Smith, only to go back to Couch's agent to renegotiate their deal. Smith had said publicly that he wanted to whip the Browns' asses bad on this day, if only to show them they should have used their pick on him.

That night, the Cleveland Indians were playing the Boston Red Sox in game four of their best-of-five play-off series. The Indians had won the first two games of the series convincingly, but in game three, pitcher Dave Burba suffered a sore arm in the fifth inning. Tribe manager Mike Hargrove brought in starting pitcher Jaret Wright to relieve Burba, and Wright eventually faltered and the Indians lost game three, 9–3. From a strategic standpoint, Hargrove made a huge blunder. By using Wright in game three, he was forced to bring ace Bartolo Colon back in game four on just three days' rest, something Colon had never done before. If the Indians lost game four, Hargrove was going to be forced to use starting pitcher Charles Nagy on three days' rest.

The Indians were in the midst of another glorious season. Such was not always the case for the Tribe. I was born in October 1959, and that fall, the Indians were in contention against the White Sox until the end of the season. A few months later the Indians traded Rocky Colavito to the Detroit Tigers, and the decade-long slide of losing began. From that 1960 season until I moved to Texas in 1990, the Indians won 2,307 and lost 2,626, for a winning percentage of .467. I was personally 319 games under .500 with this team, and only six times in those thirty one years did they win more than they lost. Their best season was 1965, when they were just twelve games over .500.

But after I left town, they moved into Jacobs Field and started winning. From 1995 to the 1999 season, they had won the American League Central every year and had made it to the World Series in 1995 and 1997. Though they lost both of those series—and still hadn't won since 1948—most felt that 1999 was going to be their best chance to win a world championship. The Indians had All-Stars at every position, and their pitching was considered adequate.

So it was with great optimism that the Sunday began for Cleveland sports fans. The Browns had a good chance of getting their first victory of the year, and the Indians had a chance to close out their series with Boston with their pitching ace on the mound. But there was some bad voodoo in the air that day, enough voodoo to cause even the most die-hard of Cleveland fans to sit up and take notice of the new lows in losing.

I decided to watch the game in the press box and joined Danny Coughlin, one of the sportscasters for the local Fox affiliate. Coughlin was a Cleveland legend in the sports media. He had begun as a sportswriter with the *Cleveland Plain Dealer,* then moved to the *Cleveland Press* in one of the first big contract deals for local sports media. But a few months after he signed with the *Press,* the paper folded (actually it was sold to the *Plain Dealer* and closed), so Coughlin found himself without a job. He had moonlighted as a sports talk radio host and eventually moved to TV. He was in his fifties and was one of the few local sports media guys who had a history with the Browns.

If my father thought of himself as a raconteur, then Danny Coughlin was that times ten. He knew everyone in town, and everyone knew him. He disliked working in TV, mainly because he didn't think he was very good at it. He was a print reporter at heart and longed for the days when he was writing about the Indians or the Browns with daily deadlines. "There was a time there," he once told me, "in my late thirties and early forties, when I was really good at what I did. You're in the same age range. Take advantage of it. You can lose it as quickly as you get it."

During a TV report at the first exhibition game, Coughlin reported on the high beer prices at the new stadium. "With prices like this," he said with a serious look on his face, "it's time to go on the wagon." That's what I liked about Danny. He could stick it to these new Browns and not care about the repercussions. He was the only member of the sports media to show up at my dad's wake, and he worked the room as if he knew everyone there. I brought him to my brother's bar one afternoon, and he struck up a friendship with Bill Crowley.

"What do you do here, Crowley?" he asked.

"I live upstairs, I sweep the floors, and I drink," Crowley answered.

"Well, if you ever get tired of it, give me a call," Coughlin said. "Sounds like the type of job I'm qualified for."

It looked good for the Browns in the first half. The Bengals got on the board first with two field goals, but the Browns answered with two second-quarter touchdowns. The first was a great gadget play, as the Browns faked a field goal, and the holder pitched it out option style to kicker Phil Dawson, who scored easily on the play. As an indication as to how bad the season had gone up to that point, Dawson's touchdown was the first rushing TD of the season. But just before the half, the Bengals scored a touchdown, and after the two-point conversion failed, the Browns were up 14–12.

At halftime we went out to have a smoke.

"What do you make of this organization?" I asked him.

"They are the most arrogant bunch of people I've ever dealt with. I find myself begging some kid just out of college to set up an interview with some player. And they always screw it up. How are they treating you?"

"Like a turd in a birdbath," I said. "I know they don't want me around, so I don't push it anymore."

"It wouldn't be so bad if the team wasn't so boring," Coughlin said. "If I didn't have to cover them, I doubt I'd even watch."

"Sounds like we both need a career change," I said. "The last time I saw Crowley, he was hacking something fierce. His job might be opening up soon."

"Tell your brother to give me a call if Crowley doesn't answer the bell one day. You can be my assistant."

We made it back for the second half. The Browns held on to

their lead in the third quarter and then added a field goal in the fourth for a 17–12 lead. It was looking like the Browns might have a chance. But the Browns were sitting on the ball and had lost the momentum. On a crucial third-and-two at the Bengals' 36—with just over two minutes remaining—the Browns inexplicably gave the ball to a guy named George Jones. He lost two yards, and the Browns were forced to punt.

"Who the hell was that?" I asked Coughlin.

"Never heard of him, either. The big question is, why the hell didn't they pass the ball? What a gutless call."

Coughlin was right. The Browns hadn't been able to run all season and had had even more trouble converting third downs on the ground. But more important, a team that is 0–4 and going nowhere should take some chances. They were in the Bengals' side of the field, so they had little to risk. Palmer would say later that he was trying to run the clock out.

The Browns punted into the Bengals' end zone for a touchback. Akili Smith took over with two minutes and four seconds left and eighty yards to go for the win. Surely the Browns could hold a rookie quarterback at the end of the game. But Smith made the Browns pay. He passed his team down to the Browns' 29 and then hit a fourth-and-four pass to the Browns' twenty-yard line. On the next play, Corey Fuller pulled one of his bonehead plays and was called for pass interference at the 2-yard line with twenty-one seconds left. Two incomplete passes by Smith brought the clock down to nine seconds, third and goal from the 2-yard line.

Coughlin was yelling in the press box for the Browns to call a time-out. "They've gotta tell their cornerbacks to give up the pass interference call in the end zone. It will only be brought out to the one-yard line."

As Coughlin was telling me his strategy, Smith dropped back

and lofted a pass to the corner of the end zone. Bengals receiver Carl Pickens and Browns cornerback Ryan McNeil both went up for the ball, and Pickens came down with it. All McNeil had to do was purposely interfere and the Browns would still be alive. Instead, McNeil let Pickens go up and snare the ball with five seconds left. The Browns had found a new way to lose, even to the lowly Bengals.

After the game, Corey Fuller said the losing was "starting to really wear on a brother's psyche." And shit.

"That was the worst coaching I've ever seen," I told Coughlin.

"I don't know about that. I used to cover Nick Skorich when he was coach. But that was a new way to lose. I've got to give them that."

"You think the Tribe is going to close out the Red Sox?" I asked.

"I don't know," Coughlin said. "I've got a bad feeling about that game. I've got a bad feeling."

I went to my brother's bar to watch the Indians game. They were playing in Fenway Park in Boston, and there was a big crowd at my brother's joint, even though it was a Sunday night. My brother Mark had opened his place in 1995, and his business had ridden the success of the Indians. Mark said he didn't really care if the Indians won or lost; he just wanted as many play-off games as possible. A World Series run could mean an extra $10,000 to him.

I sat down in my usual spot next to Crowley.

"You like that Bengals game, Bill?" I asked.

"You should have seen them in here," Crowley answered. "Al the Lithuanian was screaming at the TV, calling that black quarterback for the Bengals a 'fucking Croatian monkey.' I think he lost a lot of money on it."

Of all the racial slurs I had heard in Cleveland, "Croatian monkey" was my favorite. Not a favorite in that I approved, but a favorite in its outrageousness. I had heard many white Clevelanders refer to blacks as "spooks" and "shines," words I hadn't heard in years. But "Croatian monkey" was a new one on me. It was usually reserved for NBA basketball players, and its origin was that Al the Lithuanian wanted to find a way to insult two ethnic groups at the same time. He was efficient that way, Al was.

"How's Coughlin doing?" Crowley asked.

"Still wants your job," I answered. "He says he wants to switch with you. He sweeps up here and drinks, you do the ten o'clock sports. Think you can handle that?"

"I'm not usually sober at ten," Crowley said, and then let out a big hacking laugh. He was pleased with himself, being clever and all after a full day of drinking.

As the game started, the Indians grabbed a quick 1–0 lead in the first inning. It was the last lead they would have for the game. Colon came out in the bottom of the first and gave up a two-run homer to John Valentin. In the second the Tribe scored once to tie the score. And then the floodgates opened. The Red Sox scored five in the second, three more in the third, five more in the fourth.

The patrons in my brother's bar were screaming at the twenty TVs. It was 15–2 in the bottom of the fourth. People were pounding the bar, yelling motherfucker this and motherfucker that at their beloved Indians. The season that held so much promise was beginning to unravel, quickly and in a very ugly way. I was beginning to get giddy. I mean, I wanted the Indians to win, but Christ, if you're gonna get spanked, this was the way to do it.

Crowley was laughing his ass off. "Look at all these assholes," he whispered. "Now, don't get me wrong. I like to see the Indians win as much as anyone. But these people have no life. Christ, it's only a game."

I thought it funny for Crowley to point out that people watching the play-off game had no life. To most people who hung out at the Time-Out, Crowley was the one with no life. But at least Crowley had the life he wanted. He had a place to sleep, he had a job, and he had all the booze he wanted. Everyone I knew in their forties wanted for everything. Crowley wanted for nothing. No wonder Danny Coughlin wanted his job.

By the time the carnage was over, Boston had scored twenty-three runs on twenty-four hits, both all-time play-off records. The Indians scored some meaningless runs at the end, with the final score being 23–7. Crowley had passed out in the seventh inning and woke up after midnight. The game was over and the bar was empty.

"Where are all the great Cleveland fans?" Crowley slurred. "Where'd everybody go?"

"Home, bubba, the place you need to go."

"One more drink, Dannyboy. One more on me."

"I think you've been cut off."

Sheila the bartender nodded in the affirmative.

Crowley got up to leave. "I may be a drunk," he said, "but at least I'm not one of these nuts. When you get my age, you don't care about any of these teams anymore. I've been watching them since I was a kid and they always fucking lose. Why does anyone watch these assholes?"

"I think we all want some hope, Bill. Just a little bit of hope."

Crowley made his two left turns and went upstairs. I left soon after. I came back the next night to watch game five. The Indians kept it close for a while, but eventually lost, 12–8. The winning margin of victory was a grand slam by Boston's Troy O'Leary. It was another ugly way to lose. After being up two games to none, the Tribe had been outscored 44–18 in the final three games. No one at my brother's bar seemed to care anymore. The enthusiasm had been beaten out of them.

Within a month Mike Hargrove was fired for his handling of the pitching rotation. The team's batting coach, Charlie Manuel, an affable southerner from Virginia, was hired as his replacement. Manuel had an unusual speaking crutch during interviews with the media. After every other sentence, Manuel would say "and things of that sort." I guess Charlie was too polite to say "and shit."

I turned forty on Halloween, which landed on a Sunday. The Browns were playing the Saints in New Orleans, and earlier in the summer I had thought about traveling to the Big Easy for my birthday. It was going to be a guys-only trip, all my friends and brothers, one big jakefest and the Browns to boot. But after my father died, the lethargy set in and I just didn't feel like going. Besides, none of my friends' wives would let them go, and I didn't relish going down there by myself.

I planned a quiet night for Halloween. I really loved the holiday as a kid, getting dressed up, getting candy, getting birthday presents; it was a day of excess for me. But in recent years, Halloween had been hijacked by adults. Baby boomers had come to see Halloween as their only chance of the year to act wild, and I wasn't the type to want to join in. I felt the same way about New Year's Eve. When the amateurs came out to play, I stayed inside.

I also wasn't real thrilled at how my birthday had become a sort of mating-ritual night for homosexuals. I know it isn't politically

correct to say this, but I was getting tired of going to bars on Halloween and watching drag queens humping each other. I personally didn't care what they did; I just wasn't all that interested in
watching.

I went to my brother Brian's house for dinner and went out
trick-or-treating with his three kids. Later I met Lance for a few
drinks. He was chasing around a twenty-two-year-old waitress, a
nitwit of a woman with big tits. When she went to the bathroom,
I asked Lance how he kept it up all these years. He was forty-
three now, yet he acted like he was twenty-five.

"Don't you get tired of them?" I said. "I mean, don't you get
tired of having nothing in common with them?"

"What we have in common is that they like to get laid and I
like to get laid."

"No, I'm serious. Do you ever have a conversation with any
of these women?"

"I don't care about that anymore. I'm serious now. I spent all
my life looking for some perfect woman, and now I look for
someone I can have a good time with. I get what I want from
them, and they get what they want from me."

"What do they get from you?"

"My pleasing personality."

Miss Nitwit 1999 came back and I walked home. I decided
Lance was full of shit. He dated these women because they
believed all of his bullshit. And he had a flat stomach. Which, as
we all know by now, made his dick appear bigger.

I went to church on the morning of my fortieth birthday. This
may sound strange, given my protestations against Catholicism.

But to tell you the truth, I was bored that morning, very much alone, and without a bona fide hangover for the first time in weeks. There was also something pulling me toward church; I think I wanted to find out what my father saw in it. When he first got sick with his colon cancer four years before, he had started going to mass daily. I was very skeptical, and thought he had received some really bad news he wasn't telling his kids about. Why else would anyone go to church every day?

I talked to him on the phone one day.

"I heard you're going to mass every day," I said. "Is anything wrong? Is there something you're not telling us?"

"Like what?"

"Well, like maybe you're dying of cancer and now you're going to mass."

"You're getting cynical in your old age," he answered.

"Well, it's the first thing that popped into my head. It's not that unreasonable."

"I know you don't understand this," he began, "but I do believe in the church. I feel comfortable there. It makes me feel like I did when I was a kid, when we used to go to mass at St. Thomas. I've found over the years that I like going to church. It's a good way to start the day."

I didn't really understand, but I thought about what he said as I made my way into St. John Cantius. It was a beautiful old church, with marble columns and statues of Jesus and Mary and the saints in every nook. The altar was festooned with gold and velvet curtains. I especially liked the fact that the statues of Jesus were of the "beaten up" variety, the kind that showed the Savior with bleeding wounds and black eyes. Most churches had Jesuses that looked like Jeffrey Hunter in *King of Kings*. The statues in St. John Cantius reminded me of the churches in Mexico: dozens of saints, Virgin Marys everywhere, and Jesuses that looked like they had really suffered for our salvation.

I paid little attention to the mass, mostly because it was in Polish. My mind was spinning in the old-fashioned sanctuary, the statues staring back at me, the organ music filling the space, and the priest preaching in a language I did not understand. This was the type of service my father would have gone to when he was younger. They said the mass in Latin back then. No one knew what the priest was saying, nor did anyone care. That wasn't important. The important thing was just being there and absorbing it all.

And I did feel a comfort level being in there on my fortieth birthday. I didn't understand completely why my father felt such comfort, but I had an inkling now. The mysterious becomes more meaningful the less we try to understand. When we try to understand on an intellectual level, the meaningful becomes trivial. Better to believe and not understand than to understand and not believe. Or so I was telling myself.

I noticed some votive candles on the way out after mass. They were blue, and I had never seen them that color before. I remembered them being red when I was little. But as I approached, I saw that the color was not the only thing that had changed. The votive candles were actually little electric lights, and for a quarter, the electric light would burn for twenty-four hours. I guess these "candles" were the equivalent of AstroTurf; they did the job just about as well without the costly maintenance. I fired up one for the old man. Said one Our Father and two Hail Marys. I left it at that. Didn't want to overdo things on my first day back.

. . .

The Browns-Saints game began at 1 P.M. The Browns were now 0–7, having lost to Jacksonville and St. Louis after the Bengals game. The Saints were 1–5 (they had had a bye week), but few gave the Browns much of a chance. Saints coach Mike Ditka was on the hot seat, and the sports punditry theorized that "Iron Mike" would find a way to fire his team up and save his job. The only other interesting subplot to this game was that it featured Saints running back Ricky Williams. Ditka had traded all of his 1999 draft picks and a few more in 2000 to the Redskins for the rights to Williams. The Browns had briefly considered Williams for their top pick, but the knock on Williams was that his hands were too small and therefore he fumbled too much.

I stared at the game, but it was another boring Browns game and I fell asleep on the couch. I drifted in and out, but woke up near the end of the game when the Browns had the ball on their own 25, down 16–14, with sixteen seconds left. I remember thinking they were going to lose another one and rolled over on the sofa. But Couch completed a pass, and the Browns had the ball on their own 44 with two seconds remaining. Groggy, I sat up, rubbed my eyes, and watched the last play.

The play was your basic Hail Mary pass play, meaning the Browns would send three receivers into the end zone and hope the ball got tipped to one of them. The Browns playbook called it 258 Flood Tip, and it was a play they regularly practiced. But these plays hardly ever worked, as the defense knew what was coming, and all the defensive backs had to do was knock the ball down.

Couch went back to pass and was immediately flushed to the right by the Saints right end. Wide receiver Kevin Johnson was running downfield and slowed down a bit as he watched Couch scramble on the huge video screen above the end zone. With his back to Couch, Johnson was able to see the ball fired high in the air on the video screen. After the ball was released, Johnson turned to watch the flight of the ball. The clock now read zeros. As Johnson made it into the end zone, Saints defensive backs Tyronne Drakeford and Sammy Knight jumped for the ball together, and it squirted up in the air. Johnson alertly grabbed the ball, dragged his two feet just inside the end zone line, and fell out of bounds.

The referee signaled a touchdown. I jumped off my sofa and screamed.

It was one of the most incredible endings in NFL history. The Browns players ran onto the field and piled on Johnson and hugged Couch. The team caught its composure long enough to kick the extra point, making the final score 21–16. I sat in my house stunned.

The Browns could have run that play fifty times and not hit on any one of them. It was a play that defied description, one that defied comprehension. But wasn't this just like the Browns? Just when you had given up on them, just when you were going to write them off forever, they pull something like this. They force you to watch them again. And I knew I was a fickle fan. I had secretly been hoping they would lose all their games. Now, with one play, I was confident they could win most of their remaining games.

But I guess that's why we are fans. It took more than three years, but the Browns had finally won a football game. We were finally winners. It had been a long, long time. And it felt good.

# CHAPTER ELEVEN

# We Are Not the World

When my father used to talk about his old elementary school, St. Thomas Aquinas, always in the most loving terms, I just assumed that the school wasn't there anymore. So when I asked him one day in the summer if he was sad when his old school was torn down, he looked at me strangely.

"Oh, it's still there," he said. "They tore down the church because the diocese said they couldn't afford it anymore. But the school is still there. They merged it with St. Philip Neri some years back. But it's still there."

"When was the last time you went back?"

"Oh, I can't even remember. It's been thirty or forty years maybe."

I thought that was quite odd, a man who talked about his old school and parish in such a reverential way, but with no interest in what it had become. He had told me many times that this school and parish were the most defining institutions in his life and that his views weren't being colored by some "good old days" syndrome. St. Thomas was where he learned about life, where he gained his lifelong friendships, where he found the defining strength of both his faith and his outlook on life. But when he talked about this school, he did so as if the school no longer existed.

I asked him if he would like to go back to his old neighborhood before he died. Maybe we could walk through the school and the neighborhood; maybe it would jog his memory a bit. I thought it might be a way we could connect, maybe a way to find out a little better what was important to him.

"I have no interest in going back there," he answered.

"Don't you want to see what the school is like?" I asked him. "Don't you want to see what your old neighborhood looks like?"

"The old neighborhood doesn't exist. It's a jaboney neighborhood now."

"What about the school?"

"It's a jaboney school. Most of the kids aren't even Catholic. It's not the same."

And with that, he dismissed any notion that he might want to visit his old neighborhood. And he did so in a way I had become familiar with. It was a "jaboney" neighborhood now and a "jaboney" school. For him, the neighborhood no longer existed because black people now lived there, and the school no longer existed because black kids went there. And he was bitter about it.

I never quite got a handle on my father's racial prejudice. When we were growing up, he would not allow the word "nigger" to be said in the house, but other words like "jaboney" or "spook" or "shine" were okay. He liked to portray himself as a man of the people, a man who championed the rights of the working class. He was a liberal Democrat most of his life and had defended numerous black people in his law practice. He was outraged when, in the early seventies, someone burned a cross on our neighbor's lawn because the neighbor had invited some black kids from the ghetto to come swim in our neighborhood pool.

One of my father's favorite stories was about riding the streetcar to his job downtown one afternoon in the early fifties. He saw a black coworker sitting on the streetcar and went to sit down next to him. There was a white guy sitting in the back, a guy they called Bun-n-Run because of the jacket he wore from the bakery where he worked. After my father sat down, Bun-n-Run started yelling that my father was a nigger-lover.

"I told Bun to shut up," he told me. "What was I supposed to do, ignore this guy I worked with? Bun got off the stretcher a few stops after I got on and kept yelling, 'McGraw's a nigger-lover,' after he got off. I really didn't think much of it. I always thought Bun was crazy anyway."

For my dad, this was his "some of my best friends are black" story. He always insisted that he wasn't prejudiced, and this story was his proof. And on the one hand, I believed him. I never learned racial prejudice from my father. He did not permit it. But on the other hand, blacks were jaboneys or spooks, and unworthy of a second thought. Like many of his generation, he saw what happened to his old neighborhood after it turned black. And like most of the white people in Cleveland, he blamed the decline in the neighborhood on the color changes.

"They just wanted everything too quickly," he said of the blacks who moved into his old neighborhood. "If they had come in gradually and waited their turn like everyone else, things would have been smoother. The neighborhood would've been better off if they had just been more patient."

Of course, my father couldn't imagine that a race of people who had been put upon for hundreds of years might lose a little patience. Nor could he see the similarities between the Irish and the blacks, how they both faced discrimination when they arrived in Cleveland. And he was blind to the fact that maybe the decline in the neighborhood was because the city government pretty much abandoned the black neighborhoods once they changed over in the fifties and sixties.

He was, I believe, a classic Cleveland bigot from his generation. And in Cleveland, being a bigot is not as simple as it appears. From the moment you emerge from the womb in Cleveland, you are defined by what side of the Cuyahoga River you were born on, what parish you are from, where your grandparents came from. East Siders don't like the West Siders, Croatians don't like the Serbs, the Italians fight with the hillbillies from West Virginia. It's not so much that people in Cleveland dislike any particular ethnic group; they don't like anyone who is not like them, not from their neighborhood.

Cleveland likes to pride itself on its ethnic diversity. Every summer there is an "All Nations Festival," full of music and food and strange dances from the old country. The West Side Market is now full of Arabs and Hispanics, as well as the old Eastern European sausage stands. But all this diversity comes with a price. It produces little-minded attitudes about race and ethnicity, where many rarely leave their own neighborhood. When I moved into the Tremont neighborhood on the near West Side, some of my relatives had no earthly idea where this neighborhood was. Or why I would even want to live on the West Side in the first place.

When I was sitting in my brother's bar one day, I was talking to Max about Cleveland's racial problems. Max is a Croatian, and we would often joke about my mix of Irish and Slovenian blood. Slovenes consider the Croats to be too flamboyant and a group that doesn't work hard enough. Croats see the Slovenes as being cheap and overly concerned with money. The old joke is that when a Slovenian needs a down payment to buy his first car, he uses his First Communion money from under the mattress. Max contended my Slovenian and Irish heritage was the reason I liked drinking cheap beer.

On this day, Max recounted a trip he made with the East Side Irish American Club one Saturday afternoon few years ago. The

East Side Irish had chartered a bus to go visit the West Side Irish American Club at their new digs out in suburban North Olmsted. Even though the two clubs are only about twenty miles apart, there was a feeling among the East Siders that they needed to charter a bus to make such a long trip. Max decided to go when his friend gave him a free ticket to the party.

"When we got out to the West Side club," Max began, "the East Side Irish stood in a corner of the room and wanted nothing to do with the West Side Irish. I was probably the only one there who wasn't Irish, so I tried to introduce the two groups to each other. I tried my best, but each side of town stayed on their own side of the room.

"Even though everyone was drunk, and you would expect these micks to loosen up after a few beers, no one was talking to each other. It was so strange: these guys had chartered a bus to go visit the other club, but when they got there, they stayed to themselves. They really didn't like each other."

"Is there a moral to this story, Max, or do you just like talking about the drunken Irish?" I asked.

"The moral is this," Max said. "If the Irish don't get along in Cleveland, how can you possibly expect blacks and whites to get along?"

When the Browns opened up their new stadium in August for the first exhibition game, the Ku Klux Klan decided to hold a rally downtown. It was rather strange for the Klan to pick Cleveland, because like most northern cities, Cleveland has never had a real Klan presence. But the Klan rally was not to be about race per se.

The reason for the rally, the Klan had said, was to protest the tax dollars used to build the new Browns Stadium.

The Klan rally put an interesting spin on race relations in Cleveland. Mayor Michael White, who is black, did not fight the Klan's application for a permit, even though the rally would disrupt downtown for the first football game. But many felt that White's position was not motivated by his love of the First Amendment. White had long thought the Cleveland Police Department was racist, so his plan was to have the Klan members change their robes in a police garage and have the cops escort the Klan to the stage that was set up directly in front of police headquarters. Many in the press thought White was using the Klan rally as a photo op to show Cleveland police helping the Klan with the rally.

Mayor White appeared so adamant about having the Klan rally that he came up with an elaborate public safety plan. Despite the fact that 70,000 people would be coming to the opening of the new stadium, every street downtown was blocked off to traffic. White ordered all the bus shelters, newspapers boxes, and street signs to be removed from the area, reasoning that bus shelters and newspaper boxes might be used as weapons by protesters. The official "protest zone" in front of the stage was segregated by eight-foot-high chain-link fences: the Klan protesters on the left, the Klan sympathizers on the right, and the media in between.

I found myself in the media cage in the middle. And from the beginning, it was clear that the Klan was not there to protest the tax-supported stadium. They goaded the cops: "If you're a nigger cop, look in the eyes of that white cop next to you and know that in his heart he really hates you," said one of the Klan speakers. They called the protesters a bunch of monkeys and baboons, called any white woman who would sleep with a nigger a whore and a slut, and in general, waved the red meat of racism at the protesters.

There were not a lot of protesters. Nor were there many Klan supporters. For the most part, the Cleveland media ignored the event as best they could. Not one word of what the Klan said appeared in the *Plain Dealer* the following day.

I found myself pretty upset at the tone of the rally. It was a rather sick display of what Cleveland had deteriorated to over the years. It had come to this: white supremacists could call blacks monkeys and baboons and niggers over loudspeakers and no one flinched. In fact, it seemed like the city would rather put its head in the sand than acknowledge the racism. No one I knew supported the Klan, but no one seemed particularly upset by the rally. The prevailing wisdom was that Cleveland shouldn't let a racist rally spoil the opening of the new stadium. Football was more important than racial diatribes.

I went to my brother's bar after the rally, and a few cops were drinking beer in the afternoon. They were all very pissed at Mayor White and felt they had been set up. "He had us right where he wanted us," said one cop. "He made it look like all of us hate niggers." Another cop said there was only one way to solve the problem with Mayor White. "Sniper on a roof," he said. He was serious.

I sat down with Crowley and he asked how I enjoyed the Klan rally.

"It was quite strange," I told him. "Mayor White was up on top of a parking garage looking down on the whole thing. And then the Klan praised the mayor by saying that 'he isn't your typical nigger.' From where I sat, I wondered if he enjoyed the whole thing."

"He should use that line about not being a typical nigger as his next campaign slogan," Crowley said. "A lot of white people would vote for him."

The first black kids I ever met in my life were on our Little League football team. I was the quarterback, and Lewelyn Brookins was our running back, the only black kid on our team. We had two basic plays: Lulu Fly Right and Lulu Fly Left. There would be an unbalanced line to the right or left, and I would pitch to Lewelyn Brookins to the side of the field that had the blockers. Lulu would then run down the field, usually for a touchdown. He was bigger and faster than the rest of us, and even though our offense was very predictable, the play worked just about every time.

We saw Lewelyn as a curiosity. Behind his back, some of the Italian kids on our team would call him racist names, but no one disliked him. (I first learned about sex from Lulu. "You gotta put your thing in her cookie," he told me one day at practice.) He scored touchdowns for us, after all, so race became secondary. Winning football games was important to us, and Lulu was an important part of that. It was an early lesson that I learned. After you blocked and tackled someone, you found out he wasn't much different from you. You could knock the crap out of someone, and it didn't much matter if he was black or white, or Croatian or Slovenian for that matter. It didn't much matter what neighborhood he lived in. You score touchdowns, and you have value.

If there is one lesson that sports imparts to kids and later to the adults who play the game, it is that you are judged by what you do. You also learn that you can try to beat someone and even try to hurt him, and still be friends after the game. I think this is something that women of my age group have missed out on through the years. I have worked for a number of female bosses who could not get past spirited arguments in the newsroom. It is a generalization, to be sure, but there is an amount of truth to it. Women I have worked for held grudges, and I think a large part of that is that women have never had the experience of fighting hard against each other on the football field and then putting that aside and being friends afterward.

And sports in general, especially at the pro level, are among the least racist segment of our society, much like the military in that respect. Granted, more minorities need to be hired for front-office and managerial jobs. But on the field there isn't a coach alive who will bench a player because of race. Too much is on the line, too much money involved to make player decisions based on race.

Not that there isn't segregation in the locker room. Black players tend to hang out with black players, and whites with whites. But the segregation is based more on position than on race. Football players attend meetings by position, have their lockers together because of position, and practice together by position. On most teams, offensive and defensive players barely know one another, because 90 percent of their time is spent with the other players at their positions and their coaches. Thus, offensive linemen, many of whom are white, hang out with one another. Defensive backs, most of whom are black, do the same. They are like any other segment of society: they hang with the guys from their own neighborhood.

Not to say that there weren't some racial overtones on the Browns during the season. When Chris Palmer decided to bench some of the veteran players after the season was determined to be a total loss, some grumbled about racism. But Palmer for the most part replaced aging black players who weren't performing with younger black players who had some potential. Some of the older black players thought Palmer was insensitive to the black athletes on the team, but in reality, Palmer was doing what all coaches do. He was playing the guys who he thought were best in the long run. Race had nothing to do with it.

I never saw Lewelyn Brookins after that one season. Even though we lived only a few miles from one another, we never hung out together after practice or played with each other. It didn't have anything to do with race. He just didn't live in my neighborhood.

On October 26, 1999, I went to the Tree House bar down the street from my house in Tremont to watch *Monday Night Football*. It was a horrible game, one of many that *MNF* had been saddled with during the season. The Pittsburgh Steelers were playing the Atlanta Falcons, and before the season started it looked like a good game, on paper. But the Falcons, who played in the Super Bowl the previous year, had lost their star running back, Jamal Anderson, to a season-ending knee injury. And Steelers quarterback Kordell Stewart, whom the Browns had made look like an All-Star in their season-opening loss, was having a dismal season.

Neither team was having an easy time moving the ball, and I left early in the fourth quarter with the Steelers leading 13–0. There were about a dozen people in the bar when I left, a fairly typical crowd for a Monday night.

About an hour after I left, a young black kid name Tekili

Williams and his friend Franklin B. Smith walked into the bar wearing ski masks. Williams walked behind the bar, demanded money from the cash register, and then pistol-whipped the bartender. What Tekili Williams didn't know was that three off-duty cops—two of them with their guns—were sitting at the bar.

The cops pulled their weapons and ordered Williams to drop his gun. Smith ran out of the bar (he was later caught a few blocks away), but Williams continued to point his weapon at the officers. They repeatedly told him to drop the gun, but he fled to a back room at the bar and tried to kick out the window of a locked back door. The cops chased after him, and again asked him to drop his weapon. Tekili fired a shot at the officers. The officers fired back, hitting Williams nine times. One shot hit Williams in the head, killing him. He was seventeen years old.

Not only did this police shooting seem justified to me, I thought that the cops were heroes. It all seemed pretty obvious. A guy comes into a bar, pistol-whips the bartender, and then is asked several times to drop his weapon. The cops fire on him only after he fires on the police. But like everything in Cleveland, the incident became a racial issue. The cops were derided in the black community for killing a teenager, and Mayor White opened an investigation to try to charge the cops with unlawful use of their weapons. A popular police commander was fired by the mayor a few months short of retirement because the commander attended a rally in Lincoln Park supporting the officers.

The fact is, Tekili Williams never had a chance. Not in the bar during the gunfight, but in his life. He was a high school dropout, and his seventeen-year-old girlfriend was pregnant. He bought into the whole rapper lifestyle, with tattoos of "Lawless" and "A Thug's Life" on his abdomen. He had been charged several times with receiving stolen property and spent some time in a state reformatory. Part of me felt sorry for the kid, because growing up poor and black in Cleveland doesn't leave one with many career choices. But anyone who walks into a bar with the intent to rob the place isn't very smart and deserves what he gets. Everyone in Cleveland knows that the most common place to find an off-duty cop is in a bar.

A couple days later I came out of the little market on my block and overheard some black kids talking about the crime. They were talking about how the cops shot Tekili Williams in the back. Not only that, but the kids were convinced that the cops shot him nine times in the back.

There were three of them, each about fifteen years old. I couldn't help jumping in. I'm sure they saw me as just another one of those rich white people who had moved into their neighborhood, but I couldn't believe what I was hearing.

"You guys really think he was shot in the back?" I asked.

"The brother never had a chance, man," one of the kids answered. "You know those cops was just waiting for something like this."

"You don't shoot some kid nine times," another one said.

"But he went in there trying to rob the place," I said. "Don't you think you're putting your life in your hands if you try to rob a bar?"

"Them white cops shouldn't shoot nobody just 'cause they're trying to rob somebody," the kid said. "If he was a white robber, they wouldn't be shooting him."

"You think white cops want to shoot black kids?" I asked.

They all started laughing. "It's what they do, man, it's what they do," one kid said.

We started talking a bit more. The three kids lived at the projects down the street. Two of them had dropped out of school. I asked them if any white people lived in their projects. Not in a few years, they said. I asked them if they had any white teachers in their school. Not many, they said.

"You think white people care about what happens to you?" I asked.

They laughed again. "White folks don't know nothin' about me, and they don't give a shit, either," said one.

"How do you know so much about what white people think?" I asked. "Do you know many white people?"

"You're the first white man ever talked to me like this," said one.

"Like what?" I said.

"Asking me what I think."

I realized then how little things had changed in Cleveland. When I was a kid, I didn't know any black people. These kids didn't know any white people. After I left them in front of the market, I was pretty depressed. These kids thought of me as a racist who was trying to keep them down. I couldn't blame them, either. Growing up black in the Cleveland projects means you have pretty much no education and little chances. Kids like Tekili Williams were probably closer to the norm than we would care to admit.

The day after the shooting, the Tree House owner replaced the floor-to-ceiling windows that had been shot out by the gunfight. That night, someone came by and threw bricks at the expensive smoked glass, shattering all the windows. "R.I.P. Thug Love Sugar Bear" was painted on the front windows of the bar.

·  ·  ·

I am not by nature a prejudiced person. I say that not to pat myself on the back or try to be better than other people. Racial attitudes are just more complicated than that. But I guess the reason I have fought hard against being racist is the effect of growing up in Cleveland. When I hear many of my old friends and acquaintances getting pissed about all the niggers and spics and hillbillies around them, I have a hard time accepting it. These are the same people whose grandparents faced discrimination when they came off the boat from Europe.

I had lived in Texas since 1990. You would expect the racial attitudes in Texas to be much worse than in a city like Cleveland. The opposite is true. Blacks and whites in the South have been dealing with each other for several hundred years. Of course, many of those years were of the master-slave variety or were in the Jim Crow era. But still there is a history, one of sharing cultural institutions. Blacks and whites eat in the same barbecue joints, drink and listen to music in the same blues clubs. And though they worship in different churches, both groups are predominantly Baptist. I'm not being Pollyannaish here, but I've noticed that the northern stereotypes of racial relations in the South are way off base.

The problem in Cleveland is that blacks and whites have no real history. Most blacks came to Cleveland—mostly from Tennessee—before and just after World War II. They came to a city that was accepting all sorts of ethnic groups but at the same time was casting a wary eye at all these newcomers. It is a paradox that envelops the city. We are ethnically diverse, the city leaders like to point out. The flip side of that is that we don't like anyone different from us.

Not to say that I have been immune to racist attitudes. When

I was a cabdriver in Cleveland, I would not pick up black male passengers downtown. Soon after I started driving, two cabdrivers were killed when they picked up black males who robbed them. I fell prey one night when I picked up two young black men and found myself in the Cedar Road projects with a gun to the back of my head. High-minded ideals of racial equality quickly leave you when your safety is involved. I was not proud of my decision to leave black guys on the curb, but I would do it again.

I found through the years as a journalist that race is the most overblown part of my job. As part of reporting, I would have to size up people quickly, often in less than an hour. Who those people were, and what kind of influences they had in their lives, were an important part of understanding who they were and how they formed their opinions. Whether they were male or female was important, and their occupation and education level were up there too. Did they grow up in a small town or a big city? Were they highly religious or not? All these factors played a role in sizing up a person quickly. I found through the years that race was the least likely predictor of who a person was, and a waste of my time to pursue.

And I think my attitude grew in part out of my father's attitude toward life. When you overly identify with a group, you lose a part of who you are. Weak people look outside themselves for their identity, my father taught me, the strong ones forge their own. When you wave the banner of being white or black, or Irish or Slovenian, you diminish yourself in the process.

That's what made deciphering my father's racial attitudes so difficult. He enjoyed reading James Baldwin and was conversant in the writings of Martin Luther King and Malcom X. He embraced the era of the black athlete; he loved Bill Russell of the Celtics and thought Tim Duncan of the San Antonio Spurs was among the best basketball players he had ever seen. When Latrell Sprewell choked his coach, P. J. Carlesimo, and white fans around the country were calling Sprewell a typical ghetto thug, my dad defended him. "Carlesimo is a punk coach," he said, "and he had it coming to him."

But much of my father's views toward the black race was for his own amusement, mostly of the stepinfetchit variety. I have a feeling he liked Sprewell because he got a kick out of his cornrows. He used to dance and sing as if he were one of the Pips, of Gladys Knight fame, doing his version of "Midnight Train to Georgia."

When I asked my dad one day to sum up his racial attitudes, he paused for a minute. "I'm not prejudiced against any group," he said. "I hate them all. But I never disliked anyone because of their race. I learned to dislike them for who they were."

I was watching a rerun of *The Drew Carey Show,* a sitcom based in Cleveland, and the character of Oswald Harvey was sitting at the bar. He has about five full beers in front of him when Kate walks up. Oswald explains that he is depressed and wants to get as drunk as possible and as quickly as possible. Kate looks down at him and says, "If you had your shirt off and were polishing your gun, you'd look just like my father."

In *The Drew Carey Show,* beer drinking is the common theme that binds all the characters together. They drink when they are at Drew's house, they meet and drink beer at the Warsaw, their favorite bar, they even make beer in their garage. I believe this is an accurate portrayal of life in Cleveland. I don't know of another city in the country where everyone drinks so much. Maybe it's just the crowd I'm hanging with. All I know is that I am drunk about five or six nights a week, and I am having a tough time reigning it in.

As October rolls into November, and the cold and damp winds off Lake Erie cut right through you, Cleveland can be a very depressing place to live. My neighborhood was fun and vibrant in the summer, people hanging out on street corners and music blaring from open windows. But now it is dirty and barren and foreboding; people are already shutting themselves in for the winter. The only thing that is the same is that the brothers from the projects still walk by my house every afternoon to pick up their fortyouncers of malt liquor.

I have found that I have trouble with my drinking when I am bored or if I am depressed, and I have both these days in spades. I am very much alone in my little Tremont apartment, my daughter back in Texas at school and my dad in his grave. I have stopped going out to Browns headquarters, as the team is not only boring on the field but mostly uninteresting off as well. I have stopped seeing most of my brothers and sisters and their families; I tell them I am busy writing, but I am doing little of that. I guess I would rather talk to strangers in bars than to have to deal with anyone I really care about.

My life has taken on a predictable schedule. Sunday nights I go to the Tree House, where Packy Malley—who was a few years behind me at Ignatius—bartends and holds court. Monday nights I watch football at the Time-Out, Tuesdays are for bowling. On Wednesdays I usually go see Maxse down at Major Hooples in the Flats. On Thursdays I call up Lance and we barhop around Tremont or the Flats. I get to the Time-Out on Friday for happy hour and drink with Crowley until neither of us can stand it anymore. I try to stay in on Saturday night, but usually end up at some joint in the neighborhood around midnight.

I cannot stand to be alone with myself. That is my rationalization for going out so much. And when I sit alone with a Bud, smoking one Camel Light after another, I hear his voice. Stay out of the saloons, for chrissakes, they waste your time. Get your personal life together. Don't waste your talent. I hear him quoting Milton, and I see the fear on his face in the hospice bed. Enough of the idolaters and the whoremongers already. Let's get out of here, Danny. I want to go home. I want to go home.

His voice rattles around in my head, his words echoing in my brain seemingly at random. I listen to them all; I heed none of them. I have another drink.

A good football team serves a very important purpose in Cleveland. During the most depressing time of year, when the weather is biting cold and people bide their time until spring, it serves as a diversion. Gives everyone something to talk about at work. Gives them an excuse to go out drinking. Gives them something to do when their lives suck.

After the miracle win against the Saints, the town was reenergized. Browns tackle John Jurkovic had told me that you couldn't judge the team by the first half of the year. There were just too many personalities to mesh, too many new players who needed to gain experience. "If we don't play .500 ball in the second half of the year," Jurkovic said, "then most of us on this team won't be around next year."

After the Saints, the hated Baltimore Ravens were coming to

town. The fans were psyched; this was a grudge match if there ever was one. Art Modell's team was coming into our house, and we thought we could beat his team. The Ravens were as bad as the Browns, we all thought, and the emotional win over the Saints, combined with the emotional nature of this game, would carry us to victory. It was a victory the city of Cleveland had to have.

But the Browns players didn't really understand what this game meant to the city. For them, it was another game on the schedule, one of sixteen. For some reason they came out flat for this one and got blown away. The final score was 41–9, and once again, the Browns made a rather spare quarterback look like an All-Pro. This time it was Tony Banks who cut them up. After the ninth week of the season, the Browns had but one victory, and none at home.

The following week the Browns got lucky in Pittsburgh. In another low-scoring and boring game, the Browns found themselves down 15–13 late in the fourth quarter. Couch got the ball at the Browns' 20 with 1:51 to go, and he moved them to near midfield quickly. Couch completed a pass over the middle, and a Pittsburgh defender was called for roughing the passer, tacking on another fifteen yards. Palmer decided to take a chance and let the clock run out before sending the field goal unit on the field. With no time left, Phil Dawson hit from 39 yards into a stiff wind. After the debacle against the Ravens, things were looking up. The Browns had now won two of their last three.

Everyone in town expected the fans and the media to give the team a free ride in their first year. But the new Browns were having as much trouble off the field as they were on. The problem was one of class, not the type that Carmen Policy talked about when discussing his first-class organization, but the social-class disparity in the new stadium. The fans were getting pissed about the seemingly strong-arm tactics of Browns security. The team had banned banners at the new stadium, even ones that supported the team. The music being played at home games is perceived by many as being too loud, and promotional announcements are endless.

But these were specific complaints. The more substantive argument behind them was that the new Browns Stadium had turned into a place for the elite, the cell-phone-wielding corporate types who were only interested in being seen at the game, not cheering for the Browns. The feeling among most fans was that the home field advantage Cleveland had with the old team—driven by the crazy antics in the Dawg Pound—was being eaten away. The fans felt their spirit had been taken away.

Carmen Policy addressed the problem in an interview in the *Plain Dealer*. The problems, Policy contended, came from "a singular source that is very vocal and also has a different agenda from the majority of the fans.

"We are changing as a nation, the way we do business, the way we live," he continued. "I think we have to get with it. The yuppies complain about those die-hard fans barking like canines. So our staunch die-hard fans have to be a little more tolerant of the geeks.

"We have this cadre of concerned fans that have a special attachment to the Dawg Pound that feel we're violating a sacred trust by permitting families in the Dawg Pound. As if it's a sacred right to throw up on each other, urinate on your neighbor. We're actually being chastised for defiling the concept of the Dawg Pound."

After the Pittsburgh game, under pressure from the fans, the Browns relaxed their restriction on banners. Only about twenty fans bothered to bring banners to the Carolina game, and the crowd was lethargic. The crowd was very white, very much of the corporate type, and many were families. Fans were wary of misbehaving because the Browns had threatened to take away season tickets from anyone who got out of line. It was obvious that the geeks, as Policy put it, had won. They were the ones with the money.

I asked Doctor Deadhead at bowling on Tuesday night what he thought of Policy's comments. "He sounds like a little prick to me," he said. "No one tells me how to act at a Browns game. I'd like to go up to Policy's luxury suite and puke on his suit. And piss on Al Lerner's shoes."

If you get the feeling that my brother's bar is full of a bunch of Archie Bunker racist types, that's not entirely true. Our old neighborhood had changed a lot in recent years, with more and more black families moving in. But the immigration has been gradual, and my brother has embraced this new group of families coming into his business. The black families that come to his bar are working-class like everyone else, and they want to have a cheap meal and a few beers while their kids play video games. No different really from anyone else. Some of the old-timers resent the black faces they see around them, but the younger crowd doesn't even notice. It is actually one of the few integrated blue-collar joints I have seen in Cleveland.

But there are times when I am amazed by what I hear. A case in point is a conversation I had in November with a guy I'll call Jerry.

After my father died, my brother Mark and I were having a

few beers and discussing my dad's legacy. We thought it might be nice to do something in his memory, perhaps using some money from his will to do something lasting. Mark had long heard complaints from parents that there was no place in the neighborhood for kids to play; the nearest playground was a few miles away. The elementary school down the block from his bar—Oliver Hazard Perry—had a lot of land and no playground. The school was mostly black kids, and 80 percent qualified for free or reduced lunches, one of the best measures of the poverty rate.

I had gone to kindergarten at the school, and my mom and her brothers and sister had graduated from there. We decided that it might be a good idea to try to raise money for the playground, kicking in a little of our own money, but getting most of it through fund-raising parties and from charitable foundations. We approached the principal of the school and she was elated.

We saw little opposition. I mean, who would be against building a playground for kids? As an added bonus, Mark thought it would be good public relations for his bar, and he would be able to increase his profile in the political and business communities.

Jerry was a guy in his early sixties who had graduated from Perry. As we planned our first fund-raiser at the Lithuanian Hall on 185th Street, I thought Jerry might be a good guy to endorse what we were doing. He was about the oldest graduate of the school we knew, lived in the neighborhood, and was a regular at my brother's bar. I asked him if he wouldn't mind coming to the fund-raiser and saying a few words.

"I don't support this playground thing at all," he said. "I think you guys are making a big mistake."

"What's wrong with it?" I said.

"It's all nigger kids at that school," Jerry said. "That school is nothing like the school I went to. They've ruined it."

I thought I was listening to my father. "Don't those kids deserve a place to play?" I told him. "Besides, the white kids that live in the neighborhood and go to the Catholic schools can use it, too."

Jerry just shook his head. "Any money you raise for this will be like throwing it down a rat hole. Those kids will destroy what you build in less than a year."

I decided to take a different tack with him. Jerry was planning to retire to Las Vegas in a few years and would be selling his house. I pointed out that a young family would be the most likely buyer, and having a playground close by might add value. If you can't appeal to a bigot's heart, then try for his wallet.

Jerry was having none of it. "Like I said, I think this is a stupid idea. You can take those kids out of the ghetto, but you can't take the ghetto out of those kids."

I gave it a rest. I moved over to the end of the bar where Crowley was sitting, pissed as hell at what I had just heard. Crowley laughed at me. "You must be the most naive asshole I know. I can't believe you write for a national magazine and you're surprised by this. You know how people are. You, of all people, should know how this town works."

I asked Crowley how he felt about the playground. After school each day, some of the latchkey kids in the neighborhood would try to get out of the cold and hang out in my brother's bar. Crowley would give them some popcorn and quarters for the video games before shooing them out. Crowley tried to act as if having the kids around bugged him—he said the bar was "turning into a fucking Chuck E. Cheese"—but he had a soft spot in his heart for them.

"I don't know who would be against building a playground," Crowley said. "Even shine kids need a place to play."

Orlando Brown is one of the meanest guys in the NFL. He's 6'7" and weighs about 350 pounds. While Couch was firing the Hail Mary pass against the Saints, Orlando Brown was giving a fore-arm to the back of New Orleans defensive lineman Jared Tomich, who was lying on the ground at the time. The referees didn't see Brown's cheap shot—if they had, the play would have been nul-lified and the Browns would have lost—but the league honchos did. They fined Brown, who calls himself Zeus, $5,000.

This is how Orlando Brown explained that play: "I've always been one of the top dirtiest players in the league. That was one of my moves there. Now I do it in the last two seconds of the game, and they just blow it up. I never knew it was wrong to do that. I thought if a guy falls down, you can do what you want to him."

Brown grew up in the ghetto of Washington, D.C., and had risen above his troubled past. He was an undrafted free agent out of college, and through hard work had become a millionaire in the NFL. Before their first season, the Browns made Zeus the highest-paid offensive lineman in football, stealing him away from the Baltimore Ravens for $27 million over six years. But for all the money they had paid, the Browns were disappointed in the season Zeus was having. Tim Couch was getting sacked more than any other quarterback in the league, and defensive linemen were running by Zeus and the rest of the Browns' high-priced offensive line.

I never went near Zeus's locker in the back left corner of the locker room. I tried to talk to him once, and he scowled at me. When a man that big grunts and scowls at you, it is best to get out of the way.

On December 19 Zeus moved from merely being a mean

offensive lineman to a place in NFL infamy. The Browns, with a record of 2–12, were at home playing the Jacksonville Jaguars. In the second quarter referee Jeff Triplette flagged the Browns offense for offsides. He threw the flag toward the line of scrimmage—which was customary—but the flag, weighted with BBs, shot into Zeus's face mask. No one thought much of it at the time—those of us in the press box thought it was a minor injury, like an eye poke—and Zeus went to the Browns sideline. But before the next play could start, Zeus ran out on the field, shoved Triplette to the ground violently, and then stood over the referee, shaking his fist.

I was sitting next to Danny Coughlin. "Have you ever seen a player go after a ref like that, Danny?" I asked.

"I've never seen anything like it," he said. "I've been watching this team for more than thirty years. No one has ever pushed a ref like that. I can't even think of anything like this in any other sport."

Zeus was immediately ejected, and two of Lew Merletti's earpieced goons escorted him out of the stadium. Zeus kicked at yard markers as he was led out, and Coughlin and I speculated what might happen to him. The Browns had only one more game left and then a bye week. Certainly Zeus would be suspended for the next game and probably for a bunch of games in the following season. He had assaulted a ref in front of 70,000 people. "He's going to be gone for a long time," Coughlin said. "I wouldn't be surprised if they suspend him for four or six games next year. Hell, they might even go for the whole season."

Immediately after the Zeus's referee knockdown, the media and fans all thought the Browns would make a clear statement about the severity of the incident and handle it accordingly. Whether the team would suspend or fine Zeus—some even speculated they should release him—was up for debate. But surely the team should do something. Carmen Policy had made it very clear that the new Browns would not tolerate bad behavior from their fans. No fighting, no pissing in the sinks, no lewd behavior in the Dawg Pound. Surely they would hold their players to the same high standard. But in the days following the incident, it became clear that Policy was not going to take the lead in punishing Zeus.

After the game, Chris Palmer was visibly distraught. He apologized to Triplette and the Browns fans. "I've tried to work with the player and his emotions during the course of the year, and obviously I've failed that situation." Palmer was so mad he couldn't even say Brown's name. Zeus was "the player."

But Palmer must have been taken to the woodshed after those comments, for the next day the team was in serious spin control. Zeus was now in the Cleveland Clinic receiving round-the-clock care for a bruised eye. Palmer and Policy met with the media and said that Zeus might lose sight in his right eye. The reason for the blowup, they said, was that Orlando Brown's father had been blinded by glaucoma, and Zeus went after Triplette because he was fearful he, too, would be blinded. He was said to be "scared to death" in the hospital. The Browns offered no doctor to confirm such a dire diagnosis, citing their policy not to let their medical staff comment on player injuries. Then Palmer reversed his field on his view of his offensive tackle. "At this time, I have not changed my view of Orlando Brown," the coach said. "I do not have problems handling the player."

A day before, Palmer had failed in his handling of Brown, and now he had no problems handling him. And for good measure, he told us he had not changed his view.

The following day Zeus invited selected media to visit him at the hospital for a carefully orchestrated press conference. Before he came out of his hospital room, however, he was careful to tape his metal eye patch to his face. Zeus then sat down to read a prepared statement, but almost tearfully said he couldn't read it. The statement was read by his wife instead, a garden-variety apology to the team, the fans, and the league. There was no doubt in my mind that the statement was written by lawyers or the Browns PR staff, and not Zeus. All the verbs were conjugated correctly.

Zeus wouldn't answer any media questions, saying the pressure might worsen his condition. His agent, Tom Condon, told the reporters that he and Zeus were very concerned about "permanent vision problems." Condon, who admitted he hadn't talked to Brown's doctors, then intimated he and his client might sue the NFL for the effects of the eye injury.

The Orlando Brown incident certainly presented the Browns with a moral dilemma. But there were also some financial considerations involved. Zeus's base salary for the 1999 season was just $420,000, and being suspended for the last two weeks of the season would cost him about $49,000. His salary in the 2000 season, however, jumped up to $2.12 million, making each game he might be suspended the following year worth $125,000. A six-game suspension in the 2000 season would set Zeus back $750,000. If the Browns decided to suspend him they would lose a player in whom they had invested millions of dollars. If the Browns decided to release him, Orlando Brown's $7.6 million signing bonus would count against the salary cap.

It was clear the Zeus had suffered an injury from the weighted flag flying into his eye, though the severity of the injury was not quite so clear. But it was crystal clear that Orlando Brown had no right to charge the field and push the referee to the ground. When asked if the team would punish Zeus on their own, Policy said it was a league matter. And as I listened to the Browns officials pass off any responsibility for dealing with Orlando Brown, I couldn't help feeling that Carmen Policy had missed a chance to show the Cleveland fans how this organization was indeed going to be different from the rest. Policy had repeatedly told the fans that the team would only employ players with character, players who were not involved in criminal mischief or of poor moral fiber that had been plaguing professional sports. Policy could have stood up and been counted as someone who would put into practice what he had been preaching. Instead he seemed more concerned about the pissing habits of his fans. And shit.

After the Super Bowl, the NFL reinstated Orlando Brown. He lost two weeks of pay. Prior to the 2000 training camp, the Browns asked Zeus to sign a waiver saying he would not sue referee Jeff Triplette over the incident. He refused. Claiming he could not engage in any physical activity without seeing white spots in front of his eyes, Zeus did not participate in pre-season workouts. Coach Palmer told the media it was doubtful Zeus would be able to play in the Browns' second season. And Zeus had consulted with O. J. Simpson lawyer Johnny Cochran to explore any possible lawsuits against the league and the Browns.

The Orlando Brown story would not be complete without relating one incident in the locker room the day after the game. I figured there might be some action, so I made my way out to Berea. When I walked in the door of the locker room, I saw Corey Fuller going apeshit.

*Plain Dealer* reporter Tony Grossi had been asking players if they were afraid of Zeus, a story angle that I thought was kind of stupid. Hey, but when you have to fill space every day, you find yourself asking stupid questions. Ty Detmer said he was not afraid of Zeus, saying no one thinks Zeus is "legitimately crazy." One for Zeus's sanity. Grossi then moved to Corey Fuller and asked him the same question. Fuller started screaming at Grossi, motherfucking him this way and that, saying he'll never help Grossi with an article again. The Browns PR guys immediately moved Fuller out of the locker room, lest he motherfuck any more members of the media. Motherfucked media members, after all, do not write positive stories.

But Fuller wasn't through. He came back into the locker room and sat calmly at his locker. As the media gathered around him, Fuller started a full-scale rant, at one point implying that violence in the movies was responsible for Zeus's tirade on Triplette. "Yeah, he lost it," Fuller said. "But is he crazy? No. Is he a bully? No. One thing that people don't realize is when all you've been trained to do all your life . . . It's like a guy in the army. He's trained to go off into war and battle. He doesn't know anything else."

And then Corey Fuller said something real curious. "We come out of the inner city," he said. "Just because we get to this place and y'all give us millions of dollars to play this game, it doesn't change who you are."

I looked down at my notebook. If I read his quote right, it appeared Corey Fuller was saying you could take the man out of the ghetto, but you couldn't take the ghetto out of the man. I guess everything comes full circle in this town. Maybe blacks and whites in Cleveland could find some common ground, after all.

# CHAPTER TWELVE

# Praying in the End Zone

There is nothing that drives me more batty than pro athletes thanking God every time they toss or kick their various balls through or between the various apparatuses in their games. I don't mind guys practicing their religion as they see fit. I support the Constitution in that way. But I just wish they would keep these displays to themselves. This kneeling and thanking the Lord in the end zone is killing me. Browns running back Terry Kirby likes to do that. Maybe it's because he has gotten there so few times this year.

And then there are the guys that point to the sky each time they do something they deem spectacular. Tim Couch likes to do that when he throws a touchdown pass. I suspect that someone died in his family and he is pointing to the approximate place he thinks heaven is. But isn't that a somewhat limited view of religion? Is God really up there? Is that where my dad is? Up there somewhere? I don't think so. I think he is looking over my shoulder right now making sure this sentence is properly conjugated.

The worst guys are the ones who thank the Lord for helping them win their games. I always wanted one of the TV guys doing the interview to shoot back this question at them: "If God helped you win, are you saying that God was responsible for your opponent losing?" You can't have one without the other. The world is interconnected in that way. God cannot help us vanquish our opponents without having a hand in smiting them down as well.

The most curious form of God's hand moving in professional sports is the role he plays in free agency signings. When Reggie White signed with the Green Bay Packers a few years back, he did so at the direction of the Lord. But it is rather odd how the Lord works. He always directs the athlete to the team that offers the most money. On the other hand, God seems to have little role in trades. I have never heard a jock thank the Lord for orchestrating a trade. The only exception to this may be the Cleveland Indians players who were traded to other teams during the mid-seventies.

I think this end zone praying thing is getting out of hand. After the 1999 season, the NFL banned celebrations in the end zone involving more than one player. The impetus for the new ruling was the St. Louis Rams' "Bob 'n' Weave" celebration, which was no doubt offensive to Paul Tagliabue. But the league didn't address what it would do if more than one player prayed after a touchdown. I find this troubling. And perhaps the NFL is missing a licensing deal here. Maybe they can set up an "official" altar in the corner of each stadium, where prayers can be said without upsetting the group-think policies that the NFL likes to adhere to. Throw a Nike headband on Jesus and call it a sponsorship deal. I think football is coming to this, I really do. The NFL is a religion in some quarters, and putting an official, licensed Jesus in the end zone would help confirm its status as such.

If you think I'm getting a little crazy about this stuff, you are right. Seven months in Cleveland watching death and football will do that to a man. I find myself babbling worse than my father on marijuana, making about as much sense as Corey Fuller at a press conference. If Ty Detmer were to give a diagnosis, he would proclaim me "legitimately crazy." Doctor Deadhead says there is nothing wrong with being crazy. "Keeps everyone off guard," he says. As time goes by, Doctor Deadhead makes more and more sense.

A wife of a friend of mine says I have to learn to find "release" in God. If you give yourself over to God and Jesus, she says, the Lord will guide your actions and you'll have nothing to worry about. I told her it sounded like shallow happiness to me. She said there was nothing shallow about God. I don't know about that. I think God likes the concept of shallow happiness. When life fails around us, when we have no clue to where our life is going—and when you lose someone you really love—you can grin your way to heaven. Tim Couch can point the way. Right up there, above Cleveland Browns Stadium.

I have spent a lot of time trying to make sense of my dad's death. It is not easy to do. There is the Elisabeth Kubler-Ross school of thought that says we have to go through the various stages of grief—denial and isolation, anger, bargaining, depression, and acceptance. I think I missed some of them. I definitely went through the isolation and depression. I can't say that I was ever angry or tried to bargain him back. The acceptance part—well, at this point, I just don't know.

It is easy to try to put our emotions in little boxes and pretend that there is an acceptable way to deal with a parent's death. But when all is said and done, I find that I am just plain sad most of the time. I miss just talking to him. Grabbing the phone and joking around. Listening to the old stories I've heard twenty times before. Nothing more than that. Despite the problems we had had through the years, I always enjoyed his company. He made me laugh, and he made me think. And he was always complicated. He kept everyone off guard. He was, as my niece Karen would say, colorfulish.

I will not miss the pomposity or the pressure he put on me. In that way, death is liberating. He made life tough on all of us, sometimes to our betterment, but often to our detriment. He wasn't easy to live with, nor was he the loving father in the classic sense of that term. But most of the time he cared, and did his best. Not always what I wanted, mind you, but what was best.

Someone asked me if I would miss my father over the holidays, as that is the time most people think that the shock of death comes roaring through. Not in the case of Dick McGraw. He was the most belligerent during the holidays. When the family would gather on Christmas Eve, he would sit in his chair with a scowl on his face. After each present was opened, he would yell at the gift-getter to pick up the wrapping paper. At one Christmas dinner, as my father was leading prayer, he asked my stepbrother Michael why he wasn't praying. Michael yelled that he was an atheist. My father pounded his fist on the table, let loose a few choice words, and left the house. We always joked that he was just looking for an excuse to get out of the house on Christmas.

And maybe that's what it boils down to. I don't have some romantic and sappy view of who my dad was. He was a lot of things, good and bad. But he was a complete person. He lived life hard and he held his beliefs firm. And he lived his life with a complete confidence that I rarely saw in other people. Some who didn't like him saw this as arrogance. I saw it as a strength.

So what did I learn, coming back to Cleveland and watching him wither away? I learned that death is not easy; it is a very hard thing to do. I learned that success in life is not measured by accomplishments, but by who you are. I found that I could be stronger than I previously thought possible; I also learned that my demons of weakness were still very much inside of me. And I learned that my brothers and sisters and nieces and nephews and cousins and aunts and uncles were a source of strength. I had spent a good deal of my life running away from my family, and I now knew there was nothing to fear.

But mostly I learned this important lesson. If you live your life with confidence, you don't have to give a flying fuck what anyone else thinks. I think back to that day long ago when my father got in the ambulance for the last time, that smirk just radiating off his face. He knew where he was going, and he knew that what he was doing was going to be tough. But he didn't give a fuck. He went out on his own terms, and I was proud of him for that.

The week that Orlando Brown wigged out, my daughter, Meredith, came to spend her Christmas break with me. Her being around pulled me back from the edge. You can't go out drinking every night when you have a nine-year-old getting up at seven in the morning demanding breakfast. I finally felt some purpose in my life that had eluded me for many months. I was beginning to see why my dad always had lots of kids around him. They force you to pay attention to them, taking your mind off your own small troubles.

We went sled riding and visited her cousins, and I began to get back into a routine. I didn't want to celebrate Christmas, but she made me get a Christmas tree. We decorated it with some ornaments she had made in school. She was at the age when Santa Claus was just about on his way out, so it was fun to see her question the whole thing.

"If Santa Claus is real, then how does he make it around the world in one night?" she asked me on Christmas Eve. "He couldn't possibly do it, all those houses."

"Well, I really don't know how it works," I answered. "I've never seen him. But maybe it has something to do with magic. I really don't know how else it could work."

"I know it couldn't be you," she said. "You don't have enough money to afford all the presents every year."

"I know," I answered. "No way I could get all the stuff. Not on my salary."

"One of my friends at school says that Santa Claus was invented by Coca-Cola," she said. "That's why he's red and white. Those are Coca-Cola's colors."

"Why would Coca-Cola make up Santa Claus?" I asked.

"It's a sponsorship deal, Dad."

I assured her that Coca-Cola wasn't licensing Santa Claus. As she fell asleep, I thought how much things had changed. Kids were now falling asleep on Christmas Eve with visions of marketing deals dancing in their heads.

The next morning, as she eagerly opened her presents, she gave me a look. "You're Santa Claus, aren't you?"

"Why would you say that?"

"Because there is no way that Santa would wrap the presents so bad. You wrapped them, didn't you?"

I started laughing and she started crying. It was one of those moments when you can see your kids growing up. I remembered when I learned that my dad was really Santa Claus. I had seen a football hidden in the closet and then saw it under the tree. I didn't let on for a few years. I thought the presents would dry up if I let them know that I knew.

We watched the tape of my dad singing. She studied him singing, rewinding it over and over again, studying him, watching his every move. Then she said something that I will remember all my life.

"Let's go to church," she said.

"You really want to go to church? Why?"

"We're the only ones in our family that doesn't go to church. Our whole family is Catholic except for us. Grandpa was a Catholic and we should be, too. It's what our family does, Dad. It's a part of our family."

We went to church that Christmas Day and I've been taking her ever since. Not that I believe in any of it. It's still a mystery to me. But it's what we do. It's part of the family.

My bowling average had steadily increased during the season. I was up to 149 and no longer at the bottom of the league. I had moved solidly into the bottom third. Doctor Deadhead's advice had worked. Stop thinking, and just roll the fucking ball. Drink a beer and do it again. Bowling in Cleveland was a lot like going to church. You did it because that's what people did in Cleveland. It was part of the family.

I had decided this Tuesday before Christmas would be my last with the team. I would be going home soon, back to Texas, and had to finish up all the packing and moving. Doctor Deadhead didn't let me buy a drink during the entire night, and I was sad that I would be leaving these guys. With all the racial prejudice running around Cleveland, my bowling league was the most harmonious. The league was mostly Puerto Rican, hillbilly, and regular old ethnic white boys, but everyone got along. No one got mad when the Puerto Ricans played their salsa music, no one cared if the hillbillies played country-western. And no one got mad at Doctor Deadhead for playing his Journey or Boston. He was the keeper of the porno cards, after all.

I bowled a 183 in my last game. We lost the game, but I felt pretty good about my effort. We settled into Dickey's bar and had a few last beers.

"You never did buy a ball or shoes, you asshole," Doctor Deadhead said.

"The longer I put it off, I just figured I'd ride it out for the rest of the year. I can procrastinate with the best of them."

"I'm having a party on Thursday," Lance said. "Why don't you come over? Lots of poontang."

"I've got my daughter in town, so I really can't. I've got to spend some time with her."

"You know, I just can't picture you as a father," Lance said. "I keep picturing you when we lived down at the Backhouse and were running all those whores through our house. Remember when those chicks were over and they needed to call in sick for work? You told them to call in with leukemia. That one chick was so stupid she almost did it."

"One of my shining moments," I said. "But the father thing, well, it does change you. You think of someone else. But it's funny. I don't think my dad ever really pictured me as a father, either. He said when he thought of me, he always pictured me as nine years old. He said I was the most fun back then. We would sit around and make fun of the neighbors."

"You miss him?" Doctor said.

"I guess. Having my kid with me this week has made me look at things a little differently. I guess she's having a little trouble in school because she's mad that I'm gone. So I'm just kind of interested in getting back home now."

"It's funny that you think of Texas as being home," Doctor said. "You don't want to live in Cleveland anymore?"

"I love Cleveland and I hate it, too. I guess since my dad died, this isn't really home anymore. I thought it was home when I moved up. But home is where my kid is. And I've got to get back there."

And with that, I made my leave. I had to pick up my daughter at my brother's house. As I was leaving the bar, Edwin walked up. He extended his hand. "*Toma punueta,* Dannyboy. Best of luck to you."

"And a lick me sow to you, my friend."

Professional sports at the end of the century have a problem. The sports media aren't writing about it, and the teams stick their heads in the sand. The problem is that they are losing their fan base, and if they don't address the problem soon, they are heading for big-time trouble.

At first glance the business side of sports couldn't be better. The TV rights deals are being measured in billions of dollars, and teams are selling for record prices. How could there be a problem in sports when a team like the Cleveland Browns goes for $530 million? And while attendance in the four major sports—hockey, basketball, baseball, and football—has dropped slightly in recent years, most teams are still playing to houses that are 90 percent of capacity. So whenever I bring up the problems with pro sports to those in the league offices, they scoff at me and call me a doomsayer.

The problem is twofold. Kids now don't play sports like we did when we were younger. There are too many other things to do. Kids have a hundred cable channels and video games and the Internet to keep them occupied. There aren't twenty other kids on the block to get together for a baseball or football game. As a result, they just don't have the affinity for the major sports like we did as kids. The number of kids playing Little League baseball has declined for the past three years, the first time there's ever been a decline for three consecutive years. Likewise, the number of people playing basketball, baseball, and softball on an informal basis is also down. The results are already being felt in the athletic shoe business and the sporting goods industry, both of which are in a deep slump.

So kids aren't playing sports so much anymore? What does that have to do with whether they go to games or not, whether they watch them on TV? That brings us to the second problem. Ticket prices have increased so much in recent years that it has become increasingly difficult for families to afford to go to games. Since 1991, ticket prices for the NBA, NFL, and MLB have risen on average more than 80 percent. The prices for all products, measured by the Consumer Price Index, has risen only 25 percent during the same time.

So kids aren't playing the sports, and most families can't afford to go. Is it any wonder that TV ratings are down substantially during the past decade? The TV people claim that every facet of network television has lost audience share over the past decade because of the myriad choices on cable and the Internet. But something has to give soon. The networks can't keep paying more money for smaller audiences.

In recent years Nike and Reebok have cut back drastically on signing athletes to endorse their shoes. And big consumer products companies—like Coca-Cola—are scaling back their sports marketing deals. The reason is that pro sports are increasingly drawing a wealthier and wealthier fan base. Coke needs to sell to everyone, not just the rich.

The economics are on the verge of not working anymore. Teams must increase ticket prices to keep up with player salaries. That keeps younger families away from the ballpark. Less interest across a broad spectrum of fans leads to lower TV ratings. Lower TV ratings will eventually lead to less revenue. The key point here is that pro sports aren't replacing their fan base as their older customers die off. The kids are watching the WWF. They could care less about *Monday Night Football.*

This isn't to say interest in pro sports is going to drop off drastically in the next few years. But the trends don't look good. Any business that prices itself out of the market is in danger of losing its customers. It's basic business theory. Sports are not immune from that.

Not to say Al Lerner is going to the poorhouse anytime soon. He's going to make his $530 million back by refinancing all the credit card debt in Cleveland. And everyone gets a free T-shirt or autographed football.

There was one last game left in this piss-poor season. The Indianapolis Colts were in town with a 12–3 record. The Browns hadn't won since the Pittsburgh game and were now 2–13. But the Browns were two plays away from being winless. If Orlando Brown had been called for the penalty against the Saints, and Couch hadn't got a break with the roughing-the-passer call, this team would be winless.

After Orlando Brown's meltdown in Jacksonville, Tim Couch

was injured while being sacked by Tony Brackens. It appeared at the time that Couch had broken his ankle, but it later proved to be just a sprain. Still, he wasn't going to play against the Colts. Couch had already been sacked fifty-six times during his rookie season, a league high and franchise record. Once again, Browns fans could thank the NFL for allowing us to keep the team records.

The Browns had one thing to play for on the day. If they lost, they would have the worst record in the league and be assured of the first pick in the 2000 draft. Detmer was going to start at quarterback behind a makeshift offensive line. I fully expected him to be spending the day running for his life.

For the fans, most just wanted this horrible season to be over. The Orlando Brown pushing incident and subsequent cover-up by the Browns had left a bad taste in everyone's mouth. The most optimistic fans had thought this team to be challenging for a play-off spot on this last week of the season; instead they were more than likely going to wind up with the worst record in the league. Many fans stayed home. It was the first home game of the season with snow, and the corporate crowd evidently decided that a cold stadium and a losing team weren't worth showing up for.

As the game started, Coughlin and I were paying close attention to the number of punts by Chris Gardocki. He need twelve to break the NFL all-time record for punts. In a season of futility, this was one you could be proud of. Gardocki only got six during the game. Once again, the Browns proved to disappoint.

But a funny thing started to happen. The Browns were playing well. Detmer was scrambling and didn't get sacked all day. The offensive line—without malcontents Lomas and Orlando Brown—was moving the Colts defense around. At the half, the

Browns were actually winning, 14–13. By the end of the third quarter, they were winning 28–19. The key was Detmer. He was cool under pressure and was moving the ball in a methodical, if unspectacular, way. We all wondered what kind of season it would have been had Palmer not yanked Detmer out of the starting lineup after the Pittsburgh game.

"These guys can't even lose the way they're supposed to," I told Coughlin. "All they have to do is lie down and get the top draft pick. They can't even do that right."

"You'd think these guys could figure that out," he said. "But that's the way it is in Cleveland. We can't even lose in the right way."

The Colts scored a touchdown in the fourth quarter to cut the lead to 28–26. After exchanging punts, the Browns had the ball on their own 12-yard line. All they had to do was run out the clock. On the first rush they gained two, and on the next play they lost four. It was third and twelve, and no one in the stands wanted to see them run again. This was a team that had nothing to lose—besides the draft pick—and they needed to show some balls out there. I was beginning to get into the game for the first time all year. The snow was swirling around, and the fans were cheering louder than they had all year.

It was time for a pass. Roll Detmer out and throw the ball. If they got the first down, they could keep the Indiana offense off the field. But Palmer did what he had done all year. He played it safe and ran Terry Kirby off right guard. He gained only six yards and the Browns had to punt.

"Why is Palmer being such a pussy?" I asked Coughlin.

"He's thinking about that draft pick. This game means nothing. He's doing everything he can to lose."

We decided to go down to the field. With five minutes to go

in each game, the Browns PR department would herd the entire press box down to the west end zone. The reason for the mass exodus from the press box was that the media could get into the locker room more easily from the field. I had gone down on the field a few times, but after a few locker room press conferences, and the nonsense said at such, I had passed more often than not.

We got down on the field for the two-minute warning. The Colts had driven from their own 43 to the Browns' 36. Colts quarterback Peyton Manning kept dumping the ball off to his wide receivers or rookie running back Edgerrin James off tackle. Soon the Colts were at the 20, then the 8, finally the 3. The Browns had used up all their time-outs, and the Colts ran their field goal unit out with seven seconds to play, down by 2 points. Their kicker, Mike Vanderjagt, had to make the equivalent of an extra point to beat the Browns.

How perfect this had turned out. In the worst season in the history of the franchise, the Browns could lose their record fourteenth game on the last play of the season. What a way to end this thing. Losing in the last second.

I decided that I needed to do something appropriate to the situation. I was standing right under the goalposts, and the ball would be kicked into the netting behind me. My plan was to push the security guards out of the way and run out of the stadium with the ball. It would be my way of paying back Lew Merletti for kicking Doctor Deadhead out of the stadium.

"I'm going to catch the ball, Danny," I told Coughlin.

"What?"

"Yeah, I'm going to catch the ball and run out of the field. Try to get in the way of those guards when I run out."

"You're nuts, McGraw," he said. "You'll never get out of here."

Vanderjagt was lining up the kick. I moved closer to the netting, ready to catch the ball as it ricocheted back toward the field.

"Say a prayer for me, Danny," I said.

"Which one you want?"

"Hail Mary's always treated me well."

And with that the kick was up. The snow was swirling and the ball tumbled high in the air, end over end, right through the uprights. I felt my way back toward the netting, never taking my eye off the ball. Everything seemed to be moving in slow motion. I felt like Burt Reynolds in *The Longest Yard*.

The ball was falling to earth. The clock read nothing but zeros. I had positioned myself perfectly. The ball hit the net about halfway up, and I extended my hands toward the ball. I felt the point of the ball on my right palm and moved my other hand to grab it. I pulled the ball into my gut, just like my dad had taught me in the backyard, thirty years before. I could see him throwing me the ball. Pull it into your gut, and don't run until you have the ball. Catch the ball with your body and not with your hands. Don't fight the ball, pull it toward you.

I was ready to make my move. But like Earnest Byner had done in Denver against the Broncos, I forgot something. I forgot the ball.

I had fumbled.

The security guard gave me a dirty look and picked up the ball. Coughlin put his arm around my shoulder and shook his head. "I thought you had good hands," he said. "I want you to work on that when you get back to Texas."

And so it ends as it started. We Clevelanders know how to lose, and we know how to make a grand and stupid gesture when we need to. It's what we grow up learning and it's what we know. And as I walked out of that silent and dreary stadium, the snow swirling and players praying in the end zone, I pointed up to the sky. This fumble was for you, Dad.

A mindless grin creased my face. We had lost again, but I didn't care. Shallow happiness was the order of the day.

And shit.

# *Acknowledgments*

More than anything else, this book is about a family, my family, one that is as dysfunctional as they come, but at the same time, one that is supportive and loving in its own strange and inimitable way. As we watched my father fight cancer, my own family showed their resilience and ability to pull together, gathering strength we didn't know we had, and showing the class and dignity that would have made my father proud. I was wary of some of my family members before this effort, but the experience has brought me closer to them.

I would especially like to thank my brothers and sisters, who gave their time and effort to this project in their own unique ways. My brothers Brian and Mark—one older, one younger—gave me insight into my father's life I hadn't known before, and showed me how to deal with adversity with courage and humor. They are not just brothers now; they are good friends. My sisters—Kathleen, Sheila, and Mary Margaret—were tough and compassionate, and I now know why my father had such a special place in his heart for them. They were caring, they never felt sorry for themselves, and they dealt with death in such a way that put other people first.

To my brothers' and sisters' spouses—Mary, Lisa, Craig, Rich, and Pat—thanks for allowing the McGraw family to overwhelm your lives during the course of a very tumultuous year. Likewise, I would like to thank my stepmother Theresa for allowing me extraordinary amounts of time to see my father when we all knew time was a very precious commodity. I would also like to thank my eight stepbrothers and sisters and their spouses for rallying during a very difficult time.

I had to move to Cleveland from my home in Fort Worth, Texas, for eight months to write this book, and my wife, Teresa, and my daughter, Meredith, adjusted their lives to permit me to do this work. There were many hardships along the way, but somehow we were able to muddle through. Without their support and understanding, I would not have been able to do what I had to do.

I would like to thank my agent, Jim Donovan, for believing in this project from the second I proposed it to him, and for working tirelessly on my behalf. My editor at Doubleday, Shawn Coyne, also understood the subtleties of this book from the start, and I benefited greatly from his wisdom and understated nudges. As a first-time author from Cleveland, I had doubts that Coyne—a Pittsburgh native and Steeler fan—could handle this book without having a spring pop out of his head. But he proved—that despite the handicap of his place of birth—he was able to understand the ravings of a Browns fan and translate my writings into simple sentences that even Steelers fans could understand. I also need to thank Doubleday's Chris Min, who made me see the importance of making the trains run on time, and doing so in a way that was neither harsh nor fawning.

There were numerous people in Cleveland who helped me find my way. My brother's bar—Mark's Time-Out Grill—proved to be a haven for all sorts of psychological and metaphysical healing, and I thank all the staff and regulars who welcomed me with open arms. Special thanks to Sheila, Anna, Chris, Yo, and Greg, who put up with their boss's brother hanging out a little bit too much. And to Max, Jocko, Ralph, Joe, Al, Horst, Joanie, and all the other denizens of the Time-Out, well, thanks for keeping the beer flowing and the conversations lively. And to Bill Crowley, well, thanks for being yourself and indulging me with a friendly ear and your interesting observations. You may be an irascible old drunk, Crowley, but you are not an asshole. That much needs to be said.

To the Dickey family, thanks for welcoming me with open arms into your bowling alley for the Tuesday night men's league. And to Doctor Deadhead, thanks for teaching me the Zen approach to bowling, and for bringing the porno playing cards every week. Doctor Deadhead is a true renaissance man, and he knows when to buy the beers and to keep the party going. Along the same lines, thanks to Lance for remembering the past, to Packy Malley for the good conversations at the Tree House on Sunday nights, and to my friends at the Wreck Room in Fort Worth, who survived a tornado and kept me in good spirits while I tried to finish this book. And special thanks to Tom Finn, who came up with the last paragraph.

I would not have been able to write this without the help from my employers at *U.S. News & World Report,* who granted me a leave of absence and welcomed me back after all was finished. I would like to especially thank Gordon Witkin, chief of correspondents for *U.S. News,* who facilitated my leave and ran interference for me on all those sticky personnel issues.

To the Cleveland Browns public relations staff, thanks for allowing me some access to the team even though the brass didn't want me around. I also appreciate the help I received from the sports boys over at WJW-TV, especially Tony Rizzo, Danny Coughlin, and John Telich. They never took themselves too seriously and were fun to be around. I would also like to thank the staff at the Hospice of the Western Reserve, who showed me that dying can be done with dignity and with real care for those on their way out.

I have held many jobs in journalism through the years, and have learned much from many different people. But had I not found myself sitting next to Jeff Harwood at the *Lake County News-Herald* a decade ago, I would not be where I am today. Harwood taught me that journalism is not a craft practiced by Ivy League weenies who are looking for a TV gig, but by real people who are truth-seekers, storytellers, and mischief-makers. I thank him for teaching me what I know, and for being a true friend even though we live 1,200 miles apart.

Lastly, I would like to thank my father, Richard J. McGraw. He embraced this project with his whole being, and had fun with it. As I look back now on his life and mine, forever intertwined, I realize how much I learned from the man. He introduced me to the wonders of great books and good writing, to biting humor and compassion for others, and to sports and religion. But mostly he taught me how to be a man and how to be a good father. I miss him every day and wish we had more time together.

—DAN MCGRAW